Software Runaways

Other Books by Robert L. Glass:

Prentice Hall and Yourdon Press:
Software Reliability Guidebook, 1979*
Software Maintenance Guidebook, 1981*
Modern Programming Practices: A Report from Industry, 1982*
Real-Time Software, 1983*
Software Communication Skills, 1988*
Measuring Software Design Quality (with David N. Card), 1990*
Software Conflict: Essays on the Art and Science of Software Engineering, 1991
Building Quality Software, 1992
Measuring and Motivating Maintenance Programmers (with Jerome B. Landsbaum), 1992
Software Creativity, 1995
An ISO Approach to Building Quality Software (with Osten Oskarsson), 1996

IEEE Computer Society Press:
In the Beginning: Recollections of Software Pioneers, 1998

Computing Trends:
The Universal Elixir and Other Computing Projects Which Failed, 1977, 1979, 1981, 1992
Tales of Computing Folk: Hot Dogs and Mixed Nuts, 1978*
The Power of Peonage, 1979*
The Second Coming: More Computing Projects Which Failed (with Sue DeNim), 1980*
Software Soliloquies, 1981
Computing Catastrophes, 1983, 1991
Computing Shakeout, 1987
Software Folklore, 1991
Software 2020, 1997

* out of print

Computing Trends books are available from 1416 Sare Rd., Bloomington, IN 47401

Software Runaways

Robert L. Glass

**To join a Prentice Hall PTR Internet mailing list, point to
http://www.prenhall.com/mail_lists/**

ISBN 0-13-673443-X

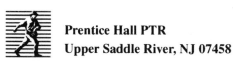

**Prentice Hall PTR
Upper Saddle River, NJ 07458**

Library of Congress Cataloging-in-Publication Data

```
Glass, Robert L., 1932-
    Software runaways / Robert L. Glass
        p.  cm,
    Includes index.
    ISBN 0-13-673443-X
    1.Software failures--Case studies. I. Title
QA76.76.F34G54    1998                                    97-29566
005--dc21                                                 CIP
```

Editorial/production supervision: *Mary Sudul*
Cover design: *Anthony Gemmellaro*
Cover design director: *Jerry Votta*
Manufacturing manager: *Alexis R. Heydt*
Marketing manager: *Dan Rush*
Acquisitions editor: *Paul Becker*
Editorial assistant: *Maureen Diana*

©1998 Prentice Hall PTR
Prentice-Hall, Inc.
A Simon & Schuster Company
Upper Saddle River, New Jersey 07458

Prentice Hall books are widely used by corporation and government agencies
for training, marketing, and resale.
The publisher offers discounts on this book when ordered in bulk quantities.
For more information, contact: Corporate Sales Department, Phone: 800-382-3419;
Fax: 201-236-7141; E-mail (Internet): corpsales@prenhall.com
Or write:
        Corporate Sales Department
        PTR Prentice Hall
        One Lake Street
        Upper Saddle River, NJ 07458

ISBN 0-13-673443-X

Printed in the United States of America
      10 9 8 7 6 5 4 3

        Prentice-Hall International (UK) Limited, *London*
        Prentice-Hall of Australia Pty. Limited, *Sydney*
        Prentice-Hall Canada Inc., *Toronto*
        Prentice-Hall Hispanoamericana, S.A., *Mexico*
        Prentice-Hall of India Private Limited, *New Delhi*
        Prentice-Hall of Japan, Inc., *Tokyo*
        Simon & Schuster Asia Pte. Ltd., *Singapore*
        Editora Prentice-Hall do Brasil, Ltda., *Rio de Janeiro*

This book is dedicated to

my professional friends and colleagues,
those pioneering software practitioners
who have struggled through the barriers in their paths
to make our era truly
the Computing Era

may none of YOUR projects
become runaways!

Contents

Foreword

by Alan Davis

Bob Glass has done it again. One of the most prolific and insightful writers of our industry has once again found the energy to create a book that, like all the other books he has produced, might actually alter how we perceive ourselves and how we pursue our technological growth.

For at least a decade, the software industry has heard the advice "do a post mortem." This advice is to spend a few days after a software project completes analyzing what went right and what went wrong during the project. The advice falls on deaf ears usually. However, it is only through analyzing our successes and failures that we can possibly improve. As the software industry continues to tackle problems that are just beyond our proven capability, it becomes ever more important to look back at our (individual and collective) experiences with success and failure.

Failures are of course more sensational than successes. They cry out to us more loudly with "lessons to be learned." They are full of stories that shout "Don't Do it This Way!" The case studies that Bob has collected for this book are by far the most sensational and most profound of our time. Hopefully, our society will find ways to learn from the experiences reported on these pages. I have always been an avid Bob Glass reader. This book helps me see why. Bob examines and comprehends our industry so well. And he is unselfish in sharing his insights with us.

One of the most refreshing aspects of this book is that the editor does not dwell on "the sky is falling" themes. Instead, he fills us with hope, with optimism, with the belief that most software projects undertaken by humankind *are* successful. The software industry in general and software developers specifically have been trusted to preserve our lives, our assets, and our future. Bob Glass continues to enlighten us and help us accept this responsibility in a more mature and respectable manner. I know that you will find this book as enlightening, educational, and insightful as I did.

Preface

I've always been interested in computing projects that failed. There seems to be a much more indelible lesson to be learned from failures than from successes.

Some of you readers may know that I once wrote a column for a leading computing newspaper under an assumed name, and the content of the column was fictionalized failure stories. (I wrote it under an assumed name and fictionalized the stories, because I suspected that my employer at the time wouldn't appreciate my washing its dirty linen in public!) Those columns eventually became a book (*The Universal Elixir and Other Computing Projects That Failed*) and then grew to fill another (*The Second Coming: More Computing Projects That Failed*). They also became the basis for talks I frequently presented at chapters of my computing professional society, the ACM.

Buoyed by that success, I did it again (*Computing Catastrophes*, true stories of mainframe computing projects and companies that failed) and again (*Computing Shakeout*, true stories of microcomputer projects and companies that failed). I was on a roll. Failure was my fate!

But the last of those books was (self-) published in 1987, over a decade ago. It wasn't that I lost interest in failure; it was simply getting harder to find good failure stories! The frequency of early-day failures, and the shakeouts in the mainframe and microcomputer industries, had largely ended. Computing had become an almost boringly-successful field.

Some would, of course, take issue with that statement. Those who cry "software crisis" promote the belief that the software field is full of failure, with far too few successes in between. But that's not how I see it. In spite of the time I've spent finding and publishing failure stories, I believe that software is the dramatic success story of our age, the spark that ignites the Computing Era. There have been failures, of course; but what makes them interesting is partly that there aren't that many of them. It's what journalists and software people call "exception reporting"—we tend to focus on the things that go wrong, because they're more interesting or important than the run-of-the-mill things that go right.

Well, I'm at it again! I've been gathering stories about software runaways for about 10 years now, and I have enough of them to put together yet another book. This book contains stories about the Denver Airport Baggage Handling System, the FAA Air Traffic Control System, the Internal Revenue Service Modernization effort, and a baker's dozen or so other examples of software projects that got way out of control, most of them crashing and burning (usually figuratively rather than literally!). Once a failure nut, always a failure nut!

One of the things I do as I accumulate stories for a book is to analyze the lessons they teach us. It's a good way to create an outline for the book, for one thing, and it's also a way to make sure that there's value added for the reader; these are not only fun stories to read, but the lessons make the reading a learning experience.

What I'd like to do in this preface is highlight for you some of the learning experiences from the material that follows. I think there are some particularly interesting things happening in our field, as reflected in these failures, and they don't always agree with what our textbooks and our research papers, and our newspapers and our televisions, are telling us.

First, let's get the predictable out of the way. Here are some things I discovered that match what our traditional sources of information tell us:

1. Most of the runaway projects are (or were) huge. It is well known in the field that huge projects are much more troublesome than smaller ones. These stories support that finding.

2. Most runaway projects result from a multiplicity of causes. There may or may not be one dominant cause, but there are always several problems contributing to the runaway.

3. Many of the runaway projects were lauded early in their history as being "breakthroughs," significant advances over the systems they were replacing. It appeared that visibility into the possibility of failure did not emerge until the project was well under way.

But the unpredictable is much more fascinating. Here are some characteristics of these runaway projects that none of my reading (and I suspect yours as well) prepared me for:

1. Technology was just as often a cause of failure as management. The literature, especially in the software engineering field, tends to say that major failures are usually due to management. But for nearly half of these 16 failure stories the dominant problem was technical.

2. There were two especially surprising and dominant technical problems. The first was the use of new technology. Four of the projects, fully expecting to be breakthroughs because they were using the latest in software engineering concepts, instead failed because of them! One used a megapackage approach to replacing its old, legacy software, betting the company on the approach—and losing. Another used a Fourth Generation Language ("4GL," a problem-focused programming language) for a large project, and found (after the work was complete!) that it was not capable of meeting performance goals for the (on-line) system. Yet another tried to port an existing mainframe system to client/server, and found the complexity increase got out of hand. And the fourth put together so many new technologies that the project foundered from their sheer weight (that didn't prevent some of the project's principals

from proclaiming the project a success in their company's house organ!).

3. The second dominant technical problem was performance. Many of these runaway projects were in some sense real-time (that in itself is a pertinent finding), and all too often the as-built systems simply were too slow to be useful. This is particularly interesting because most academic curricula now downplay the importance of system efficiency, with the thought that brute force hardware speed has done away with the need for more subtle software solutions. This data, at least, suggests that the field may have overplayed that hand.

In summary, I would like to say this: software runaways don't occur often in our field, but when they do they are increasingly visible. Many of the stories in my book were mentioned one or more times on TV and in general, print media news reports. And a surprising number of these projects, as evidenced both by the research findings I cite and by the stories I have collected, were flawed because of the technical (not just the management) approach. There are some words of warning here for those who embark on major software projects; none of us would like to see our best efforts become the headline story on the nightly news!

Robert L. Glass
1416 Sare Rd.
Bloomington, IN 47401

Spring 1997
(two and a half years from what may become the
Mother of All Software Failure Stories,
the Year 2000 Date Crisis)

About the Author

Robert L. Glass has meandered the halls of computing for over 40 years now, starting with a three-year gig in the aerospace industry (at North American Aviation) in 1954-1957, which makes him one of the true pioneers of the software field.

That stay at North American extended into several other aerospace appearances (at Aerojet-General Corp., 1957-1965 and the Boeing Company, 1965-1970 and 1972-1982). His role was largely that of building software tools used by applications specialists. It was an exciting time to be part of the aerospace business—those were the heady days of Space Exploration, after all—but it was an even headier time to be part of the Computing Field. Progress in both fields was rapid, and the vistas were extraterrestrial!

The primary lesson he learned during those aerospace years was that he loved the technology of software, but hated being a manager. He carefully cultivated the role of technical specialist, which had two major impacts on his career: (a) his technical knowledge remained fresh and useful, but (b) his knowledge of management—and his earning power(!)—were diminished commensurately.

When his upward mobility had reached the inevitable technological Glass ceiling (tee-hee!), Glass took a lateral transition into academe. He taught in the Software Engineering graduate program at Seattle University (1982-1987) and spent a year at the (all-too-academic!) Software Engineering Institute (1987-1988). (He had earlier spent a couple of years (1970-1972) working on a tools-focused research grant at the University of Washington).

The primary lesson he learned during those academic years was that he loved having his Head in the academic side of software engineering, but his Heart remained in its practice. You can take the man out of industry, apparently, but you can't take the industry out of the man. With that new-found wisdom, he began to search for ways to bridge what he had long felt was the "Communication Chasm" between academic computing and its practice.

He found several ways of doing that. Many of his books (over 20) and professional papers (over 60) focus on trying to evaluate academic research findings and on transitioning those with practical value to industry. (This is decidedly a non-trivial task, and is largely responsible for the contrarian nature of his beliefs and his writings.) His lectures and seminars on software engineering focus on both theoretical and best-of-practice findings that are useful to practitioners. His two newsletters, *The Software Practitioner* and *PERC* (*Practical Emerging Research Concepts in Information Technology*), trod those same paths. So does the (more academic) Journal of Systems and Software, which he edits for Elsevier. And so do the columns he writes regularly for such publications as Communications of the ACM, Journal of Systems and Software, Managing System Development, and ACM SIGMIS's Data Base. Although most of his work is serious and contrarian, a fair portion of it also contains (or even consists of!) computing humor.

With all of that in mind, what is his proudest moment in the computing field? The award, by Linköping University of Sweden, of his honorary Ph.D. degree in 1995.

PART

1

Introduction

It is only possible to succeed at second-rate pursuits—like becoming a millionaire or a prime minister, winning a war, seducing a beautiful woman, flying through the stratosphere, or landing on the moon. First-rate pursuits—involving, as they must, trying to understand what life is about and trying to convey that understanding—inevitably result in a sense of failure. A Napoleon, a Churchill, a Roosevelt can feel themselves to be successful, but never a Socrates, a Pascal, a Blake. Understanding is forever unattainable. Therein lies the inevitability of failure in embarking upon its quest, which is none the less the only one worthy of serious attention.

—Malcolm Muggeridge,
from his "Woman's Hour" radio broadcast, August 5, 1965, and later quoted in many places including Ed Yourdon's book Death March.

The bulk of this book is made up of war stories—in-depth yet interesting analyses of software runaway projects, often prominent ones, extracted from the literature. That literature includes popular-press accounts (e.g., the *Wall Street Journal*), computing-press accounts (e.g., *InformationWeek*), and academic accounts (e.g., a Harvard Case Study). But before we get to those war stories—that will happen in Chapter 2—there are some words of introduction that are needed. We will answer the definitional question "What is a software runaway?" in Section 1.1. We will deal with the claims that software practice is a discipline in crisis in Section 1.2. We will talk about some related but different ideas—what happens when projects find themselves in "crunch mode," and what constitutes a "death march" project, in Section 1.3. And to close this chapter, we will present some fascinating findings of a research study that explored the notion of software runaways, and drew some diverse and important conclusions about them.

1.1 WHAT IS A SOFTWARE RUNAWAY?

Press reports of systems failures caused by software are often spectacular. "Company XYZ," they say, "is M months behind schedule and D dollars over budget in producing system SYS, and it looks inevitable that the project will be canceled, costing the company BUX dollars overall." And when you look at M and D and BUX, they are represented by really large numbers, the kind with lots of zeroes after them.

The main thrust of this book is to present the stories of some of those XYZs and SYSs, including how they screwed up at the M and D level, and how many BUX were really lost. As you will see in that material, XYZs represent some of the better-known companies in the business of producing systems, and the SYSs include some highly-visible projects that appeared more often in the press than their developers could ever have imagined or wished.

But before we get into those stories, there is—as we say in the software business—some initialization to be performed. That is, it is important to put those stories into an overall context. Setting that context is the role of these initializing, introductory sections.

First of all, what is a software runaway? It is

> a project that goes out of control primarily because of the difficulty of building the software needed by the system.

The implication of "out of control" is that the project became unmanageable; it was not possible to manage it to meet its original target goals, or to come even close to them. If those goals are thought of in terms of schedule—and this is the most likely kind of runaway—then the project consumed close to double its allotted estimated time or more. If the goal was cost, and usually projects that go well over budget also exceed cost targets, then the project consumed close to double its estimated cost or more. If the goal was a reliable product that met its functional requirements, then the product could not meet those targets, and in fact, all too often, failed to meet any targets at all because the project had to be canceled.

Our definition differs from a somewhat better-known definition. KPMG's says

> A runaway project is one which has failed significantly to achieve its objectives and/or has exceeded its original budget by at least 30 percent [KPMG 1995].

As you can see, the KPMG definition of runaway is far more inclusive than ours. That is, if a project is somewhat over cost targets, 30 percent or more, by the KPMG definition that would be a runaway, whereas by ours it would not (it would have to exceed by 100 percent to meet ours). Using the KPMG definition, there would be a lot more runaway projects than we would include. The reason we mention the KPMG definition at all, given our difference with its quantitative representation, is that it comes from the only research studies we are aware of on runaway projects. In 1989 and again in 1995, KPMG performed a survey of runaway projects to determine their frequency, their causes, the remedies tried, and the effect of the runaway on the enterprise where it happened. We will present those research findings in subsequent sections of this chapter.

Why are we so fussy about the definition of runaway? The reason is this: It is now 1998, and we are only 40 something years into the history of the software field. At this primitive, early stage, the most common problem in building software systems is not the construction of them itself, but rather the estimation of the costs of that construction. Why is there such a problem of estimation? Because the software field has not made a conscientious effort to develop histories of past project costs. Because the construction of software is an extremely complex task—some say it is the most complex task ever undertaken by human beings.

Because of the lack of history and the amount of complexity, a barrier was produced that no amount of mathematical techniques and no amount of savvy, individual expertise has been able to overcome. It is all too common for a software project to fail to meet its cost and schedule targets, because those targets themselves were simply (and grossly!) wrong.

It is our belief that a runaway project is one that fails for a reason more profound than poor estimation. That is why we have raised the barrier beyond the KPMG 30 percent figure—we want to make sure that those projects that we call runaways are so called because the development effort itself got out of control, regardless of whether the original estimates were close to the correct figures or not. Often, a project can exceed bad cost targets by more than 30 percent without being a troubled or failed project. It is our intent not to include such projects under our runaway umbrella, even though the KPMG study would.

REFERENCE

KPMG 1995, "Runaway Projects—Cause and Effects," *Software World* (UK), Vol. 26, No. 3, Andy Cole of KPMG.

1.2   THE CRIES OF SOFTWARE CRISIS

It has been common over the last decade or so to see a mention of the "software crisis" in computing literature and sometimes even in the popular press. Although different writers seem to use the term to mean different things, the most common definition of software crisis is this:

> Software is always over budget, behind schedule, and unreliable.

It is important to me, however, to say here at the outset of this discussion that

> I do not believe in the existence of a software crisis.

It is important that I take that position fairly early in this book, because otherwise it would be easy to conclude that the author of a book on software runaways felt that those runaways were symptoms of, and examples from, the software crisis. And nothing could be further from the truth.

There are lots of runaways, of course. This book will tell those stories. But it is my belief that the incidence of those runaways represents a tiny percentage of all the software projects ever attempted.

It is interesting to note that there have been many estimates provided by those who do believe in a software crisis as to the frequency of such projects. But there is a fundamental problem with those estimates, they differ all over the map! The most famous numbers, derived from a Government Accounting Office study, were that upwards of 98 percent of projects failed ("less than 2 percent of the software contracted for was usable as delivered"). But there was a serious problem with those numbers—the GAO study was of several projects that were in trouble—that's why the GAO studied them—and thus it is not surprising (nor very informative!) that 98 percent of software projects that are in trouble eventually fail. (For a refutation of the misuse of the GAO numbers, see [Blum 1991].)

Many authors and speakers have repeated that GAO finding, without really appreciating that the study was about something different from what they thought it was. But even those who have not repeated that 98 percent number have come up with huge percentages of failed software projects—I have seen numbers such as 60 percent, and 48 percent, and 35 percent, in various places in the literature. It is my personal belief that there is no more reason to believe those numbers than to believe the GAO 98 percent number. The fact of the matter is, no one has really sufficiently performed a survey to tell us what percentage of software projects fail. In fact, hardly anyone has come up with an adequate definition of failure, which of course would be necessary before that survey could have any meaning. Note the difficulty we have already encountered in this book in defining "runaway," surely an easier term to define than "failure" since a runaway is in a sense more spectacular.

I am particularly incensed about these cries of software crisis and their fraudulent quantifications for two reasons:

1. There is an implication in the cries of crisis that software practitioners are the original Mr. Bumble, unable to program their way out of a paper bag.

2. There is an implication also that software practice is, in general, full of failure, and that few successes have been achieved.

My own belief is that those implications are terribly wrong. When I look around, I see a world in which computers and their software are dependable and indispensable. They make my plane reservations, control my banking transactions, and send people into space—with enormous dependability.

Why, then, are there so many crying crisis? Because they have something to gain by doing so. Some vendors cry crisis in order to sell products or services that they claim will offer a cure. Some researchers cry crisis in order to obtain funding for research projects that they claim will also (eventually) offer a cure. Some academics cry crisis in order to motivate the acceptance and reading of their professional papers that suggest a cure. Hardly a disinterested collection of people.

There is, in fact, a funny thing about the cries of crisis (if a problem with such serious implications could ever be funny). Most of those who cry crisis and are trying to sell or promote something are offering a better technology for building software. But most of the case studies of software failure find that poor management technique, not poor technology, is the cause of the problems. Thus even if there were a software crisis, the offerings of these people would not—and could not—solve the problem.

In fact, the findings of the KPMG study mentioned earlier, and our own findings in this book, will show that, more recently, technology is becoming a more common cause of software failures. But the real irony is this: Most of those technology-based failures are caused, in fact, by the very technologies that others have proposed as solutions. The same tendency toward hype that allows these people to cry crisis in the first place also allows them to make excessive and erroneous claims for the benefits of those technologies. There are stories later in this book where projects became runaways *because of* the use of such technologies as formal methods, expert systems, and fourth generation languages. Far from becoming cures, sometimes those technologies become albatrosses, dragging a project down toward defeat.

The cries of crisis, in fact, represent something of a "blame the victim" mentality. We have already noted that, when software projects fail to achieve cost and schedule targets, it is often those targets themselves that are at fault. Thus software practitioners, laboring to achieve impossible goals, and all too often putting in tons of voluntary overtime to try to meet them in spite of their impossibility, end up being blamed for a problem that was out of their control from the beginning of the project. Study after study of software estimation in practice has shown that most often cost and schedule targets are set by marketers or customers, next most often by managers, and least often by the technologists who will do the work. Without control of their own destiny, practitioners still get blamed when things go wrong.

Because of all of the above, I would like us all to pause, at this point in the reading of this book, for a moment of appreciation. Here's to all those pioneering software practitioners who have struggled through the barriers in their paths to make our era truly the Computing Era, the half-century or so in which computing has been the dominant force in our society. May they be appreciated for their efforts, and lauded for their successes!

REFERENCE

Blum 1991, "Some Very Famous Statistics," the *Software Practitioner,* March 1991, Bruce I. Blum.

1.3 "CRUNCH MODE" AND THE "DEATH MARCH" PROJECT

Colorful terminology is de rigueur for computing people. We invent new terms and new acronyms at the drop of a hat. It has gotten so bad that we've even invented a term for that profusion of terms— "Computerese" is the word we've coined for the specialized language in which computer people discuss things.

"Runaway" is one such term; "software crisis" is another. In this section, I'd like to talk about two more, related, terms—"Crunch Mode" and "Death March."

Crunch Mode is a term used by John Boddie in his book of the same name [Boddie 1987]. It is a term describing the status of a project. A project that is in crunch mode is there due to a threat to its reaching its original targets (cost, schedule, functionality, . . .), and the project team is working very hard to try to overcome that dilemma. "We're in crunch mode, and I won't be home 'til after midnight," a software specialist might say in a call from the office to his life partner. The life partner probably won't be surprised—crunch mode tends to last for days, weeks, or even months, depending on the duration of the project itself, and the degree to which it is off-target. The term crunch mode itself was not invented by Boddie. It was invented by the software practitioners who found themselves under the gun to finish the project they were working on.

Death March is a term used by Ed Yourdon in his book of the same name [Yourdon 1997]. It is a term that also describes the status of a project. A project is a death march if the parameters for that project exceed the norm by at least 50 percent. (The parameters might include schedule, staffing, budget, and functionality.) "This is a death march project, and I hope to avoid becoming a part of it," a software specialist might say in a call from the office to his life partner. The life partner probably has heard all of this before; unfortunately, all too many software projects these days are death marches, and the life partner probably knows—perhaps more than even the software specialist—that avoiding participation is unlikely. The term death march was not invented by Yourdon. It was invented by people who found themselves involved in projects for which the only hope of achieving those unreasonable targets was to work far harder and far longer than normal. Unfortunately, as Yourdon points out in the preface of his book, death march projects have become the norm, not the exception.

So what's the difference between all these terms? Obviously, they are all dancing around the same general subject. But there is a difference:

1. Crunch mode is used to describe a project that has an extremely tight schedule. It speaks to the pressures being felt by the project participants.

2. Death march is used to describe a project that has a nearly impossible schedule. It speaks to the oppressive smell of potential failure surrounding the project participants.

3. Runaway is used to describe a project nearing or after its termination. It speaks to the failure of the project to stay within its boundaries. Often it speaks about a project that has either already failed (usually in a spectacular way), or is about to.

A typical project to which these terms might apply could progress in the following way: The project looks from the outset to be crunch mode because someone has promised project results that are too much, too soon. As the project gets underway, project participants all too soon find themselves on a death march, trying to achieve these increasingly unachievable targets. When it becomes obvious that the project probably cannot succeed and will fail in a major way, the project becomes a runaway.

Not all projects that are death marches fail, of course (remember that the death march is the normal way of running a project these days, according to [Yourdon 1997]. Although some of those death marches become runaways, others will become successes). But all of them, successes or failures, will have functioned in crunch mode.

Most people, given their choice, would not want to participate in a death march, would not want to find themselves in crunch mode, and would never, ever, want to be on a runaway. But project managers have found a way to entice people into participation. They use a process called "signing up" (described in [Kidder 1981]), that dangles so many benefits[1] in front of the prospective participant that they simply can't say no.

Why do we have such terms and such projects? The fact that these terms are needed by the computing field speaks of the intense pressure in our era put on project completion. Usually systems projects are managed by schedule—that is, the responsible manager examines project progress against a predetermined schedule of events,[2] and all too often that schedule is unreasonably short, and those events are thus late in occurring. Because we know so little about accurate schedule estimation, and because estimates are usually made by the people who are least able to make accurate estimates (e.g., marketers and customers), it is simply the norm that schedule targets, and thus cost targets, are unreasonably short. Thus project achievement of them is at best problematic. This is, of course, not a problem unique to the systems and software field. Given the intense competitive pressures of the last half of the 20th century, workers in all fields find themselves under the gun to do more than they can in too short a time. The problem for systems and software is worsened, however, by the fact that the field is so young, and because we know so little about it compared to other fields, we are really never quite sure that an unreasonable schedule is, in fact, THAT unreasonable.

REFERENCES

Boddie 1987, *Crunch Mode*, Yourdon Press, 1987, John Boddie.

Kidder 1981, *The Soul of a New Machine*, Little-Brown, 1981, Tracy Kidder.

Yourdon 1997, *Death March*, Prentice Hall, 1997, Ed Yourdon.

1. Software personnel are motivated by things such as challenging projects and/ or a chance to use new technology rather than the more traditional ones of power or money.
2. The schedule is often made up of "milestones." If these milestones are extremely detailed, they are sometimes called "inch-pebbles."

1.4   SOME RELEVANT RESEARCH FINDINGS

Research in the computing field is all too often focused on theory to the exclusion of practice. That is, computing researchers are very interested in developing new algorithms, new data representations, or new formal methods, but very seldom are they interested in the formalization of best practices or the learning experiences that can be derived from worst practices.

That is an important failure of the computing research field. It is well known in other fields that practice sometimes leads (is more advanced than) theory; I will not belabor the point here (it is belabored elsewhere, such as in [Glass 1989] and [Glass 1990]!), except to point out that the invention of the steam engine preceded the development of the theory of thermodynamics, and the invention of the airplane preceded the development of the theory of aerodynamics. In a newly-emerging field—and what field in our time is more "newly-emerging" than software?—there is a great deal that theory can learn by studying practice (some theorists even say that "theory is the formalization of practice"), and computing theorists are not taking advantage of that possibility.

All of that is prelude to this good news and bad news:

1. The bad news is that there are few research studies of runaway projects. There are case studies of individual runaways (that is what this book is primarily about), usually appearing in the popular computing press rather than the theoretic literature, but there has been little organized research attempting to study runaways in more breadth in order to grapple with the lessons that might be learned from doing so.

2. The good news is that there is one such recent study, and it is an excellent one. It is published in what to most of us jingoistic Americans is an obscure journal, but nevertheless it is a superb study of the trends in, reasons for, remedies attempted, and aftermath of software runaway projects [KPMG 1995].

In fact, that research study is actually about two such studies. Not only do we have the findings of the study published in 1995, but that study also reflects on the findings of the same study performed by the same organization in 1989. In other words, we not only can learn some things about contemporary software runaway projects, but we can learn some things about the trends in such projects.

In reporting on the findings of these studies, I would like to divide their discoveries into three categories. The first is *predictable* findings. The software engineering literature contributes considerable insight into what to do, and what not to do, during a software project. The predictable findings reflect what we already know from that literature. (It is important, of course, for research to study those predictions in order to determine what can be supported by empirical findings and what cannot. Those that cannot should be quickly relegated to the category of "old wives' (or husbands') tales," and not passed on through the literature any more.

The second category I would call *surprising* findings. There are usually fewer surprising findings than predictable ones, but in a sense surprising findings are more important than predictable ones, since they provide us with new insight into our field. And, in the case of the KPMG study, there are actually *more* surprising findings than predictable ones.

The third category I will call *trends*. Because the study was conducted in both 1989 and 1995, the author of [KPMG 1995] had a unique opportunity to present us with observations that take into account the lapse of six years between the studies.

The predictable findings are:

1. Many of the runaway projects are (or were) "overly ambitious." It is well known in the field that large projects are problematic.

2. Most of the projects failed from a multiplicity of causes. There may or may not have been a dominant cause, but there were several problems contributing to many of the runaways.

3. Management problems were more frequently a dominant cause than technical problems. But see the list of surprising findings below.

4. Schedule overruns were more common (89 percent) than cost overruns (62 percent).

The surprising findings are:

1. Survey respondents thought that there would be more runaways in the government and financial sectors, and fewer in service and manufacturing. But the survey findings found all such sectors equally susceptible.

2. Respondents were optimistic about the trend in runaways; 42 percent believed they would decrease in number, while only 8 percent felt they would increase.

3. The use of packaged software did not help in reducing the incidence of runaways. Of the runaway projects studied, 47 percent consisted of mixed custom and packaged software; 24 percent were custom software; and 22 percent were packaged software.

4. Runaway projects showed their true colors early in the project history. More than half started showing symptoms during system development, and 25 percent showed those symptoms during initial planning.

5. In spite of the above, visibility into the existence of a runaway came first of all from the project team (72 percent); only 19 percent were spotted initially at the senior management level.

6. Technology is dramatically increasing as a cause of runaways. "Technology new to the organization" was the fourth most common problem in the runaway projects. See this topic discussed also under trends, below.

7. Risk management appears more and more frequently in the software management literature. But 55 percent of the runaway projects had not performed any risk management, and of those 38 percent who did (some respondees did not know whether it was used or not), half of them did not use the risk findings once the project was underway.

The trends are:

1. Companies were much more reluctant to discuss runaway projects in 1995 than they were in 1989. The number of respondees in the newer study was half that of the earlier one,

in spite of the fact that the survey population (about 250 major organizations) was roughly the same.

2. Technology is a rapidly increasing *cause* of runaway projects. Whereas in 1989 only 7 percent reported it as a cause, in 1995 the figure was 45 percent. (Interestingly, only 16 percent of respondents felt the technology was "wrong" for the job.) [KPMG 1995] concludes "Technology is developing faster than the skills of the developers." (This conclusion will be questioned in what follows.)

It is important to say several things about this study as we consider these predictable and surprising findings and trends:

1. The definition of runaway used in this study is different from that used in this book (this was discussed earlier in Section 1.1). Far more projects would be considered runaways by the definition used in the KPMG study ("a project that has failed significantly to achieve its objectives and/or has exceeded its original budget by at least 30 percent") than by the more restrictive definition we use ("a project that goes out of control primarily because of the difficulty of building the software needed by the system," where "out of control" is taken to mean "schedule, cost, or functionality that was twice as bad as that sought").

2. The survey was conducted only in the UK (there were 250 major enterprises contacted). In this book, on the other hand, most of the projects discussed are American. We are not saying that we know of any differences in runaway projects caused by country of origin; we are only saying that we would prefer to put that fact on the table in case it is discovered to be important by later studies.

3. The surprising trend in technology as a problem may be the single most important finding of the survey. As noted above, the KPMG study concludes that the problem usually lay not with the technology, but rather with the ability of the software practitioners to utilize it. Our analysis of the runaways in this book suggests a different conclusion. Although our sample is

considerably smaller than that of the KPMG study, it is clear from the projects we examined that (a) new technology was also a frequent cause of problems, and (b) the reason was that the technology was used prematurely or inappropriately. For example, one project used a 4GL that was clearly inappropriate for the large project on which it was attempted (performance was inadequate for the large number of users projected), and another made a point of using several different advanced technologies (formal methods, expert systems, etc.) and failed because those technologies were not yet ready for the kind of large project use on which they were attempted. Our conclusion is that it is often the technologies themselves (particularly either their inability to scale up or the lack of a track record of scaling them up) rather than the technologists, who are primarily at fault when technology fails and a runaway ensues.

There are two other conclusions that might be drawn from our own runaway reports in this book that are not found in the KPMG study. They are:

1. Early on, those responsible for our runaway projects often bragged about the "breakthrough" nature of the project, either in terms of its business relevance or its technical (computing) advances. There seemed to be little or no understanding by those making such claims of the perilous course they were undertaking. (In fact, for one of our runaways, a report appeared in the computing literature bragging about the project *after* it was known to have become a runaway!) In some ways this contradicts one of the conclusions drawn in the KPMG study: that many runaways are "misconceived to start with." Or perhaps it is not a contradiction—the projects were, in fact, misconceived; it was just that certain key players didn't know it yet! (This, in fact, matches the KPMG finding that runaway projects were spotted more often at the team level than the management level.)

2. Of all the technology problems noted earlier, the most dominant one in our own findings in this book is that

performance is a frequent cause of failure. (This was not noted at all in the KPMG study.) A fairly large number of our runaway projects were real-time in nature, and it was not uncommon to find that the project could not achieve the response times and/or functional performance times demanded by the original requirements. This is an important finding; it has become popular now to say that with the rise in speed of marketplace computers, there is no longer a need for software people to take responsibility for product performance. This saying is manifested in several ways, the most important of which is that there is little in computer science or information systems education having to do with improving software performance, or providing for it in the first place. Since poor performance may be difficult to overcome once it has been built into a project (by using an interpretive 4GL or 3GL, for example, instead of a 3GL with an optimizing compiler), this lack could be contributing to the incidence of runaways.

3. There was one other problem in our runaways that was not mentioned in the KPMG study. A significant number of the runaway projects were in an application domain that might be called "movement of goods." As you will see in the stories of Chapter 2, there were two warehousing applications and one baggage handling application among our collection. The KPMG study, by contrast, felt that there was no one business sector that was more likely to have runaways. (It may be that the difference here is one of semantics; KPMG was talking about what might be called "industries," and we are discussing something below that level that we would call "domains." It may well be that there is no difference in likelihood across sectors (industries), but there is across domains.) It will be interesting to watch for this difference in future such studies (we hope there will be lots of them!).

There is one more, perhaps the most important, idea to utilize from the KPMG study. One of the primary findings of the study was that of identifying the "six top problems" that arose during runaway projects. Those six top problems become the organizational, outlining device we use in Chapter 2 of this book. Using those six findings as section numbers in the chapter (2.1 through 2.6), we slot the runaway war stories that we have found into those causes. (You will note that we have also identified a Section 2.7 to cover causes "Other" than those identified by KPMG. This is largely an opportunity to list the runaways that failed from performance problems.)

And now, enough of this initialization, this introductory material. The context for our war stories has been set. Let us turn to those stories themselves for the primary lessons, and the most fascinating material of this book.

REFERENCES

Glass 1989, "The Temporal Relationship Between Theory and Practice," *Journal of Systems and Software*, July 1989, Robert L. Glass.

Glass 1990, "Theory vs. Practice—Revisited," *Journal of Systems and Software*, May 1990, Robert L. Glass.

KPMG 1995, "Runaway Projects—Causes and Effects," *Software World* (UK), Vol. 26, No. 3, 1995, Andy Cole of KPMG.

PART 2

Software Runaway
War Stories

Frankly, one of the challenges facing Microsoft is that many of its employees have not suffered much failure yet. Quite a few have never been involved with a project that didn't succeed. As a result, success may be taken for granted, which is dangerous . . . When you're failing, you're forced to be creative, to dig deep and think hard, night and day. Every company needs people who have been through that.

—Bill Gates, in "The Importance of Making Mistakes,"
USAir Magazine, July 1995.

Here they are, the war stories we have been promising you in this book about software runaway projects. As an organizational scheme, we divide these war stories into several categories identified in the research study discussed in the previous section. In that study, it was found that runaway projects could be categorized by their primary cause. These causes, in order of decreasing importance, are each preceded by the section number assigned to them in this chapter; they are:

- ◆ 2.1 Project Objectives Not Fully Specified—51 percent

- ◆ 2.2 Bad Planning and Estimating—48 percent

- ◆ 2.3 Technology New to the Organization—45 percent

- ◆ 2.4 Inadequate/No Project Management Methodology—42 percent

- ◆ 2.5 Insufficient Senior Staff on the Team—42 percent

- ◆ 2.6 Poor Performance by Suppliers of Hardware/Software—42 percent

(Percentages are estimates; the research study presented them in graphical form, and the numbers themselves were not present in the paper).

We add another category to this chapter:

- ◆ 2.7 Other—Performance (Efficiency) Problems

This latter category was not present in the research study. However, as we examined the various war stories that we will present, and assigned each to one of the above sections based on its dominant cause, we discovered some war stories that simply didn't match the prime causes found in the research work. "Other" is the catch-all we invented to cover those stories; they consist primarily of software runaways caused by performance problems. That is, the software was unable to run fast enough to meet user needs.

Except for the "Other" category, the war stories that constitute this book fit comfortably within the organizational framework resulting from the research study. And that, in turn, suggests that, for the most part, our war stories reflect the software runaway patterns discovered by the research.

In the material of each section that follows, we will say a little bit more about the runaway cause that constitutes the section title and then present our runaway stories that fit that particular cause.

Enough introduction! On with the stories.

2.1   *PROJECT OBJECTIVES NOT FULLY SPECIFIED*

There is little doubt that project requirements are the single biggest cause of trouble on the software project front. Study after study has found that where there is a failure, requirements problems are usually found at the heart of the matter.

Requirements problems occur when:

1. There are far too many of them. Huge projects fail far more often than smaller ones.

2. They are unstable. The users cannot decide what problem they really want to solve.

3. They are ambiguous. It is not possible to determine what the requirements really mean.

4. They are incomplete. There is insufficient information to allow a system to be built.

There are other possible problems with requirements, but the above list covers the most common ones. And, in fact, the first two rise head and shoulders above the others. Huge projects as well as projects whose requirements cannot be pinned down dominate the list of project runaway causes.

In a sense, nearly all of the runaway war stories in Chapter 2 have requirements problems. But in assigning the war stories to the categories obtained from the research study discussed in Section 1.4, there were three projects that suffered most clearly from requirements trouble. They are the Denver International Airport Baggage-Handling System, the Florida Welfare System, and the FAA Air Traffic Control System.

At Denver, those responsible for the system tried to scale a relatively simple system into a far more complicated one, thereby causing a spectacular schedule overrun that made the nightly news and the newspapers more often than any other software project failure story in history! In the final analysis, those scaled-up-to-huge requirements, unstable due to these changes, had to be scaled back to the original system in order to be able to make the project work at all.

In Florida, the responsible people tried to use a centralized system from another state as the basis for a decentralized project in Florida, leading to a host of problems with increasingly ugly contractual, and political implications.

At the FAA, it was once again a mismanaged requirements story but with a different verse. The requirements for the originally proposed system were so huge that it is still unclear if such a system could be built. De-scoping the massive project to a more modest but achievable target appears now to be the way out of the morass. Only time will tell. We use two very different articles to tell the FAA story; as presented in the second of them, it is noted that several people who look at an event may see it quite differently.

With that as an introduction, let's move directly to these war stories.

2.1.1   *BAE AUTOMATED SYSTEMS (A):*
DENVER INTERNATIONAL AIRPORT
BAGGAGE-HANDLING SYSTEM

No airport anywhere in the world is as technologically advanced as the Denver International Airport.[1]

It's dramatic. If your bag (got) on the track, your bag was in pieces.[2]

In November 1989 ground was broken to build the Denver International Airport (DIA). Located 25 miles from downtown Denver, Colorado, it was first major airport to be built in the United States since the opening of the Dallas-Fort Worth Airport in 1974. In 1992, two years into construction, the project's top managers recommended inclusion of an airport-wide integrated baggage-handling system that could dramatically improve the efficiency of luggage delivery. Originally contracted by United Airlines to cover its operations, the system was to be expanded to serve the entire airport. It was expected that the integrated system would improve ground time efficiency, reduce close-out time for hub operations, and decrease time-consuming manual baggage sorting and handling. There were, however, a number of risks inherent in the en-

1. Fred Isaac, Federal Aviation Administration regional administrator, quoted in "Denver Still Working Out Kinks as Its First Birthday Arrives," *USA Today* (February 28, 1996), p. 4b.
2. Fred Renville, United Airlines employee quoted in "Denver Still Working Out Kinks as Its First Birthday Arrives," *USA Today* (February 28, 1996), p. 4b.

This article and the one that follows were originally published as a Harvard Business School case study.

Assistant Professor Ramiro Montealegre and Research Associate H. James Nelson of the University of Colorado at Boulder, Research Associate Carin Isabel Knoop, and Professor Lynda M. Applegate prepared this case as the basis for class discussion rather than to illustrate either effective or ineffective handling of an administrative situation. Some names have been disguised.

deavor: the scale of the large project size; the enormous complexity of the expanded system; the newness of the technology; the large number of resident entities to be served by the same system; the high degree of technical and project definition uncertainty; and the short time span for completion. Due to its significant experience implementing baggage-handling technology on a smaller scale, BAE Automated Systems Inc., an engineering consulting and manufacturing company based in Carollton, Texas, was awarded the contract.

Construction problems kept the new airport from opening on the originally scheduled opening date in October 1993. Subsequently, problems with the implementation of the baggage system forced delays in the opening of the airport another three times in seven months. In May 1994, under growing pressure from shareholders, the business community, Denver residents, Federal Aviation Administration (FAA) commissioners, and the tenant airlines and concessionaires, Denver mayor Wellington Webb announced that he was hiring the German firm Logplan to help assess the project. Logplan characterized BAE's system as "highly advanced" and "theoretically" capable of living up to its promised capacities, services and performances," but acknowledged mechanical and electrical problems that "make it most improbable to achieve a stable and reliable operation." Logplan suggested that it would take approximately five months to get the complete BAE system working reliably. It also suggested that a backup system of tugs, carts, and conveyor belts could be constructed in less than five months.

In August 1994, Mayor Webb approved the construction of a backup baggage system. At the same time, he notified BAE of a $1200-a-day penalty for not finishing the baggage system by DIA's original October 29, 1993 completion date. Webb also demanded that BAE pay for the $50 million conventional tug-and-cart baggage system. Gene Di Fonso, President of BAE, knew that his company could demonstrate that flaws in the overall design of the airport and an unsystematic approach to project changes had affected implementation of the integrated baggage system. He wondered whether he should just cancel the contract and cut his losses, or attempt to negotiate with the city for the support required to finish the system as specified, despite the severe deterioration in communication and rising hostility. Could the problems with the automated system be overcome with the dedication of additional resources? Given that the system represented a significant departure from conventional technology, would reducing its size and complexity facilitate resolution of the problems that plagued it? And, if the city could not be persuaded to accept a simplified system, would the tenant airlines, particularly those with hubbing operations that had been promised more advanced functionality and better performance, be likely to follow suit?

Building the Most Efficient Airport in the World

Until about 1970, Denver's Stapleton Airport had managed to accommodate an ever-growing number of airplanes and passengers. Its operational capacity was severely limited by runway layout; Stapleton had two parallel north-south runways and two additional parallel east-west runways that accommodated only commuter air carriers.

Denver's economy grew and expanded greatly in the early 1980s, consequent to booms in the oil, real estate, and tourism industries. An aging and saturated Stapleton Airport was increasingly seen as a liability that limited the attractiveness of the region to the many businesses that were flocking to it. Delays had become chronic. Neither the north-south nor east-west parallel runways had sufficient lateral separation to accommodate simultaneous parallel arrival streams during poor weather conditions when instrument flight rules were in effect. This lack of runway separation and the layout of Stapleton's taxiways tended to cause delays during high-traffic periods, even when weather conditions were good.

Denver's geographic location and the growing size of its population and commerce made it an attractive location for airline hubbing operations. At one point, Stapleton had housed four airline hubs, more than any other airport in the United States. In poor weather and during periods of high-traffic volume, however, its limitations disrupted connection schedules that were important to maintaining these operations. A local storm could easily congest air traffic across the entire United States.[3]

The City and County of Denver had determined in the mid-1970s that Stapleton International Airport was in need of expansion or replacement. In July 1979, a study to assess the airport's needs was commissioned by the City of Denver to the Denver Regional Council of Governments. Upon completion of the study in 1983, a report was issued saying that, due to its size and geographic location, and strong commitments by United and Continental Airlines, Denver would remain a significant hub for at least one major U.S. carrier. The study recommended expansion, rather than relocation, of Stapleton International Airport onto land currently occupied by the Rocky Mountain Arsenal.[4]

Political Situation[5]

The City of Denver's 1983 mayoral politics precipitated initiatives to improve the airfield infrastructure. Three candidates were in the race: Monte Pascoe, Dale Tooley, and Frederico Peña. Pascoe, a prominent Denver attorney and former State Democratic party co-chair, seized upon the airport issue, forcing other candidates to adopt stronger positions on airport expansion than they might have otherwise.[6] Peña and Tooley, however, drew the highest numbers of votes in the general election, and were forced into a runoff. At the

3. According to James Barnes [1993], "By 1994, Stapleton was one of the top five most constrained airports in the U.S. There were over 50,000 hours of delay in 1988 and by 1997 the FAA had projected that Stapleton would experience over 100,000 hours of delay per year."
4. The Arsenal was used since 1943 by the U.S. Army as a chemical weapons production facility. In the 1950s, production stopped and by the late 1970s the Army was surveying the scope and types of contamination of the site. For more details refer to Wiely, K. and S. Rhodes: "Decontaminating Federal Facilities: The Case of the Rocky Mountain Arsenal," *Environment*, Vol. 23, No. 3, April 1987, pp 17–33.
5. Extracted from: Moore, S.T.: "Between Growth Machine and Garbage Can: Determining Whether to Expand the Denver Airport, 1982–1988," Annual Meeting of the Southern Political Science Association, Atlanta, Georgia, November 4, 1994.
6. Ibid.

persistent urging of the Colorado Forum (a collection of 50 of the state's top business executives), Peña and Tooley signed a joint statement committing themselves to airport expansion onto the Arsenal. Peña won the runoff. Committed by a public promise that could have been enforced, if necessary, by the most highly motivated members of the region's business leadership, Peña immediately restated his intent to expand Stapleton.

The City of Denver and neighboring Adams County had begun to develop plans for long-term airport development in 1984. In 1985, a new site northeast of Denver was chosen. Consummation of the airport siting issue, however, was left to Adams County voters, which had to vote to permit the City of Denver to annex property therein. The city hired a consulting firm to help organize its resources and its efforts to work through the legal process. The data that was gathered through the master planning and environmental assessment later proved useful for public education.

An "Annexation Agreement" between Adams County and the City of Denver was reached on April 21, 1988. Adams County voters approved a plan to let Denver annex 43.3 square miles for the construction of an airport. In a special election on May 16, 1989, voters of Denver endorsed a "New Airport" by a margin of 62.7% to 37.3%. According to Edmond, "Those two referendums passed largely on the merits of the economic benefits: jobs and sales tax revenues."

Economic Considerations

A number of trends and events in the mid-1980s alarmed bank economists and other of the region's business leaders. The collapse of oil shale ventures between 1982 and 1986 saw mining employment fall from 42,000 to 26,000 jobs, while service support jobs fell from 25,300 jobs to 13,700.[7] Construction jobs fell from 50,700 to 36,600 jobs, and the value of private construction plummeted from $24 billion to $9.5 billion.[8]

---

7. *Colorado Business Outlook Forum*, University of Colorado School of Business, 1990.
8. *Small Area Employment Estimates; Construction Review*, U.S. Department of Commerce, 1990.

A lackluster economy led many government officials in counties and municipalities as well as in Denver to embark upon an unprecedented policy of massive public construction to save the region from what was regarded in 1987 as an economic free-fall. A $180 million-plus municipal bond was issued for public improvements, including a new downtown library, neighborhood and major roadway improvements, and a host of overdue infrastructure investments. During the same period, the Peña administration moved decisively to confront an increasingly aggressive Chamber of Commerce leadership that was promoting airport relocation.

The determination of the "pro-New-Airport" clan was growing. The project was being marketed as a technologically advanced, state-of-the-art structure to draw businesses, import federal capital, and fund the creation of new jobs with bonded debts to overcome the short-term decline in the economy. The airport was to become a grandiose project to revive the Colorado economy and a master showcase for the Public Works Department. "The entire business community," recalled a member of the Mayor's administrative team:

> The Chamber of Commerce, members of the city council, the mayor, and state legislators, participated in informational discussions with other cities that had recently built airports. [This enabled] everybody to understand the magnitude of the project. So we studied the other two airports that had been built in the United States in the last 50 years and said, "Tell us everything that you went through and all the places you think there will be problems." We were not going into it blindly.

Forecasts of aviation activity at Stapleton by the Airport Consultant team, the FAA, and others, however, did not anticipate events such as a new phase of post-deregulation consolidation, the acquisition in 1986 of Frontier Airlines by Texas Air (the owner of Continental), significant increases in air fares for flights in and out of Stapleton, and the bankruptcy of Continental. Consequently, the level of aviation activity in Denver was overestimated. Instead of rising, Stapleton's share of total U.S. domestic passenger enplanements fell 4 percent per year from 1986 through 1989.[9]

The Master Plan

The City of Denver's approach to preparing a master plan for the airport was typical. "One hires the best consultants on airfield layout, noise impacts, terminal layout, on-site roadways, off-site roadways, cost estimating, financial analysis, and forecasting," observed DIA administrator Gail Edmond. "They brainstorm and generate as many alternate layouts as possible." Alternatives were discussed and eliminated at periodic joint working sessions, and a technical subcommittee was organized to gather input from the eventual airport users, airlines, pilots, and the FAA. "Everybody knows how to begin an airport master plan," Edmond added.

Following a bid, the consulting contract was awarded to the joint venture of Greiner, Inc. and Morrison-Knudsen Engineers for their combined expertise in the fields of transportation and construction. The consulting team, working under the direction of the DIA Director of Aviation, focused first on four elements: site selection; the master plan; the environmental assessment; and developing support by educating the public on economic benefit. The final master plan presented to the city by the team in the fall of 1987 called for the construction of the world's most efficient airport. It was to be created from the ground up with no predetermined limitations.

The plan was to allow the airport to grow and expand without compromising efficiency. Twice the size of Manhattan at 53 square miles, the nation's largest airport was to be designed for steady traffic flow in all weather conditions. It was to comprise a terminal with east and west buildings joined by an atrium structure, three concourses, an automated underground people mover, and five parallel

---

9. Furthermore, when selling the project to voters, planners at one point forecast up to 36 weekly flights to Europe by 1993. The number recorded in 1993, however, was four. The number of passengers departing from Denver was to rise from 16 million in 1985 to some 26 million by 1995. The 1994 figure, however, was about the same as the number of passengers in 1985, or half of Stapleton's capacity.

12,000-foot-long runways on which as many as 1,750 planes could take off and land daily. Its flow-through traffic patterns would allow planes to land, taxi to concourse gates, and take off again all in one direction. The ultimate buildout, projected for the year 2020, was to include up to 12 full service runways, more than 200 gates, and a capacity of 110 million passengers annually. Estimated cost (excluding land acquisition and pre-1990 planning costs) was $2 billion. By the end of 1991, the estimated cost had increased to $2.66 billion. Plans called for the project's completion by the fall of 1993.

In September 1989, Federal officials signed a $60 million grant agreement for the new airport, which was to be financed in multiple ways—by issuing revenue bonds and securing federal grants—supplemented by a sizable investment by the city. Estimated federal grants for the new airport originally totaled $501 million. Portions of these were forthcoming from the FAA, for federal fiscal year 1990 in the amount of $90 million and for federal fiscal year 1991 in the amount of $25 million. The remainder of the $501 million letter of intent was to be received on an annual basis through fiscal year 1997. The revenue bonds assumed the "Date of Beneficial Occupancy" (DBO) to be January 1, 1994, with bond repayments to begin on that date. At that time, the city determined that DIA would meet the DBO no later than October 31, 1993. A member of the Mayor's administrative team described the approach.

> What we did was plan the DBO date and then we planned an extra six months just in case there was a lag in the opening, which, in essence, allowed us to create stability in the market. The other thing we did was that we conservatively financed and filled every reserve account to the maximum. So we borrowed as much money as we could at the lower interest rate and were able to average the debt cost down, not up, as we thought it would be.

A Build-Design Project

By the time construction began at DIA in November 1989, a transfer of authority was taking place in the City of Denver. Wellington Webb was elected the new mayor. According to one of his assistants, the

Peña administration had announced that the airport would be operational in October 1993. "This was a build-design project, which means that we were building the airport [while] we were designing it," he explained. "Because of the delays early on in the project, we had to accelerate construction immediately. There was a lot of pressure and too many players. This was an airport built by committee. We had regular meetings to straighten things out, but it didn't always work."

Although the Webb administration inherited the airport project without a commitment on the part of the major carriers, the support and input of concerned airlines were absolutely key, not only financially but also in terms of input on overall airport layout, scope, and capacity, and supporting systems such as fueling and baggage handling. Denver launched the DIA program without specific commitments from either of Stapleton airport's two major tenant airlines, United and Continental, which together accounted for more than 70 percent of existing passenger traffic. Continental committed to the new airport in February 1990, United in December 1991. Fundamental changes were made to the airport layout plan and facilities (some already under construction) to accommodate the operational needs of these carriers.

The Webb administration followed the predecessor administration's emphasis on assuring that the project's greatest beneficiaries would be local businesses. The desire was to involve as many individual firms as practicable and to use Denver area talent. It was reasoned that local talent was easily accessible to the program management team (PMT), knew Denver building codes and practices, and had available the necessary professional labor pool to accomplish the design in accordance with the demanding schedule. In addition, existing law stated that 30 percent minority-owned firms and 6 percent women-owned firms had to participate in a public works program. The result was a contracting philosophy that maximized opportunities for regional businesses and the local workforce to compete for the work. At least five of 60 contracts awarded for the design of DIA went to Denver-area firms. These 60 design contracts generated 110 construction contracts. Eighty-eight professional service contracts also had to be coordinated. Many local firms had to be hired and the program was chopped up into many small projects. Involvement totaled 200 to 300 firms and reached 400 during the construction phase. Five different firms designed the runways, four the terminal. The city's emphasis on encouraging everyone to compete and yet be part of the project increased the potential for interface and coordination problems.

Denver's flat economy led the administration to keep construction money within the city. Although this benefited the city, it introduced an additional burden on administration. As many as 40–50 concurrent contracts involved many interrelated milestones and contiguous or overlapping operational areas. The estimated daily on-site work force population exceeded 2,500 workers for a 15 to 18-month period beginning in mid-1991 and peaked at between 9,000 and 10,000 in mid-1992. Adding to the human resource coordination problems was a forecasted 4,000 deliveries daily. Construction volume for six months in mid-1992 exceeded $100 million per month.

The prolonged period of assessment and negotiation prior to final approval of the project, and the financial plan selected (which required that bond repayments begin on January 1, 1994), pressured the PMT to push the project ahead at all cost. Because the project had to assume the characteristics of a "fast-track" project early in the construction startup, the compressed design period precipitated a more dynamic construction effort than might be anticipated for a "competitively bid, fixed price" program. Reliance on a design/build method for the project was, according to one DIA official, "unusual because projects this complex normally happen during separate stages. For example, you need to finish up the site selection before you begin the master planning."

Moreover, communication channels between the city, project management team, and consultants were neither well defined nor controlled. "If a contractor fell behind," a resident engineer who reported to one of the area managers said,

> the resident engineer would alert the contractor and document this. The resident engineer would document what would have to be done and what additional resources were necessary to get back on schedule and finish the

contract on time. As a public agency it was enormous, the amount of documentation that we did. I don't know how many trees we cut down just for this project. The resident engineer had about five to eight 12-drawer filing cabinets of documentation and this was nothing compared to what the area manager had. It was just incredible. There were at least four to six copies of everything.

The scheduling manager described the evolution of the tracking system that was used.

One of the biggest problems we had was keeping track of all the changes. So we developed a database system that was installed at each one of the resident engineer's trailers and each contract administrator was then charged with keeping that system up to date and feeding us disks, which we would then merge together periodically to produce an integrated report. But every party had developed their own tracking system before the start of the project. That worked well for each group, but there was no way to take each one of these divergent systems and combine it into one, comprehensive report. So when we introduced the change tracking system everybody said, "fine, that's wonderful, and I'll update it when I get to it and when I get time." It took three years to implement the tracking system.

Project Management

In a fast-moving, ever-changing environment such as the development of a new airport, the management structure must be able to rapidly produce engineering alternatives and the supporting cost and schedule data.[10] But because DIA was financed by many sources

---

10. The DIA project used the so-called "fast-tracking" method, which made it possible to compress some activities along the critical path and manage the construction project as a series of overlapping tasks.

and was a public works program, project administrators had to balance administrative, political, and social imperatives.[11]

The City of Denver staff and consultant team shared leadership of the project and coordinated the initial facets of DIA design. "The initial thought," reflected one staff member, "was that the city staff would do their thing and the consulting staff do theirs and later we would coordinate. It became evident within a very short time that we were doing duplicate duties, which was inefficient. Finally the city decided to coordinate resources."

The city selected a team of city employees and consultants and drafted a work scope document that clearly separated the city's from the consultants' responsibilities. The elements the city did not delegate to consultants included ultimate policy and facility decisions, approval of payments, negotiation and execution of contracts, facilitation of FAA approvals, affirmative action, settlement of contractor claims and disputes, selection of consultants, and utility agreements. The city delegated some elements such as value engineering, construction market analysis, claim management, on-site staff and organization, and state-of-the-art project control (computerized management of budget and schedule).

The program management team became the organization dedicated to overseeing planning and development for the new airport. Headed by the associate director of aviation, the team was partially staffed by city career service employees. To add experience and capability, the city augmented the PMT with personnel from the joint venture of Greiner Engineering and Morrison-Knudsen Engineers, the consulting team. Observed one program management team member, "This working partnership of the City of Denver and consulting joint venture team developed into a fully integrated single organization, capitalizing on the best to be offered by all participants, and optimizing the use of personnel resources."

---

11. These included considerations such as affirmative action, local participation, neighborhood concerns, civic pride, input from the disabled community, art, secondary employment benefits of contract packaging, concern for the environment, and political interest.

DIA's operational project structure comprised five different areas subdivided into smaller units. The working areas were: site development (earthmoving, grading, and drainage); roadways and on-grade parking (service roads, on-airport roads, and off-airport roads connecting to highways); airfield paving; building design (people-mover/baggage-handler, tunnel, concourses, passenger bridge, terminal, and parking); and utility/special systems and other facilities (electrical transmission, oil, and gas line removal and relocation). An area manager controlled construction within each area. Area managers were responsible for the administration of all assigned contracts and, in coordination with other area managers, for management of the portion of the overall site in which their work took place.

United Airlines' Baggage System

From the public's perspective, the "friendliness" of any airport is measured by time. No matter how architecturally stimulating a new airport structure, the perception of business or leisure travelers is often registered in terms of efficiency in checking luggage at the departure area or waiting to claim a bag in the arrival area. The larger the airport, the more critical the efficient handling of baggage. Remote concourses connected by underground tunnels present special problems for airport planners and operators because of the great distances passengers and baggage must travel. The purpose of an airport being to move passengers as efficiently as possible, moving bags as quickly is part and parcel of that responsibility. Rapid transport of frequent flyers accomplishes very little if bags are left behind.

DIA's Concourse A, which was to house Continental Airlines, was situated some 400 meters, and United Airlines' Concourse B nearly 1,000 meters, north of the main terminal. Concourse C, home to other carriers including American, Delta, Northwest, America West, and TWA, sat parallel to the other two concourses more than 1,600 meters north of the main terminal. The initial project design did not incorporate an airport-wide baggage system, the airport expecting the individual airlines to build their own systems as in most other American airports.[12] United Airlines, which

---

12. Rifkin, G.: "What Really Happened at Denver's Airport," *Forbes*, SAP Supplement, August 29, 1994.

in June 1991 signed on to use DIA as its second-largest hub airport, proceeded to do just that.

Needing an automated baggage handling system if it was to turn aircraft around in less than 30 minutes, United, in December 1991, commissioned BAE Automated Systems, Inc., a world leader in the design and implementation of material handling systems, to develop an automated system concept for its B Concourse at DIA. The contract, which included engineering and early parts procurement only, was valued at $20 million, and the task estimated to be completed in two and one-half years. "We began working at DIA under a contract directly with United Airlines," recalled DiFonso. "Obviously, United Airlines has experience with airports. They concluded that the schedule had gotten totally out of control from the standpoint of baggage and they acted to serve their own needs, basically to protect themselves. We contracted with United and were already designing their portion of the system before the city went out for competitive bidding."

BAE was founded as a division of Docutel Corporation in 1968. Docutel, which had developed Telecar (a track-mounted automated baggage system), inaugurated construction of an automated baggage system for United Airlines at San Francisco Airport in 1978. When Docutel ran into financial difficulties during this installation, United asked Boeing, a major supplier of its aircraft, to take over the company. Boeing agreed and the new company, a wholly-owned subsidiary dubbed Boeing Airport Equipment, completed the San Francisco installation. In 1982, Boeing sold the company to its senior management, which renamed it BAE Automated Systems. In August 1985, BAE became an operating unit of Clarkson Industries, a wholly-owned subsidiary of London-based BTR plc. BTR plc (formerly British Tire and Rubber) is a $10 billion conglomerate with global interests in building, paper, and printing products and agricultural and aircraft equipment.

In 1994, BAE's 365 employees worked on projects across the United States and in Europe and Australia. In-house engineering, manufacturing, and field support capabilities enabled BAE to develop, design, manufacture, install, and support every project it undertook from start to finish. BAE also provided consulting, engineering, and management services for airport projects and a variety of material handling applications.

With sales of $100 million in 1994, up from approximately $40 million in 1991, BAE accounted for 90% of U.S. baggage sorting equipment sales. Between 1972 and 1994, the company had successfully designed, manufactured, and installed nearly 70 automated baggage handling systems (worth almost $500 million dollars) at major airports in the United States, in New York, Dallas-Fort Worth, Chicago, San Francisco, Atlanta, Miami, Newark, and Pittsburgh. It had also installed systems in Vancouver and London and was selected, in 1992, as a consultant to the $550 million main terminal for the New Seoul Metropolitan Airport in South Korea.

BAE was a very self-contained, integrated company structured along two business lines: manufacturing and engineering. Its approximately 200,000 square foot manufacturing facility was capable of producing nearly all of the components required by BAE systems save motors, gearboxes, and bearings. The engineering department was structured according to major projects. Each project was assigned a project manager who reported directly to the company president.

Implementing an Integrated Baggage-Handling System

BAE had already commenced work on United's baggage system when the PMT recognized the potential benefits of an airport-wide integrated baggage system. Moreover, as one DIA senior manager explained, "airlines other than United simply were not coming forward with plans to develop their own baggage systems." Airport planners and consultants began to draw up specifications and the city sent out a request for bids. Of 16 companies contacted, both in the United States and abroad, only three responded. A consulting firm recommended against the submitted designs, on the grounds that the configurations would not meet the airport's needs.

BAE was among the companies that had decided not to bid for the job. BAE had installed the Telecar system at a number of other airports and the basic technologies of the Telecar, laser barcode readers, and conveyor belt systems were not new. What was new was the size and complexity of the system. "A grand airport like DIA needs a complex baggage system," explained Di Fonso,

> Therefore the type of technology to be used for such a system is the kind of decision that must be made very early in a project. If there is a surprise like no bidders there is still time to react. At DIA, this never happened. Working with United Airlines, we had concluded that destination-coded vehicles moving at high speed was the technology needed. But quite honestly, although we had that technology developed, its implementation in a complex project like this would have required significantly greater time than the city had left available.

A United project manager concurred: "BAE told them from the beginning that they were going to need at least one more year to get the system up and running, but no one wanted to hear that." The City of Denver was getting the same story from the technical advisers to the Franz Josef Strauss Airport in Munich. The Munich Airport had an automated baggage system, but one far less complex than DIA's. Nevertheless, Munich's technical advisers had spent two years testing the system and the system had been running 24 hours a day for six months before the airport opened.

Formulating Intentions

As BAE was already working on United's automated baggage handling system and enjoyed a world-wide reputation as a superior baggage system builder, Denver approached the company. BAE was asked to study how the United concept could be expanded into an integrated airport system that could serve the other carriers in the various concourses. BAE presented the City of Denver with a proposal to develop the "most complex automated baggage system ever built," according to Di Fonso. It was to be effective in delivering bags to and from passengers, and efficient in terms of operating reliability, maintainability, and future flexibility. The system was to be capable of directing bags (including suitcases of all sizes, skis, and golf clubs) from the main terminal through a tunnel into a remote concourse and directly to a gate. Such efficient delivery would save precious ground time, reduce close-out time for hub operations, and cut time-consuming manual baggage sorting and handling.

Although an automated system was more expensive initially than simple tugs and baggage carts, it was expected that it would reduce the manpower which was required to distribute bags to the correct locations. Bags unloaded from an aircraft arriving at a particular concourse would barely be touched by human hands. Moved through the airport at speeds up to 20 mph, they would be waiting when passengers arrived at the terminal. To prove the capability of its mechanical aspects, and demonstrate the proposed system to the airlines and politicians, BAE built a prototype automated baggage handling system in a 50,000 square foot warehouse near its manufacturing plant in Carrollton, Texas. The prototype system convinced Chief Airport Engineer Walter Slinger that the automated system would work. "[The City of Denver] approached us based on one core concept," recalled Di Fonso. "They wanted to have a fully integrated, airport-wide baggage system. The city had two major concerns. First, they had no acceptable proposal. Second, United was probably going to go ahead and build what it needed and the rest of the airport would have been equipped with something else." Di Fonso continued,

> When we arrived on the scene, we were faced with fully defined project specs, which obviously in the long run proved to be a major planning error. The city had fallen into a trap, which historically architects and engineers tend to fall into as they severely underplay the importance and significance of some of the requirements of a baggage system, that is, arranging things for the space into which it must fit, accommodating the weight it may impose on the building structure, the power it requires to run, and the ventilation and air conditioning that may be necessary to dissipate the heat it generates.

In April 1992, BAE was awarded the $175.6 million contract to build the entire airport system. According to Di Fonso, company executives and city officials hammered out a deal in three intense working sessions. "We placed a number of conditions on accepting the job," he observed.

> The design was not to be changed beyond a given date and there would be a number of freeze dates for mechanical design, software design, permanent power requirements and the like. The contract made it obvious that both signatory parties were very concerned about the ability to complete. The provisions dealt mostly with all-around access, timely completion of certain areas, provision of permanent power, provision of computer rooms. All these elements were delineated as milestones.

Denver officials accepted these requirements and, in addition, committed to unrestricted access for BAE equipment. Because of the tight deadlines, BAE would have priority in any area where it needed to install the system. Di Fonso elaborated,

> When we entered into the contract, Continental Airlines was still under bankruptcy law protection. The city was very concerned that they would be unable to pay for their concourse. They only contracted for about 40 percent of the equipment that is now in Concourse A, which was the concourse that Continental had leased. Beyond that, Concourse C had no signatory airlines as leaseholders at the time. The city, therefore, wanted the simplest, most elementary baggage system possible for Concourse C. The outputs and inputs were very, very crude, intentionally crude to keep the costs down because the city had no assurance of revenue stream at that point in time. The city did not get the airlines together or ask them what they wanted or needed to operate. The approach was more along the lines of "we will build the apartment building and then you come in and you rent a set of rooms."

Project Organization and Management

No major organizational changes to accommodate the new baggage system were deemed necessary, although some managerial adjustments were made on the DIA project. Design of the United baggage system was frozen on May 15, 1992, when the PMT assumed managerial responsibility for the integrated baggage system. The direct relationship with BAE was delegated to Working Area 4, which also had responsibility for building design efforts such as the people-mover, airside concourse building, passenger bridge main landside building complex and parking garage, and various other smaller structures. The area manager, although he had no experience in airport construction, baggage system technologies, or the introduction of new technologies, possessed vast experience in construction project control management.

BAE had to change its working structure to conform to DIA's project management structure. Di Fonso explained,

> There was a senior manager for each of the concourses and a manager for the main terminal. The bag system, however, traversed all of them. If I had to argue a case for right of way I would have to go to all the managers because I was traversing all four empires. In addition, because changes were happening fast at each of these sites, there was no time to have an information system to see what is concourse A deciding and what is concourse B deciding. We had to be personally involved to understand what was going on. There was no one to tie it all together and overlap all these effects because the basic organization was to manage it as discrete areas. It was pandemonium. We would keep saying that over and over again. Who is in charge?

For the first two years of the project, Di Fonso was the project manager. Then the project was divided into three general areas of expertise—mechanical engineering, industrial control, and software design. Mechanical engineering was responsible for all mechanical components and their installation, industrial control for industrial control design, logic controller programming, and motor control panels, and software design for writing real-time process control software to manage the system.

The major adjustments were operational. At the time the contract with BAE was signed, construction had already begun on the terminal and concourses. Substantial changes had to be made to the overall design of the terminal and some construction already completed had to be taken out and reinstalled to accommodate the expanded system. Installation of the expanded system was initially estimated to require more than $100 million in construction work. Walls had to be removed and a new floor installed in the terminal building to support the new system. Moreover, major changes in project governance were taking place during the baggage system negotiations. In May 1992, shortly after the baggage system negotiations commenced, the head of the DIA project resigned.

The death in October 1992 of Chief Airport Engineer Slinger, who had been a strong proponent of the baggage system and closely involved in negotiations with BAE, also exerted a significant impact on the project. His cooperation had been essential because of the amount of heavy machinery and track that had to be moved and installed and the amount of construction work required to accommodate the system. His replacement, Gail Edmond, was selected because she had worked closely with him and knew all the players. Her managerial style, however, was quite different from Slinger's. A Public Works manager recalled his first reaction to the change: "[The airport] is not going to be open on time." A United Airlines project manager summarized Edmond's challenge thus:

> Slinger was a real problem solver. He was controversial because of his attitude, but he was never afraid to address problems. He had a lot of autonomy and could get things done. Gail was in a completely different position. Basically, she had a good understanding of how the project was organized and who the key players were, but she didn't know much about the actual construction. Also, the city council didn't give her anywhere near the autonomy and the authority that Slinger had and she had to get approval from the council on just about all decisions. They really tied her hands and everyone knew it.

Di Fonso echoed the project manager's assessment:

Walter [Slinger] understood that one of the things we had to have was unrestricted access. I think he clearly understood the problem the city was facing and he understood the short time frame under which we were operating. He was the one that accepted all of the contractual conditions, all the milestones of the original contract. He really had no opportunity to influence the outcome of this project, however, because he died two months after the contract was signed. I think Gail did an excellent job [but] she was overwhelmed.[13] She just had too much. The layers below focused inward, worrying about their own little corners of the world.

"Not only did we not get the unrestricted access that was agreed upon," Di Fonso emphasized, "we didn't even have reasonable access." Ten days after Slinger's death, a BAE millwright found a truck from Hensel Phelps, the contractor building Concourse C, blocking her work site. She asked someone to move the truck or leave the keys so it could be moved. According to a BAE superintendent, "she was told that "This is not a BAE job and we can park anywhere we please: is that clear?" Elsewhere, BAE electricians had to leave work areas where concrete grinders were creating clouds of dust. Fumes from chemical sealants forced other BAE workers to flee. Di Fonso pleaded with the city for help. "We ask that the city take prompt action to assure BAE the ability to continue its work in an uninterrupted manner," he wrote. "Without the city's help, the delays to BAE's work will quickly become unrecoverable."[14]

To further complicate matters, the airlines began requesting changes to the system's design even though the mechanical and software designs were supposed to be frozen. "Six months prior to opening the airport," Di Fonso recalled, "we were still moving equipment around, changing controls, changing software design."

In August 1992, for example, United altered plans for a transfer system for bags changing planes, requesting that BAE eliminate an

13. In addition to her role as Chief Airport Engineer, Edmond kept her previous responsibilities as Chief of Construction and Acting Director of Aviation.
14. *Rocky Mountain News*, January 29, 1995.

entire loop of track from Concourse B. Rather than two complete loops of track, United would have only one. This change saved approximately $20 million, but required a system redesign. Additional ski-claim devices and odd-size baggage elevators added in four of the six sections of the terminal added $1.61 million to the cost of the system. One month later, Continental requested that automated baggage sorting systems be added to its west basement at an additional cost of $4.67 million. The ski claim area length was first changed from 94 feet to 127 feet, then in January 1993, shortened to 112 feet. The first change added $295,800, the second subtracted $125,000, from the cost. The same month, maintenance tracks were added to permit the Telecars to be serviced without having to lift them off the main tracks at an additional cost of $912,000. One year later, United requested alterations to its odd-size baggage inputs—cost of the change: $432,000.

Another problem was the city's inability to supply "clean" electricity to the baggage system. The motors and circuitry used in the system were extremely sensitive to power surges and fluctuations. When electrical feedback tripped circuit breakers on hundreds of motors, an engineer was called in to design filters to correct the problem. Although ordered at that time, the filters still had not arrived several months later. A city worker had canceled a contract without realizing that the filters were part of it. The filters finally arrived in March 1994.

A third, albeit disputed, complication was related to Denver's requirement, and city law, that a certain percentage of jobs be contracted to minority-owned companies. The City of Denver had denied BAE's original contract because it did not comply with hiring requirements, whereupon BAE engaged some outside contractors in lieu of BAE employees. Di Fonso estimated that this increased costs by approximately $6 million, a claim rejected by the Mayor's Office of Contract Compliance. Then, in September 1993, BAE's contract negotiations with the City of Denver over maintenance of the system occasioned a two-day strike of 300 millwrights that was joined by some 200 electricians. BAE negotiated with Denver for maintenance workers to earn $12 per hour on certain jobs that the union contended should be worth $20 per hour. As a result, BAE lost the maintenance contract.

Project Relations

Much of the effort for implementing the baggage system was directed within one of the four working areas. "The relationship with the management team was very poor," recalled Di Fonso.

> The management team had no prior baggage handling competence or experience. This was treated as a major public works project. The management team treated the baggage system as similar to pouring concrete or putting in air-conditioning ducts. When we would make our complaints about delays and access and so forth, other contractors would argue their position. The standard answer was "Go work it out between yourselves." With contractors basically on their own, this led almost to anarchy. Everyone was doing his or her own thing.

Another perspective was offered by a project manager from Stone & Webster, a consultant to the PMT, reflecting on the work done by BAE: "This contractor simply did not respond to the obviously incredible workload they were faced with. Their inexperienced project management vastly underestimated their task. Their work ethic was deplorable."[15] PMT management insisted that access and mechanical issues weren't the problem. "They were running cars in Concourse B all summer (1993)," Edmund observed. "The problem was that the programming was not done and BAE had full control of the programming."[16]

Lawsuits and a Baggage System

In February 1993, Mayor Webb delayed the scheduled October 1993 airport opening to December 19, 1993. Later, this December date was changed to March 9, 1994. "Everybody got into the panic mode of trying to get to this magical date that nobody was ready for,"

---

15. *Forbes*, ASAP Supplement, August 29, 1994.
16. *Forbes*, ASAP Supplement, August 29, 1994.

a senior vice president for BAE recalled. In September 1993, the opening was again postponed—this time until May 15, 1994. In late April 1994, the City of Denver invited reporters to observe the first test of the baggage system, without notifying BAE. Seven thousand bags were to be moved to Continental's Concourse A and United's Concourse B. So many problems were discovered that testing had to be halted. Reporters saw piles of disgorged clothes and other personal items lying beneath the Telecar's tracks.

Most of the problems related to errors in the system's computer software, but mechanical problems also played a part. The software that controlled the delivery of empty cars to the terminal building, for example, often sent the cars back to the waiting pool. Another problem was "jam logic" software, which was designed to shut down a section of track behind a jammed car, but instead shut down an entire loop of track. Optical sensors designed to detect and monitor cars were dirty causing the system to believe that a section of track was empty when, in fact, it had held a stopped car. Collisions between cars dumped baggage on tracks and on the floor; jammed cars jumped the track and bent the rails; faulty switches caused the Telecars to dump luggage onto the tracks or against the walls of the tunnels.

After the test, Mayor Webb delayed the airport's opening yet again, this time indefinitely. "Clearly, the automated baggage system now underway at DIA is not yet at a level that meets the requirements of the city, the airlines, or the traveling public," the mayor stated. The city set the costs of the delay at $330,000 per month. Recognizing that his reputation was staked on his ability to have a baggage system performing to a point at which the new airport could be opened, Mayor Webb engaged, in May 1994, the German firm Logplan to assess the state of the automated baggage system. In July, Logplan isolated a loop of track that contained every feature of the automated baggage system and intended to run it for an extended period to test the reliability of the Telecars. Jams on the conveyor belts and collisions between cars caused the test to be halted. The system did not run long enough to determine if there was a basic design flaw or to analyze where the problems were. Logplan recommended construction of a backup baggage system, and suggested using Rapistan

Demag, a firm it had worked with in the past. Construction of a backup system was announced in August 1994. The system itself cost $10.5 million, but electrical upgrades and major building modifications raised the projected cost to $50 million.

In the meantime, the City of Denver as well as many major airlines, hired legal firms to assist with negotiations and future litigation. "We will have enough legal action for the rest of this century," a city administrator mused. The City of Denver had to communicate with such parties as the United States Federal grand jury, Securities Exchange Commission, and the General Accounting Office. The federal grand jury was conducting a general investigation concerning DIA. The SEC was investigating the sale of $3.2 billion in bonds to finance DIA's construction, and GAO the use of Congressional funds.

Di Fonso, reviewing Mayor Webb's letter and requests that BAE pay a $12,000-a-day penalty for missing DIA's original October 29, 1993 completion date, as well as assuming the costs of building the $50 million conventional tug-and-cart baggage system, summed up the situation thus: "We have gotten to the point with the city that literally we are not talking to each other. Consultants recommended a backup baggage system, and the minute that the decision was made, the city had to defend it. We are left out in limbo."

2.1.2   BAE AUTOMATED SYSTEMS (B): IMPLEMENTING THE DENVER INTERNATIONAL AIRPORT BAGGAGE-HANDLING SYSTEM

In September 1989, U.S. Federal officials authorized $60 million to construct a new, highly technologically advanced airport for Denver, to be called the Denver International Airport (DIA). In April 1992, BAE Automated Systems presented the City of Denver with a proposal to develop the "most complex automated [and integrated] baggage system ever built," according to CEO Gene Di Fonso. On August 22, 1994, City of Denver Mayor Wellington Webb notified BAE that it would have to pay a $12,000-per-day penalty for not finishing the baggage system by DIA's original October 29, 1993 completion date. The mayor had also ordered the construction of a conventional tug-and-cart backup baggage system for which he expected BAE to pay $50 million. The City of Denver insisted on holding BAE legally and financially responsible for failing to finish the original system.

BAE, blaming delays on lack of site access and permit delays for which it held the City of Denver responsible, went public on September 7 with a $40 million claim against the city. The essence of BAE's counterclaim was that the entire airport was behind schedule and constant design changes had prevented BAE from installing its system. A major issue had been the city's alleged inability to meet agreed-upon deadlines to build the space that would house different elements of the baggage-handling system. The claim also accused the city of breaking contractual promises to make the BAE system the top priority by allowing other contractors' jobs to take precedence.

When the airport finally opened in late February 1995, it was 16 months behind schedule and close to $2 billion over budget. The first flight to land at the airport, nearly three years after BAE was retained to build the automated integrated baggage system, encountered not one state-of-the-art integrated baggage handling system, but three.

Back to Square One

On August 31, 1994, the *Rocky Mountain News* reported that in an effort to avoid legal action the City of Denver had proposed a "stand still" agreement whereby major parties (the city, United Airlines, and BAE) would waive certain previous agreements and rights until the new airport was opened and operational. "Of course," the reporter emphasized, "the legal departments of these parties are going to be busy until the end of this century with this case."

The moratorium nevertheless broke the deadlock. Problems had arisen between the City of Denver and United Airlines around the design of the backup baggage system. United Airlines objected to the manual system, saying it would not accommodate the airline's heavy schedule. United offered a plan to modify the automated system to deliver bags to the planes and rely on tugs and carts to deliver most of the baggage for arriving passengers. United and the City of Denver, unable to agree who should pay for the modifications, approached BAE executives, who indicated they would not continue without a signed contract from the City of Denver.

Both United and Continental Airlines had geared up for protracted negotiations and possible litigation. The law firm retained by United pointed out that it was hired to negotiate the proposed backup baggage system at DIA—not to initiate litigation procedures. Continental, which had engaged a law firm for "assistance with both DIA and Stapleton issues," maintained that the last minute baggage system was a breach of contract for which it could sue the city or choose to cancel its lease of DIA gates. United urged the city to bring in mediators "because of the deteriorating relationship with BAE."

As a result of the negotiations, the original contract was broken into two pieces: the United contract; and the remaining piece of the city contract. Under the new contract, United used BAE's system to serve its Concourse B. It also took over and used at reduced speed two loops of track that served Concourse C. It isolated its operation from the BAE system that served Concourse A. The number of cars was reduced from 3,100 to 2,300 and the spacing between cars extended. The rest of the baggage system was designed around conveyor belts and propane-powered tugs and carts. Warning lights were installed in the baggage tunnels to guide the tugs.

The negotiations also brought about a change in the organization structure. United immediately hired a construction manager with full decision-making authority and contracted with a consulting company for further assistance. BAE hired its own consultant to develop and write test plans and prepare commissioning documents.

"When we changed from working directly for the city to working for United," Di Fonso recalled:

> it was like the sun came up. We were now working for people who fully understood the technology and its needs. We signed the contract with United in September 1994. Five months later we opened this airport. The contract with United required us to make $35 million worth of changes. That's an example of what can be done when people are working together as opposed to against one another.
>
> We formed a team; everybody had the same goal; we developed a schedule. Anytime we hit a problem—a building interference, a code—they would clear it up almost immediately. We never had to wait more than 24 hours for a problem to be resolved, as compared to sometimes waiting two or three months for a problem to be resolved by the City. That's how dramatic the change was.

Integrated testing continued through the fall and winter of 1994. In January 1995, a full-scale, three-hour, 10,000 bag practice run of the substitute baggage system was completed without any problems.

Open for Business

On the sleety, snowy, icy morning of February 28, 1995, the DIA opened with ceremony, the thunder of jet engines, and a sense of relief. The first scheduled passenger arrival, United Flight 1474 from Colorado Springs, was to land at 6:05 a.m. Former mayor and then Secretary of Transportation, Federico Peña, and current mayor, Wellington Webb, the two politicians responsible for the new airport, were on hand to greet the first passengers in the presence of a large crowd that included 1,725 journalists. The waiting was finally over. The airport opened with five runways and 88 gates (20 fewer than Stapleton), at a cost of $5.2 billion and an $18.80 average per-passenger airline fee—the nation's second highest. The airport's opening also offered the possibility of political relief for Mayor Webb, who was running for re-election that spring.

As the first flight approached the terminal, a switch controlling the movement of the enclosed passenger walkways reportedly malfunctioned at the gate where dignitaries waited for the airplane. The historic load of passengers had to wait an extra ten minutes while the plane was backed out and moved to another gate. Their luggage, however, arrived as they finished the hike from the gate to the luggage claim. Despite minor problems, including one of six lines breaking down for short periods, BAE's automated baggage system worked well. Nor did airlines served by the backup system report any major difficulties.

The baggage system was almost back to the original plans, with United, the airline that carried the most passengers at DIA, using an automated baggage delivery system and others using a conventional system. United's $300 million system, which comprised 22 miles of rollercoaster-like track, 3,500 cars, and 55 computers that could handle up to 30,000 pieces of luggage per day, controlled more of the airport rights of way than originally planned.[17] A simplified automated system served United's Concourse B. Continental used a tug-and-cart system on its Concourse A but was expected to shift to the automated system in the future. Other airlines were operating a very conventional, highly labor-intensive system. Airlines on Concourse C would have an automated system only if BAE installed new track, and United granted rights for access. Given that the backup system was designed to be "100 percent independent" of BAE's system, United's baggage consultant explained, "There's no longer an integrated baggage system. What we have is three baggage systems."

---

17. Robert Davis, "Denver Still Working Out Kinks as Its First Birthday Arrives," *USA Today* (February 28, 1996).

2.1.3   *FLORIDA FIASCO (FLORIDA WELFARE)*

by Bruce Caldwell with Chuck Appleby

When Hurricane Andrew hit southern Florida last summer, the state's welfare agency was caught flat-footed with a brand-new but badly flawed computer system that was already overwhelmed by the size and complexity of the state's public assistance programs. Like the storm itself, the results were devastating: While hundreds of thousands of people received benefits to which they were not entitled, tens of thousands of others desperately in need of food stamps waited in long lines for days.

Last week, the state's inspector general issued a report blasting the state's welfare agency for mismanagement of the Florida On-line Recipient Integrated Data Access system (widely known as FLORIDA) and a cover-up of the problems. The system processes eligibility claims for several million recipients of Aid to Families with Dependent Children, food stamps, and Medicaid. A mammoth mainframe-based system designed to support 84 databases, 1,390 programs, more than 12,000 terminals and PCs, and 5.5 million on-line transactions a day, FLORIDA was supposed to save the state hundreds of millions of dollars by reducing payment errors and agency staff requirements. Instead, it has doled out hundreds of millions of dollars in overpayments, spurred mass resignations and dismissals at the state Department of Health and Rehabilitative Services (HRS), and kicked up a storm of controversy.

But it is those who truly need state benefits who have suffered the most. "I had homeless clients who had to walk 12 miles back and forth three days in a row in the dead of summer last year only to be told their food stamps were not available," recounts Cindy Huddlestone, director of litigation for Florida Legal Services Inc. in Tallahassee. Even before Andrew, such delays were common, she says, because the number of people in need of assistance had already outstripped the system's capacity.

This article was originally published in InformationWeek, April 26, 1993. Copyright 1993 by CMP Publications, Inc., 600 Community Drive, Manhasset, NY 11030. Reprinted with permission.

Since 1989, when the contract to build the FLORIDA system was awarded to Dallas-based EDS Corp., the recession and Hurricane Andrew have more than doubled the number of people receiving welfare benefits in Florida, and both HRS and EDS blame many of FLORIDA's problems on the unexpected jump in caseloads and budgetary restrictions that prevented the agency from hiring more caseworkers. But many observers believe the FLORIDA system was flawed from the start.

Good Intentions

In 1983, the Florida Legislature mandated the creation of an integrated computer system to help manage the state's 14 separate public assistance programs. Some critics charge that goal was seriously compromised in 1985 when the federal government, which pays for 90 percent of all state welfare automation projects, stipulated that to remain eligible for its funds, the states must base such projects on systems that are already in operation in other states.

The federal requirement was prompted by earlier failures, such as in Washington, where the state spent $20 million in the 1980s to develop an automated welfare system from scratch only to end up with a system that was slower than the old manual system.

Complying with the federal requirement, Florida inexplicably decided to predicate its design for a *distributed* system on an Ohio project that used *centralized* computers to serve two counties. To accomplish that miracle of computer engineering, the state turned to EDS, which in 1989 was awarded a three-year, $85 million contract, and which proceeded to begin transferring several million lines of Cobol code from Ohio to the project in Florida.

By early 1990 the finger pointing had begun. EDS claimed that HRS was demanding real-time data access, an impossibility with the distributed architecture, which was designed for overnight batch processing. HRS says that was just a red herring; what really concerned EDS was that it would be unable to deliver the original design on time and within budget. In any event, HRS agreed to switch to a centralized mainframe system, provided EDS guaranteed adequate capacity.

Bickering over systems changes and upgrades continued—EDS threatened a work stoppage at one point—until May 1992, when EDS and HRS agreed to part company. EDS, according to a spokesman, was all too happy by that point to forego two one-year contracts worth $19 million to run the new system.

HRS officially took delivery of the FLORIDA system in June; two months later, Andrew hit. Without electricity, FLORIDA was useless to citizens whose homes and lives were brutalized. It was little better once power was restored. Victims of the disaster faced the same confusion and inaccuracy that confronted earlier aid recipients.

Attempts to increase FLORIDA's capacity brought new troubles. In November, suspicions that favoritism played a role in IBM's selection for a $5.1 million contract to upgrade the system prompted a grand jury investigation into HRS's computer procurement practices. In connection with the investigation, Judy Mitchell, an HRS manager of the FLORIDA project, resigned, and Tom Johnson, deputy assistant secretary for management systems at HRS, was fired. The state attorney declines comment on the probe.

The storm around FLORIDA whipped to fever pitch in February, when Gov. Lawton Chiles, citing projections of a $173 million Medicaid shortfall, pushed for new taxes. The state Legislature was on the verge of going along, according to state Sen. Charles Crist, head of the ethics committee, when it was discovered that FLORIDA had erroneously sent Medicaid cards to some 235,000 people who were no longer eligible. The improperly issued cards were used to obtain more than $28 million in health care services between last August and February. That sparked a probe by the Senate ethics committee into why the governor's office waited several weeks to disclose the Medicaid errors.

A Toll in The Millions

HRS found human and computer error resulted in $260 million in overpayments and $58 million in underpayments during 1992. The Medicaid overpayments in particular are directly attributable to software problems, according to an HRS spokeswoman. To top it all off, the federal government could fine the state $144 million for over-payments made with federal monies, although such fines are rarely enforced.

The FLORIDA system may also be at the root of the human errors, say observers. Caseworkers, formerly specialists in different areas of public assistance, must now act as generalists. FLORIDA does all eligibility calculations, which frees recipients from being shuffled from caseworker to caseworker, but also means that if FLORIDA makes a mistake, the caseworker is unlikely to catch it unless he or she has specific knowledge of the assistance program.

Chiles, who won the governor's office in 1990 on a platform of welfare reform, has now taken direct charge of the matter. He has ordered the agency and EDS into mediation to work out their differences, pressured former HRS secretary Bob Williams to resign, and replaced Williams with Lt. Gov. Buddy MacKay, who will oversee a massive restructuring of the agency. MacKay, in turn, has called for the resignations of all 41 top managers at the agency.

That still leaves FLORIDA, which limps along with its software problems unresolved. "When they get it running right," says Huddlestone, "it will be fantastic, a real improvement in delivery of services." But, she sighs, "they have a lot of glitches to work out."

2.1.4 ANATOMY OF A RUNAWAY: WHAT GROUNDED THE AAS

by Stephen Bourlas

When the U.S. Federal Aviation Administration announced the Advanced Automation Program in 1981, it promised to modernize air-traffic control using sophisticated computer systems. Fifteen years and billions of dollars later, the centerpiece Advanced Automation System has become the "figurehead" of everything that has gone wrong with air-traffic modernization, according to Drew Steketee, senior vice president of a pilot's lobby, the AOPA. "Very, very little has been accomplished," Steketee said.

Ken Mead, then-director of transportation issues for the General Accounting Office, told the Senate subcommittee on aviation in August 1995, "The impact of delays has been significant: long-awaited safety and efficiency benefits have been postponed, costly interim projects have been started to sustain existing equipment, and FAA's credibility has been eroded."

Sector Suites

The problems in the first 13 years of the AAS project revolve around the development of software for the new workstations—called sector suites—that were to be deployed by 1989. The Initial Sector Suite System was to have been deployed on 3,000 workstations at 23 enroute facilities, which guide air traffic between airports. The FAA planned to replace its 220 Tracons (terminal radar-approach control facilities) with the 23 en-route facilities. Tracons control air traffic for a radius of 35-40 miles from an airport; once a plane leaves a Tracon's space, it is picked up by an en-route facility, which guides the plane along one of the air highways striated between 18,000–40,000 feet.

Eliminating the Tracons was a major rationale for the development of the ISSS. The plan was to connect the sector suites to the

This article was originally published in IEEE Software, January and March 1996. Used with permission.

IBM host computers via local area networks. The host computers would retain responsibility for radar and flight data processing. Not only would these sector suites allow controllers to more quickly pick up potential air-traffic problems, but they could direct the planes along more efficient routes, saving considerable fuel.

The initial estimate was that perhaps 1.5 million lines of code would have to be written.

The cost for the ISSS piece of the AAS was never broken out, but it was a substantial part of the total, which was announced as $2.5 billion in 1983, with deployment in 1990–91. Both the dollar estimates and deadlines grew over time. In 1988, they went to $4.3 billion and 1994–95. Through fiscal 1995, Congress had given the FAA $2.6 billion for the AAS, $300 million less than had been requested.

The sector-suite concept has since been criticized for being technically so ambitious that it could never be realized. Valerio Hunt, who was the AAP program manager between 1981 and 1986, now admits that "the concept was admittedly grand," but said there were plenty of serious problems in the implementation phase, after he left the FAA in 1986. Hunt was succeeded for a few years by an interim replacement, who in turn was succeeded by Mike Perie, who was eventually posted to the FAA's Seattle regional office in 1994. Perie did not return phone calls about the AAP. Nevertheless, it is possible to piece together the AAS's troubled history from Congressional and General Accounting Office reports.

Prolonged Competition

The ISSS design competition between Hughes Aircraft and IBM, which IBM eventually won, lasted four years. During this time, neither the FAA, the air-traffic controllers, nor the airlines had much input into the design plans. In 1993, during hearings before the House subcommittee on aviation, acting FAA Administrator Joseph Del Balzo admitted that the design competition had been flawed. "During the design competition phase," he said, "we were unable to bring to bear the user's expectation on the details for fear of limiting or inhibiting technological solutions. In retrospect, design competition made sense, but we let it go on too long."

Jack Fearnsides, senior vice president at Mitre Corp., and director of its Center for Advanced Aviation Systems, has watched the air-traffic modernization program for years. According to Fearnsides, the design competition kept getting extended as the contractors tried to match technology against a projected 10-year development life cycle. "At the end of the design phase, there was not a real "fly-off,'" he explains, using a term that is applied to military procurement competitions for aircraft. "The technological risk was put into the acquisition phase."

In fact, Fearnsides said, had today's software and affordable work-stations been available in the mid-1980s, IBM and Hughes could have mocked up the sector suites, which would have gone a long way toward avoiding the problems which were to follow.

Implementation Problems

When IBM finally won the contract in 1988, and after the FAA shook off a legal challenge from Hughes, IBM Federal Systems was off and running, but the problems were far from over.

For one thing, the FAA was pushing for unprecedented reliability, demanding that system downtime be no more than three seconds a year, which translates into 99.99999 percent reliability—the so-called "seven nines." At the 1993 hearings, Gerald Ebker, then the president of IBM Federal Systems, told the subcommittee that the seven nines was "more stringent than on any system that has ever been implemented." He said that an IBM analysis "indicates it is achievable" but stopped short of saying it had or would be achieved. But in the process of trying to get seven nines, he explained, "the last nine has cost a great deal."

The FAA also required console features the air controllers did not want. For example, on the old consoles, the controller turned a knob to project a vector line on the radar scope. The vector line projected an aircraft's flight pattern over time, so the controller could antici-pate any problems in its path. With ISSS, a controller had to punch in 16 keystrokes to project a vector line. The FAA also wanted to au-tomate the paper flight strips controllers use to chart the progress of a plane. The controllers wanted to maintain the paper-based system.

IBM and the FAA kept trying to reproduce the electronic flight strip with just a few easy keystrokes, but never met the objective.

The AAS contract required ISSS to sustain 210 common consoles in the same facility operating at peak load. IBM could only get 56 to dovetail for any significant length of time. One of the reasons appears to be a flawed testing regimen. The flaws in the software-testing regime were among the key criticisms in a report issued in April 1992 by the Volpe National Transportation Systems Center, a part of the U.S. Department of Transportation. By the summer of 1992, IBM had reported it was working on the ninth and final build of the ISSS. This progress report, however, turned out to be hollow because IBM had deferred testing of many key ISSS functions.

IBM, according to Fearnsides, had rushed its tests. "To meet testing deadlines, IBM tested what they had developed up until that point," he says. "In some instances, that fell short of what they were supposed to have developed."

A 1993 report from the House aviation subcommittee staff stated, "Testing milestones were skipped or shortcutted and new software was developed assuming that the previously developed software had been tested and performed." Also, testing was done by diverse organizations within IBM. The report explained: "This created confusion and inefficiency because when tests were performed, they would sometimes have to be redone because one organization was not satisfied by the other organization's test or the focus of the tests."

Six months after the Volpe report, IBM announced a 14-month delay in the ISSS program. The FAA sent IBM a "cure notice" that obligated IBM to suggest acceptable improvements in the program within 10 days, lest the FAA withhold progress payments.

The FAA ultimately accepted IBM's proposed changes, and made some of its own. For example, in March 1993, the FAA put the ISSS program manager on site at IBM and increased the software-development branch within the project office from three people to five. And, perhaps most importantly, the FAA agreed to finalize the technical requirements for the ISSS—which it had changed repeatedly—by April 1, 1993.

Program Changes

These changes came too late. By late 1992, FAA officials had already begun discussing canceling the 1983 decision to consolidate the Tracons into the 23 en-route facilities. David Hinson was appointed FAA Administrator in late 1993, and by March 1994 he had revamped the AAS management team. Hinson hired Bob Valone to replace Mike Perie. Valone had been director of the systems program office at the National Oceanic and Atmospheric Administration and had worked for Valerio Hunt at the FAA. That same month IBM Federal Systems Division was sold to Loral Corp.

Three months later, Hinson threw out major portions of the AAS, deciding that not all Tracons would be eliminated; about 170 would remain. The ISSS program was revamped and renamed the Display System Replacement. Hinson commissioned the Software Engineering Institute, which worked in conjunction with MIT's Lincoln Labs, to look at the ISSS software and answer two basic questions: How much of the ISSS software could be used for the DSR and could Loral do any better on software development? The answers were "70 percent" and "yes."

So in May 1995, the FAA awarded Loral $1.5 billion, the largest piece being $898 million for the 3,000 workstations and associated software development for the en-route facilities. The FAA insisted that Loral install a new AAS management team, a condition to which the company agreed, although the Loral senior vice president for en-route programs is Rick Padinha, who was also responsible for ISSS at IBM Federal Systems.

The first DSR is now expected to be installed in Seattle in late 1997, where it will undergo a year of testing. The much simpler DSR workstations will not have electronic flight strips and will have fewer displays than the sector suites would have had. But they will have most of "the creature comforts" originally planned under ISSS, according to FAA spokesman Jeff Thal. And, Thal said, they will have an open-systems architecture that will allow the systems to be upgraded.

FAA SHIFTS FOCUS TO SCALED-BACK DSR

Last September, air-traffic controller Larry Barbour traveled to Las Vegas for the annual convention of the Air Traffic Controllers Association. What he heard there, he said, gave him a sinking feeling. Barbour monitors the progress of the Display System Replacement program for his union, the National Air Traffic Controllers Association (which is different from the ATCA). The DSR program was launched by the U.S. Federal Aviation Administration in April, 1995, in an effort to build something usable with what was left of the Initial Sector Suite System program.

FAA Administrator David Hinson had cancelled the 10-year-old ISSS program in June, 1994, tossing out about $1.3 billion in losses. He decided, after much head-scratching and internal and external reviews, to drastically simplify the workstation software. In April, 1995, Hinson awarded the much less ambitious but still huge $898 million DSR contract to Loral, which had purchased IBM Federal Systems. Seventy percent of the software developed by IBM for ISSS would be incorporated into DSR. And in September, Loral officials brought a metal mock-up of the DSR, without software, to the ACTA convention.

Barbour's sinking feeling came on as he listened to other controllers comment on the mock-up. Some were very unhappy with the positioning of the flight-strip holders around the 15-inch CRT screen. Flight strips are used to keep track of planes which are flying in areas without radar coverage. They were to have been handled electronically in ISSS, but now that goal had been abandoned. Not only did Barbour and others find the strips cumbersome to reach, they kept falling into the laps of the controllers.

Barbour said he corralled Peter Challan and Neil Planzer, two top FAA officials who were in Las Vegas, and told them the problem. "I don't know that the system won't work," says Barbour. "I've told everybody I know about that problem. I've made it loud and clear. If it doesn't get fixed, the whole DSR project will have to go back to the drawing board."

This is the second part of the preceding article.

Mike Gough, an official in the Air Traffic AAS Requirements Branch, admits that the mock-up caused a lot of concern among air traffic controllers. "The strips did not slide, and when you grabbed one strip, sometimes six or eight others fell in your lap." But Gough says the mock-up was designed to convey a look, not a feel, and he thinks the problems will disappear once the real hardware is finished. Air-traffic controllers will be able to test the hardware early in 1996.

But it is not just the flight strips that have given some controllers pause. The software is uninspired. Barbour calls it "archaic," nothing more than what controllers have been using for the past 25 years.

Loral had told the FAA that some of the enhancements developed for ISSS could still be deployed. For example, it would be possible to give controllers a fourth line on their data block containing information on a plane's speed and headings. That could be passed electronically from controller to controller, obviating numerous distracting, time-consuming phone calls between controllers as they pass off planes to one another. But the FAA, trying to keep the software simple, declined to include that enhancement (and others) in DSR.

Stable Staff

The first of 3,200-plus controller workstations are supposed to be delivered to Seattle for a test in fall 1997. They will eventually be deployed at 21 en route air traffic control centers. They replace ancient workstations that in some instances are literally falling apart.

Challan, the FAA's en-route system's product team leader, said the fall 1997 date will be met. He says the Loral leadership is a "no nonsense, focused group of individuals." Challan joined the program in July 1995, after successfully heading up the FAA's voice switching-control system. He has a reputation as a successful manager. Challan's key lieutenant is John McKenna, who came over from the U.S. Navy after working on submarine combat programs. Also from the Navy is Cindy King, software en route manager. "We had quite a bit of churn in the fall of 1994 when we went through a huge reorganization with en route systems and DSR," she said, referring to the AAS revolving door. "We're stabilized now, though."

McKenna says that as of December there were 6,000 lines of code left to be written out of a total of 766,000. An internal critical design review of DSR was completed on September 13. FAA Administrator Hinson said in a press release on October 25, "We're very pleased with the results of this review. It is a clear indication that our decision to go forward with the DSR was the correct one, and that the contractor, Loral, is performing up to our expectations."

There have been no outside audits of the DSR work to date. In contrast, the ISSS was the subject of several critical reports from the General Accounting Office and the Department of Transportation's Volpe Transportation Center and numerous Congressional hearings. At a December, 1995, Congressional hearing on "An Industry Perspective of FAA R&D Programs," Loral executive vice president Robert Stevens was not asked a single question about DSR.

The Software Engineering Institute did review the critical design review, but the language of the report was vague. Among the recommendations: "improve error-handling design documentation; ensure consistency of design, documentation, and code to enhance maintainability; ensure that dead code is removed from the legacy components." The SEI report's conclusion said, "One key design documentation issue remains to be resolved." There is no indication if the serious and numerous software problems cited by the SEI in October 1994 had been either completely taken care of or ignored by the FAA. It is difficult to tell whether the SEI recommendations and conclusions are on the order of "sweep up after you are done" or whether they imply some level of trouble.

Reworded Specs

As for system reliability, King said the specification from the ISSS, which called for a reliability of "7/9," or 99.99999 percent reliable, has been reworked. "We have reworked the seven-nines spec. Seven nines is hard to quantify. We have stated it in more conventional terms like mean-time-to-failure and mean-time-to-repair. It is easier to measure. They give you the same results. We spent a lot of time reworking that spec."

King, McKenna, and Challan all say that Loral has made considerable improvements in its software-development process. CASE tools are being used. "Things are getting kicked back if they are not done right," says King.

Things may be getting kicked back, but some key IBM officials were never kicked out of the DSR program, as was supposed to happen when Loral won the contract. At that time, Linda Daschle, deputy administrator of the FAA, said Loral got the contract based in part on its commitment to fire the ISSS management team. However, Rick Padinha, who headed the ISSS program under IBM, was retained by Loral. He is senior vice president, en-route programs, the top DSR line manager. Jack Clemons, the key software engineer during the later stages of ISSS, is now vice president of engineering at Loral for DSR.

Judy Gan, a Loral spokeswoman, says she worries about people focusing on personalities instead of the programs Loral has put in place to insure the success of the DSR program. She also notes that Padinha reports to Bob Stevens, who in turn reports to Bob Welte, president of the Air Traffic Control Division, neither of whom were IBMers. If Loral produces, questions about personalities will quickly evaporate. One way to ensure that Loral does produce is to encourage oversight by disinterested parties.

WHY (SOME) LARGE COMPUTER PROJECTS FAIL

by Robert N. Britcher

The FAA's Advanced Automation System (AAS) began in 1981, at about the time President Reagan dismissed 11,400 striking air traffic controllers. The timing is not incidental.

President Reagan, long awed by technology (Buck Rogers had been one of his adolescent heroes), believed that, inevitably, computers would relieve mankind of the brute labor that has kept it from pursuing its dreams. Automation, he often said, would ease our lives, even solve our social problems. It would certainly protect us. He dreamed of a system of heavenly lasers that would defend us forever from nuclear attack. Within months after taking office, he authorized it: the Strategic Defense Initiative, the project everyone soon called "Star Wars." While that project never left the ground (although millions have been spent on the drawing board), the Advanced Automation System took off.

In 1981, at the dawn of airline deregulation, about 300 million passengers were taking commercial flights in the United States. It was predicted—accurately—that the number would grow to over 500 million by 1994. Today, there are over 20,000 scheduled airline flights a day; the number of passengers expected in 1997 is 546 million. By the year 2007, over 2 million passengers a day will be in flight. The number of jets in the U.S. fleet is expected to grow from 4,775 in 1996 to over 7,000 in 2007. Add in general aviation (over 180,000 planes) and military flights and you have busy skies.

On the ground, the air traffic control facilities are (and have been for some time) stressed out. The New York Tracon alone supports 7,000 flights a day. Tracons control air traffic around the terminal areas within a 60 to 90 mile radius of airports. There are over 180 such facilities, hundreds more towers, where planes are metered between the runways and the sky, and 21 en route centers. These are staffed by 17,000 controllers, about the same number today as in 1981.

On a national scale, the computer was introduced to air traffic control in 1963. The Tracons were the first to be automated. The Univac

---

This article was written especially for this book.

computers and computer programs converted analog radar signals to digital form, and presented to the controller an annotated picture of planes in airspace. The en route system followed, but it took longer to complete, largely because the en route system must process radar data and, for each flight, predict the time of arrival at each fix along its route. The present position of an aircraft is of interest, but so is its future. The second requirement takes advantage of the computer's facility as a calculator, but it also makes the system more complex. The en route system has to juggle real-time sensor data with the management of a persistent (and, as designed, labyrinthine) data base. Tower operations are largely manual. Control is still a matter of vision and voice. The large towers receive data from the computers in the Tracons and en route centers. In the 1970s, the FAA used the computerized data from the regional facilities to seed another function: traffic management, or flow control, so that the density of our domestic airspace can be summarized and trends evaluated.

The role of automation in air traffic control is modest. (With the AAS, that was to change.) This fits well with the often immediate and habitual nature of ground supervision of aircraft. In no job is immense responsibility and habit so entwined—more than in police work or neurosurgery. Cognitive scientists would have a field day with air traffic controllers. They must perceive the (computer-modeled) relationship among aircraft, racing along at over 300 miles per hour, while they simultaneously interact with a computer and talk to the pilots. The interaction of perception, judgment, and response appears to be almost autonomic. For good reason, their job is always listed at the top of the most stressful professions. And professionals they are. Controllers work 6-day weeks. In spite of the mandatory two breaks a day, some work what is called the "Quick Turn": 3 in the afternoon to 11, followed by a 7 A.M. to 3 P.M. shift. These are the young tough guys who hug those planes and passengers to their bosoms. Others, often burned out, will take only light loads. But no one works the boards for long.

The urge to replace the controllers with technology and the alarming projections of the growth of air travel were not the only motives behind the AAS. There was a more practical issue. The equipment was (is) getting old: radars, navigational aids, computers, cables, telephones, the whole gamut. The favorite word is "antiquated." Even the software was old, some said, who do not realize that old software is more reliable than new software.

But, in the end, the drivers were financial. The FAA has been under pressure from the airlines to upgrade the computer algorithms to permit "preferred" routes of flight, which could save each airline millions of dollars in fuel. According to the major carriers, today's rigid procedures, based on fixed airways, derived from a decades-old topology of ground navigational equipment, cause over 20,000 delays every day, and waste $5 billion a year. The advent of satellite navigation makes off-airway flying potentially reliable—and profitable.

The other economic issue is related to technology, specifically the unique property of software to be adapted to many environments, but it is more directly aimed at downsizing. (The two, technology and the displacement of jobs, have been cohorts for centuries.) The entire system of terminal and en route facilities, save the towers, would be consolidated. The existing facilities would be combined into some 30 or 40 area control facilities, most, if not all, in new locations. Shutting down over a hundred Tracons and en route facilities—which meant uprooting and laying off people, renovating jobs, phone lines, security operations, you name it—would save an estimated $4.5 billion in operating costs.

In summary, it was believed that the successful implementation of the Advanced Automation System would mean fewer people, less fuel, lower costs, cheaper flights, fewer delays—and (satisfying our deep American drive for technology) more automation.

Change is inevitable. But the world of air traffic control is as vulnerable to change as it gets. Change, if and when it comes, must be as imperceptible as possible. A slight shift in the position of a knob can distract a controller and create what the FAA calls an incident—when planes get too close to one another or to objects. The biggest problem in creating a new version of an old system is the transition. The air traffic control system operates all day, every day, and any change must be made while the system is running. The FAA had no clear concept of how this would be done. They set up the mission of the AAS to make transition, not just awkward, but impossible. Contrary to the sensitive character of the air traffic control system, and

especially the people who support it, the new system would be rev-
olutionary, as radical a departure from well-worn mores and customs
as the overthrow of the czars. Someone must have suspected as
much, for there were advertisements to the contrary. AAS was to be
a model for the evolution of systems. In fact, there was one incremental phase, in which the en route controllers would get new displays. This was evolution feigned. In the main, the AAS was
designed to sweep away the old and replace it with the new. If there
was a debate, the technologists prevailed. A subtle and fragile culture
would be transformed. By 1998—the planned end date for the
project—the modus operandi of air traffic controllers, maintenance
engineers, computer operators, guards, secretaries, and supervisors
would become a rumor, the stuff of anecdotes. Where they had been
and what they had done would be obliterated.

The Mission

The Advanced Automation System began, in concept, in 1981 and
ended in 1994, "terminated for convenience" by the government.
Billions of dollars were spent on it. It is hard to describe. You can't
learn anything from the name. You know it's about air traffic control
because I told you, or because you read about it in the papers. Maybe
part of the problem was the name. It sounds like the system to end
all systems.

One engineer I know described the AAS this way. You're living in
a modest house and you see the refrigerator going. The ice sometimes melts, and the door isn't flush, and the repairman comes out,
it seems, once a month. And now you notice it's bulky and doesn't
save energy, and you've seen those new ones at Sears. So it's time. The
first thing you do is look into some land a couple of states over and
think about a new house. Then you get I. M. Pei and some of the
great architects and hold a design run-off. This takes awhile, so you
have to put up with the fridge, which is now making a buzzing noise
that keeps you awake at night. You look at several plans and even
build a prototype or two. Time goes on and you finally choose a design. There is a big bash before building starts. Then you build. And
build. The celebrating continues; each brick thrills. Then you
change your mind. You really wanted a Japanese house with red-

wood floors and a formal garden. So you start to re-engineer what you have. Move a few bricks and some sod. Finally, you have something that looks pretty good. Then, one night, you go to bed and notice the buzzing in the refrigerator is gone. Something's wrong. The silence keeps you awake. You've spent too much money! You don't really want to move! And now you find out the kids don't like the new house. In fact, your daughter says "I hate it." So you cut your losses. Fifteen years and a few billion dollars later, the old refrigerator is still running. Somehow.

On the Advanced Automation System, everything was to change. Each air traffic controller would have his own workstation. He or she could operate an ensemble of computers and communications channels, software and peripheral devices, all hidden away inside the cabinetry. The workstation was the show piece of the new system. A 20 x 20-inch Sony display brought high-resolution graphics to air traffic control. Each controller could tune the splendid graphics to suit his or her situation and preference.

The original Tracon and en route computers would be replaced. There would be the new algorithms. A new digital voice system was coming along. There would be the latest in fault-tolerant computing, algorithms to protect the air traffic control algorithms, so the system would (almost) never fail. (The system could fail only three seconds a year, according to Mitre's analysis.) Although this was the most discussed requirement (later both Mitre and the FAA admitted it was not achievable), there were many extreme requirements, any one of which could undermine the successful implementation of a digital system. For example: recording video by sending computer files over a local area network because VCRs could not handle the huge Sony displays; replacing paper terrain maps with electronic renderings whose geographical markings could not be accurately certified; cutting over from one version of software to another while the system is running; distributing the processing of a single flight over dozens of computers whose synchronization could be undone by a single fault; replacing paper clearances ("flight UAL22 is cleared to altitude . . .") with electronic notes, coupled with the complete removal of printers (the FAA was zealous about having a paperless system, this system designed upon glaciers of paper. Deprived of a means to old habits, the air traffic controllers would have no choice but to adopt new ones.); a training system that was to simulate the entire system within one workstation; the capability for an entire air traffic control center to backup any other or all centers (this would have required super-computers not yet imagined, embedded in each workstation). Ada—the FAA fell in with the Department of Defense in mandating this "final and definitive language" for programming—was a requirement, especially the spirit of Ada, bearing upon its back ferocious government supervision.

The Project

The project was conducted in two phases: a design competition, which ran from 1983 to 1988, pitted IBM against Hughes; and the big prize, the acquisition phase. The design run-off included proto-typing and the development of detailed plans and specifications, very few of which made it through the acquisition phase. In the de-sign phase, years before programs would be written, years before a contractor was chosen, specifications for computer programs were written to the bit level. Systems engineers worked hundred-hour weeks to develop thousand-page specifications for programs whose loops would begin to unfold in about seven years. (By then, the orig-inal specifications had been rewritten many times.) The software de-sign was also to be completed in the design phase. It was believed that writing the design in Ada would make coding easier. But, the programmers, unschooled in the use of abstractions, delivered what amounted to code in the design phase. This was even touted by IBM, which proudly proclaimed that it had written a million lines of Ada design. Virtually none of it survived.

The FAA later admitted that the design competition, which cost the taxpayers $1 billion, was of little value. Nevertheless, it was an opportunity for the private sector to advance. Hughes and IBM brought on their experts, people who, in the prime of their careers, had helped put a man on the moon, had built weapons systems, had been heroes of another age in air traffic control automation. This was to be their greatest accomplishment, an accomplishment they would share with the dozens of subcontractors the FAA hired to watch them. Throughout the ranks, from top to bottom, in both the private and public sector, this would be their finest hour.

Things began to go wrong almost immediately. By 1986, it had become clear that the consolidation of facilities was never going to happen. It is hard to believe that anyone ever thought it would. Yet, the FAA pressed on. Just before the start of the acquisition phase, they decoupled the Tracon and the en route systems. But by then, both contractors had conceived a design that embraced both. The mission altered, the technical approach went forward as if it had not.

The outcome was decided in 1988. Hughes—having taken on many of the characteristics of its founder, Howard Hughes, who brought a Hollywood approach to the aerospace business—predictably, outscored IBM's proposal. But IBM won the job, because it was cheaper and because of IBM's long-term collaboration with the FAA. (IBM had built the en route automation system.) Hughes' protest was denied.

At $3.7 billion, the Advanced Automation System was one of the largest civilian computer contracts ever; maybe the largest. It was the largest single contract in IBM's history. From the moment it was awarded, until near the project's end, IBM patted itself on the back. The herculean efforts of thousands of people in the design competition phase fueled a years-long celebration. There was something for everybody, beginning with a great ball in Union Station, featuring Chubby Checker and "The Twist."

At its peak the project employed over 2000 people. About a million dollars a day. If you thought like the IBM project manager, this was a good deal. Many people were working and money was being made. It was going to last forever. No one considered that it wouldn't. And everyone was getting ahead. (One of the ironies of conceptual work is that it is easy to believe you are farther along than you are; only symbols are being produced.) How could it end?

The AAS project lasted longer than the siege of Troy—by four years—and the story, as at Troy, lay in the effort itself. If you want to get a feel for how it was, you can read the *Iliad*. There, for example, you can learn in Book II:

> From the camp,
> the troops were turning out now, thick as bees
> that issue from some crevice in a rock face,
> endlessly pouring forth, to make some cluster
> and swarm on blooms of summer here and there,
> glinting and droning, busy in bright air.
> Like bees innumerable from ships and huts
> down the deep foreshore streamed those regiments
> toward the assembly ground—and Rumor blazed
> among them like a crier sent from Zeus.

---

from "Bugs in the Program," 8/3/89

(A Report to the 101st Congress on problems in federal government computer software development and regulation, submitted by the Subcommittee on Investigations and Oversight.)

Dear Mr. Chairman:

"The Comptroller General reported in 1986 that the FAA Advanced Automation System—the foundation of the nation's ability to manage future air traffic—was being developed with an approach that does not adequately mitigate technical risks . . . The program has already encountered significant cost growth (at least 50 percent in the design competition phase).

"What may finally force a redefinition of this procurement system is continued failure to balance the budget. The strange policy where the Government pays twice for a system—once to buy it and again to make it work . . . cannot be sustained in an era of multibillion dollar shortfalls in the Treasury.

"Behind every successful software system, be it air traffic control or medical diagnosis, is a software manager. Like software itself, these managers must be developed.

"Adaptive intelligence in safety-critical systems may be beyond the capability of regulatory agencies to certify.

"Nothing recommended in this report will have any effect on the software problem."

The AAS must have been the most supervised project in history: this atop its enormous size and complexity, and the extreme and constantly changing requirements. One programmer described it this way: "Working on the project was like working on a car inside the garage with the motor running. Eventually, even the crickets hopping around the tires suffocate." I wonder now if we would have finished the original en route system today, with another thirty years of government rules heaped on? Surely, one thing that helped us then was our ignorance.

What I saw on the FAA's Advanced Automation System would make Sisyphus weep. Bullfinch does a nice job of describing his life in the "infernal regions": "his task was to roll a huge stone up to a hill-top, but when the steep was well-nigh gained, the rock, repulsed by some sudden force, rushed headlong down to the plain. Again, he toiled at it, while the sweat bathed all his weary limbs, but all to no effect."

Whatever commitment and discipline there was—and I believe all involved, both in the FAA and in the private sector, were deeply committed—was worn down by a battery of watchfulness that I can only ascribe to a fear of failure. In spite of the tens of millions of dollars spent on new computers for AAS, the most important piece of equipment on the project was the overhead projector. There were endless meetings attended by dozens of people—as if we were never quite sure about the whole thing. The people in charge simply lacked the confidence and the finesse of the space team: NASA, contractors, and astronauts.

The AAS was the intellectual equivalent of building a bridge over the Atlantic Ocean—all at once. The programmers knew better: they were building five bridges over the Atlantic with tools never before used in bridge-building.

If you could sit down for an hour and imagine everything you might want to know about a system and its programs, in advance of their production, and write it all down in a contract, then add it to the lists of a hundred of your friends who were asked to do the same thing, you would fall short of the requirements for workmanship and documentation levied on the AAS. For every line of software, a hundred pages were written about it. On such projects, hardly anyone programs. One test plan I saw ran to 800 pages to test five requirements for gathering online performance data. And, when it came to something as important as system availability, the documentation scaled up. None of this was done once. It was done many times. Scores of people were paid to review and critique the work, which they did with glee. Every decision resulted in more work. Nothing was replaced.

---

from Government Computer News, 8/21/89

FAA MANAGER BLAMES IBM'S ADA TOOLS

"The FAA program manager, Michael E. Perie, said last week that immature technology in the Ada Programming Support Environment supplied by IBM has delayed the AAS.

"IBM officials took issue with Perie's remarks: 'Our APSE does not impact the software development schedule.'

"The FAA also has had some 'requirements questions' regarding the contract, Perie said. 'And we're still wrestling with how big that problem is in terms of schedule and cost.'

"IBM officials disagreed: 'We're confident that if we encounter any early delays, that those would be overcome by progress made later.'

"Some of the software development problems 'are just classic,' Perie said."

---

from Datamation, 12/11/89

FAA TO ASK REVISION OF IBM

"Last summer, IBM stumbled on the third of seven builds. IBM has indicated plans to extend the fourth build from three months to six while adding one month to builds five through seven, Mullikin said."

"Build four, Mullikin said, also will be lengthened to allow IBM to rehost software from the (sic) its next-generation RISC processor.

"The original schedule did not allow for rehosting."

---

from Electronic News, 9/3/90

FAA PROJECT FACES MORE DELAYS

"The FAA's $3.5 billion air traffic control program, already 13 months behind schedule, will likely be further delayed another nine months, according to a recent report by the Government Accounting Office.

"'The 13-month extension does not consider the time required to resolve remaining requirements,' the GAO report concludes.

"'Further, little time has been allotted for resolving problems that may arise from system testing.'"

Subject: In your mail . . .

"In your mail you will be receiving a copy of a letter from Riebau to Dennis Trippel. The letter expresses a concern that IBM is modifying PU10 without FAA approval, namely by changing STNs that are fulfilling PU10 DID requirements. The letter requests Trippel to notify IBM that the applicable STNs are frozen and that any changes have to be formally submitted to the FAA for review and approval—and that exceptions must be formally submitted via the deviation and waiver process. I will be working with my representatives to determine what ramifications this may have on the mechanism that we already have in place for getting FAA approval for STN changes. I hope that whatever we work out will have little to no impact on our internal process of STN change."

"Have a nice day, Jenny"

In 1991, Harmon, a lead programmer, convinced his team to read their own source code aloud at inspections, not have it read by a disinterested party, as the procedures required. He wanted to reduce the overhead of inspections, which had become grossly over-attended and over-documented. Bloated, he called them. "They were interfering with the natural pace of programming."

Inspections have not changed much over the years. They can apply to any document: requirements, design, code, test plans, procedures. They are administered by project and conducted by peers. Management does not attend meetings. This is a take-off on Heisenberg's Uncertainty Principle, wherein observing the experiment changes it. Besides, it has been suggested, the public discovery and tallying of errors is enough to discourage making them. A separate organization, quality assurance, often placed strategically within the company or the project, approves the procedures for conducting inspections, monitors their conduct, then collects, collates, and reports statistics to management.

Inspections are often referred to as formal inspections. They do resemble a liturgy. Invitations are issued. About three days in advance, prospective participants are told the time and place of the inspection meeting and given the material to be inspected. The meeting is presided over by a moderator, who attends indoctrination sessions to prepare for the role. A presenter, a sort of ad hoc deacon who cannot be the author, reads aloud from the exhibit, usually not line-by-line. The errors and questions are scrupulously recorded by the moderator, or another. The meeting lasts about two hours. Participants must itemize the amount of time spent preparing for the meeting, reading and inspecting the exhibit, and documenting their findings. This is considered important data, because the cost of inspections is high: fifty programming statements, written in three hours, may cost twenty to forty labor-hours to inspect.

But then Harmon. The streamlining paid off—at first. Programs in his area were getting done on schedule, and they worked. There were a number of reasons for this, but he attributed his team's success to leaner inspections. He was also an honest fellow, so he reported the new method to his quality assurance department, hoping to institutionalize it. Shortly thereafter they reported it to the FAA quality assurance officer. This was in keeping with the rules of quality assurance. The contractor may define his own procedures, but, having written them down, the contractor and the sponsor quality assurance departments collaborate to penalize any violations. There are no exceptions.

In about a month, the FAA wrote a letter to IBM insisting that IBM had violated its commitment to the very methods it had created. This could result in a reduction in fee. There were several meetings involving the FAA's quality assurance officer (Riebau), and contracts officer (Trippel), IBM's software development manager, IBM's Director of Development, and scores of others. No one could agree. The matter was escalated to Mike Perie, the FAA's project manager for the Advanced Automation System, and Bill Carson, IBM's Vice-President for Air Traffic Control Systems. Here, things were clarified. The system development plan, delivered with the proposal, was considered part of the contract. And the hundreds of standards and procedures developed along the way, riders to the plan, were likewise contractually binding. Unhappily, IBM was in breach of the contract because a programmer had given voice to his own code.

After many more meetings, IBM apologized. Harmon was reprimanded, but legal actions were avoided.

A Technical Problem: The All-American State Machine

The smallness of computers and our penchant for giving everyone his own, created on the Advanced Automation System a technical problem that befit the grandness of the project.

Soon after—it seems now like moments after—the first VLSI chip rolled off the line and a few promising protocols for distributed processing had been published, the sponsors of large systems here and abroad were insisting their systems be distributed. The programmers who had just come off a decade of grinding it out on mainframes—making programs work on a single computer, albeit something fancy like a multiprocessor or an array processor—had some idea of what they were in for. But, experts were saying that distributed systems were safer, and more reliable. "The loss of one computer won't mean much; it's the family that's important," a friend said. No fool, he also said: "distributed processing appears in theory to make problems smaller, but it will make them bigger. The solution will wash over the problem with complexity."

One of the nice things about theory is you can stay close to home. In fact, it's hard to think deeply about one subject while you're musing about four or five others. So we invented polymers and didn't think too much about the effect polymerization would have on the health of chemists. The theory of distributed computing is one thing. But the theory of distributed work is another. That's where the programming comes in. Moving the work to a machine, the machine, some machines, any machine, or all machines at the right time, is no small beer, especially in the presence of failures and heavy traffic. And then clocks have a way of drifting just like programmers' thoughts. Is it easier to send work from one machine to all machines than to some, or to just one? It depends. How important is the work? Must it arrive within a small window in time? Is it transient—Can the next message be sent again with negligible effect? Must the work be synchonized across machines?

Mathematicians speak of states. (A state is a value at a moment in time.) There can be a next state and a previous state, in fact, an entire history of states. There can be incorrect states, incoherent states, contingent states, even states of no consequence. These wonderfully adaptive states can apply to the values programs produce as well as to the programs themselves. A program can be in an incorrect state temporarily, but the values it has produced are OK. Or—and this is where work involves not just the machine but the human—the values may be temporarily incorrect, but, to the human, it does not matter.

There was no standardized software product to provide control services for distributed processing at the time of the AAS design. There was nothing available like IBM's OS/360—and its descendents—which, for the mainframe, insulate the application programmer from the particulars of storage regions, channels, multiprogramming and concurrency, disk drives, tapes, communications lines, and such. To implement large-scale, real-time applications on a local area network of cooperating processors, you had to write your own control program. On the AAS, such a program was written and debugged over a dozen years. (It is in service today, adapted to other air traffic control projects; but it is not standard, and it has never been marketed as a product.) This may have been the programmers' greatest achievement; but no one anticipated the time it would take to pull it off.

Part of the AAS control program was intended to solve a most absorbing problem: replacing programs with persistent states (the half-life of the flight data of the en route system can be measured in minutes and hours) while the programs are running. There are always new versions coming along containing fixes or new features. Their insertion into the operational suite can be an intractable problem when no part of the human's work is done on paper, or when there is no completely independent digital backup system. It turns out, if the work can continue elsewhere, you can stop the machine for awhile and carefully reload, resynchronize, and reconcile new programs with old values. Otherwise, you must reconcile them while the programs are running. The latter was the case on the AAS.

No one could figure out how to do it. There were a thousand conversations about it, about how it was no big deal if you did this or that. But we simply couldn't do it. There was a backup system; but it shared programs with the primary. And the FAA insisted: no paper. "We want an All-American State Machine." The financial estimate to solve this problem was escalated to Congress. It got their attention; the ticket was in the hundreds of millions of dollars. But the fact is it could not have been done for a trillion dollars.

A Psychological Problem Dressed Up as a Technical Problem

It has been noted by everyone from the New York Times to the Vice-President of the United States that the main problem on the Advanced Automation System was "changing requirements." For those involved in large-scale computer systems, that is nothing new. No one can perfectly surmise the shape and feel of a system years in advance. Even replacing some aspect of a system you know by heart is not immune from thinking twice about it. It's in the conceptual nature of things, one. And two, we all—if we cannot explain it, at least—sense that software is a form of rapid specialization. That is, with lightning speed, we can change one "machine" into another, turn a lamp into a gate. We are no longer amazed by—in Herbert Simon's words—the "automated navigator."

The requirements churn (it was called) on the Advanced Automation System was not normal. It was the result of our enchantment with the computer-human interface, the CHI. The new controller workstation, fronted by a 20" by 20" color display, because it was capable of a seemingly endless variety of presentations, mesmerized the population of AAS like the O.J. Simpson trial mesmerized the nation. In simple arithmetic, each controller would operate a computer filled with 64 megabytes of software just to display and exchange commands with the original en route computer, which runs all of the air traffic control algorithms in about 3 megabytes. In simple psychological terms, we all went nuts.

The project was handed over to human factors pundits, who then drove the design. Requirements became synonymous with preferences. Thousands of labor-months were spent designing, discussing, and demonstrating the possibilities: colors, fonts, overlays, reversals, serpentine lists, toggling, zooming, opaque windows, the list is huge. But, it was something to see. (Virtually all of the marketing brochures—produced prematurely and in large numbers—sparkled with some rendition or other of the new controller console.) It just wasn't usable.

The display management software was designed as a single program, thousands of statements long, its task to interpret and apply hundreds of rules (in combination) aimed at mere presentation. It took years to write, and it was rewritten a dozen times. The requirements themselves were highly structured and complex, spanning the idiosyncracies of individual facilities, sectors of airspace, and controllers. Never before would the human retina play such a profound role in the design of a system—and, as it turned out, the dexterity of the human hand. (In retrospect, it may be that we were able to field the original en route and Tracon systems within a reasonable time because, on the front end, in development, we could use only punched cards—there were no CASE tools—and our programs produced data for mechanical equipment and displays that operated much as they had in the 1950s. No human factors analysis. No indecision. We could concentrate on the arithmetic—which was tough enough.)

The cost of what turned out to be a 14-year human factors study did not pay off. Shortly before the project was terminated a controller on the CBS evening news said: "It takes me 12 commands to do what I used to do with one." I believe he spoke for everyone with common sense.

The Testament

Rummaging through one of the closets at the far end of the hall on the fifth floor one day, looking for some standards document, I found an envelope left by someone who left the company—as many did after so many years advancing against stone, while the wheels of commerce were accelerating on what everyone referred to as "the outside." It contained "A Brief History of the Advanced Automation System." It was printed by hand and left, perhaps inadvertently, or perhaps with the hope that some anthropologist might some day discover it and make a pronouncement. In every important way, it is the truth.

"A young man, recently hired, devotes years to a specification written to the bit level for programs that will never be coded. Another, to a specification that will be replaced. Programmers marry one another, then divorce and marry someone in another subsystem. Program designs are written to severe formats, then forgotton. The formats endure. A man decides to become a woman and succeeds before system testing starts. As testing approaches, she begins a second career on local television, hosting a show on witchcraft. An architect chases a new technology, then another, then changes his mind and goes into management. A veteran programmer writes the same program a dozen times, then transfers. The price of money increases eight times. Programmers sleep in the halls. Committees convene for years to discuss keystroking. An ambitious training manager builds an encyclopedia of manuals no one will use. Decisions are scheduled weeks in advance. Workers sit in hallways. Notions about computing begin in the epoch of A, edge toward B, then come down hard on A + B. Human factors experts achieve Olympian status. The Berlin Wall collapses. The map of Europe is redrawn. Everything is counted. Quality becomes mixed with quantity. Morale is reduced to a quotient, then counted. Dozens of men and women argue for thousands of hours: What is a requirement? A generation of workers retires. The very mission changes and only a few notice. Programming theories come and go. Managers cling to expectations, like a child to a blanket. Presentations are polished to create an impression, then curbed to cut costs. Then they are studied. The work spikes and spikes again. Offices are changed a dozen times. Management retires and returns. The contractor is sold. Software is blamed. Executives are promoted. The years rip by with no end in sight. A company president gets an idea: make large small. Turn methods over to each programmer. Dress down. Count on the inscrutability of programming. Promote good news. Turn a leaf away from the sun. Maybe start over."

IBM Response to FAA's Cure Letter: 12/10/92

"IBM recommends . . . a new schedule, faster processors, and a new software development manager. The Chairman of the Board of IBM's Federal Systems Company (who was quoted later, 'if people could have just left it alone, we could have delivered it') will take over as IBM's AAS Program Manager. IBM will renew its efforts to test the software."

The Curtain

When the project ended it was reported in The Washington Post that there were over 3000 software defects. Other papers confirmed what everyone already suspected: the software could not be written. It was riddled with bugs. Everyone was relieved. It was the software. It was the programmers, the way they programmed, and how they were managed, how loops were divined, and the assignment of numbers to variables, how modules were laid out, and how queues were allocated, and the time spent in the lab (was it enough?). The original software development manager had been the first to go. She was defamed, first from within and then outside, according to the rules of blame, written down nowhere, but embedded deep within our unconscious. Then the test manager, the IBM project manager and his financial officer, then hundreds more left.

It was the software of course. But not in the sense we all want to believe. It was in the *nature* of software, the nature of programming; its roots tangled in the mathematics of contradiction and logic and symbol-production, plied by young tradesmen schooled in the tools of the latest process, its promise intensified by greed and ease, its complexity beyond imagining, man mingling with machine to a degree that cannot be described, felt to be immune to the laws of size— these computer programs: easy to miss within the great facilities that house them, amidst the spandrels and joists and tree-like arches and great enclosures, decorated for art's sake.

I don't know how the programmers felt about the demise of AAS. I didn't ask them. Most of them worked for years and knew about as much about the forces at work as the Fijians knew about the causes of the Second World War. They worked too hard to know. Twenty-five hour weekends. Sleep-overs. In-plant babysitting. (Ask anybody who's been a programmer on any project.) Afterwards they left, ran to other jobs, any jobs. Many are on their second or third job now. They didn't leave for advancement. They left to get away. I don't know how they endured. They did good work. In the shank of the project, the suffocating bureaucracy and the beckoning of video games their friends in other places were creating in the new age of software did not affect them. They were a cadre of disciplined programmers, who would not cut corners on writing well-documented and thoroughly-read code, who tested their bottoms off, and believed in metrics, who wrote reliable programs, when they had every reason to give in to hurriedness. Or just give in.

Coda

from the hearing before the Committee on Public Works and Transportation, Wednesday, April 13, 1994, 9:30 a.m.

The Honorable David R. Hinson, Administrator, Federal Aviation Administration:

"This Subcommittee is well aware of the troubled history of the AAS program. The review . . . reflects a range of costs from $6.5 billion to $7.3 billion for completion of the program, and slippage of implementation dates by 9 to 31 months.

"I tasked the Center for Naval Analysis with conducting an independent 90-day review. I wanted that unvarnished look from an outside group."

The project ended quietly enough. There were a few articles in the big city papers, some personnel were shifted, but, in general, civilization flowed on as usual. The CNA performed its task and made their recommendations on cue, among them the "clear evidence that electronic flight strips were unnecessary; air traffic control companies that provide this capability found it necessary to provide paper strips." The all-digital approach would not do. Too much automation, they reasoned. The FAA had insisted upon the utmost in automation. With 80% of ground control already automated, they beat the drums for the other 80%, squeezing out the remaining 20%, and redoing much of what already worked. (That is true, but so is this: put enough time and money into any project, up-front, and it will fail.)

In 1994, when the curtain fell, the FAA pressed Congress for help. Within months, Congress passed legislation permitting the FAA to waive the burdensome federal procurement regulations—over the protests of Senators John Glenn and Strom Thurmond, who argued that other government departments do just fine under the already streamlined rules. Senator William S. Cohen spoke out as well: "Regrettably, Congress bought the argument that federal procurement and personnel policies (personnel rules were reduced from 1069 pages to 41 and "integrated product teams" were put in place) have prevented the FAA from modernizing the air traffic control systems; but federal policies are not the problem. It was poor management." (Senator Cohen is mistaken, of course. Poor management? For decades, the FAA has "managed" to keep the most complex system on earth running 24 hours a day, seven days a week. I know of no more competent and committed managers. Is management the problem down the block as well, at the IRS and FBI? The IRS management is being replaced because of software project overruns. The FBI is losing Congressional support, not because of law enforcement problems, but because of two software projects. Where will it end, I wonder? How many managers in how many departments in how many nations will be replaced because they were undone by the seduction of loops?)

So, cumbersome regulations replaced software as the problem, its slate wiped clean. From now on, the FAA, unlike the Department of Defense—who must push on conservatively—can acquire systems without much oversight, so that, according to David Hinson, the past FAA administrator, the FAA can keep apace with industry. (If he meant the software industry, which is more and more taking on the character of alchemy, the problems of air traffic control may go from bad to worse.) Thus, the Advanced Automation System, failing to overhaul air traffic control automation, succeeded in restructuring the FAA. And, officially, we have learned nothing about the pitfalls of software and its use in large systems. As for IBM, it sold the Federal Systems Company to raise cash.

Epilogue

When I wrote this piece for Bob Glass, a few years back, he asked me to summarize the lessons we might learn from the AAS. He meant the lessons for practicing programmers—putting aside the limitations of programmable computers and the madness of the human condition embodied so vividly on the Advanced Automation System.

I mentioned some originally, and I would not go back on them. Surely, the problem of size and complexity is central. Although, these can easily be gotten around by misinterpreting software as a manufacturing process, composed of source statements and such, instead of the complex logico-mathematical phenomenon that it is. (On AAS, virtually all measures of effectiveness, including costs, turned on the notion of software as a collection of "lines of code.")

The two technical issues highlighted in the article also brought to the surface "limits": distributed processing, more accurately described as distributed semantics, in which meaning must cohere in the face of latency and a panoply of failure modes (as opposed to the relatively "stateless" nodes of most networks); and the "infernal CHI," as one manager called it, which became a preoccupation non-pareil.

I would add, also, the problem of programming design, which, in the late 1960s and 1970s was beginning to make inroads. It seems that there is no good way to prevent programmers from rushing ahead in the quest for intellectual control. What was once called "stepwise refinement," the gradual decomposition of structure and semantics, is not enforceable, and, if it were, it would be too easily breached. Mostly, programmers just code—as is their and their managers' preference.

There is one last thing. It is equal parts psychological and technical. Software is both a source of amusement and engineering achievement. It is easy to change, to the point of whimsy, and it allows us to do things heretofore unthinkable, like putting man on the moon. It is contradictory and miraculous. (Perhaps all miracles are contradictory.) As the genetic engineers and nano-technologists well know, get far enough down into the world of symbols and one can transform the very nature of structure and meaning.

But the miracles produced by computers and computer programming are not enough. We've gotten accustomed to them. Now we would like them to be easy: we invent tools, themselves programs, that make vendors wealthy, but seem only to complicate the already complicated, and we invent new paradigms, such as reusability and non-developed items, and commercial-off-the-shelf, to convince ourselves that programming is not so hard after all.

Not satisfied with easy miracles, we want them to occur immediately: the Department of Defense has spent millions on productivity, and private companies sling their products out the door without hesitation, as if heaping more technological side effects on a planet already choked by them were not relevant. And, to boot, the trickier the nomenclature the better: we delight in giving old concepts new names, so that software remains, perforce, a field for the young. I believe the issue has been decided: once near-science has surrendered to cant.

2.2 BAD PLANNING AND ESTIMATING

Poor estimation is the plague of most software projects. As we have mentioned elsewhere in this book, projects are often in schedule trouble simply because the estimate was far too optimistic to match the reality of the task to be performed.

But remember, in this book we are talking about runaways. And we define runaways as projects that miss their targets—be they cost, schedule, or functionality—by over 100 percent. Because of that, runaways tend to be projects on which poor estimation is only part of the problem.

That is certainly true in the two war stories that follow. In these stories, in the heap of problems encountered are unstable requirements (shades of Section 2.1 of this book!), huge projects (Section 2.1 again), new technology that doesn't scale up (we'll encounter that one again in Section 2.3), and poor management focus (Section 2.4).

But, for these stories at least, overriding all these other concerns is the ever-present, impossible schedule. In one story, the notion of "management by schedule" mentioned elsewhere in this book becomes very graphic: The project team skipped certain required practices. But "they met their schedules, and that's all that mattered because that's what they're measured on." And the other story puts it succinctly, quoting "Hofstadter's Law": "Software development always takes longer than you think, even when you take into account Hofstadter's Law."

On to these two war stories. At ON Technology, just about anything that could go wrong did. And at the Project from Hell, customers kept changing the requirements and software developers refused to change their methods. For both, trouble was unavoidable. Here it comes!

2.2.1 *PAINFUL BIRTH: CREATING NEW SOFTWARE WAS AGONIZING TASK FOR MITCH KAPOR FIRM (ON)*

The business of creating new computer software—the programs that make computers work—is one of the most complex, painstaking, even exasperating jobs around. It is as if someone is writing *War and Peace* in code, puts one letter out of place and turns the whole book into gibberish.

So difficult is the process that it can baffle even such industry stars as Mitch Kapor, the founder of Lotus Development Corp., and Peter Miller, a well-known veteran. In November 1987, the two men formed a software company with the announced intention of making personal computers much easier to use.

But the path to simplicity proved tortuous, and not until early last month did they finally turn over to their manufacturing plant their first product, a single floppy disk. The software was late and far over budget; in fact, it almost didn't make it out the door. And it bore little resemblance to their original plans.

Besides the inherent complexity of the work, there are other problems. Most software-development planning stinks: A joke in the industry is that programmers spend 90% of their time on the first 80% of a project, then 90% of the remaining time on the final 20%. And most design stinks, too: Programmers either don't understand their customers well enough or load up products with features that please themselves but perplex everyone else.

Meanwhile, companies trying to become more efficient have a problem: they have ample computer hardware but lack software. And they won't get it soon.

The difficulties faced by Messrs. Kapor and Miller and their 23 employees at the fledgling company, ON Technology Inc., go a long way toward explaining the hopes and fears that drive the $8 billion-a-year software industry. The 39-year-old Mr. Kapor agreed to give this newspaper an inside look as their initial project unfolded because he believes that software design must be improved and the development process better understood.

The story begins in the summer of 1987. Mr. Kapor had recently wound down his dealings with Lotus, where he developed the 1-2-3 spreadsheet that, in selling more than five million copies since 1983, made Lotus into one of the world's software giants and powered the whole personal-computer industry into liftoff. Mr. Kapor, who left Lotus because it was getting too big, had taken a floor of office space in a professional building but had no projects.

All he had was his horror at the difficulty of using computers. "Not a day goes by that I don't want to throw my computer out the window," he said.

Mr. Kapor chatted with Mr. Miller, who used to work at Lotus, and found that he had some ideas but no office space. They got together. They shared an interest in a new area of software, object-oriented programming. And they worried that although their secretary would know what to do if they wanted to send a letter to Joe, their word-processing software wouldn't know who Joe was, how to send him a letter, how formally to address it.

The two men decided to produce a new layer of software that would let developers build such real-world knowledge into their applications. With that idea and Mr. Kapor's name, ON quickly lured some high-profile programmers and built up to 32 people. Mr. Kapor drew on his considerable wealth to finance the project and attracted investment from two venture-capital firms that made fortunes on Lotus.

The place resembled a think tank, with people waving magic markers while arguing around whiteboards or occasionally writing papers on software theory. There was a plastic dinosaur in the lobby, carrying a sign saying, "Welcome, Insurance Salesmen, Investment Advisers, Marketing Consultants, Industrial Spies." A couple of ping-pong tables were in the back.

But the big hardware and software companies didn't see ON as benign: They worried that new, popular software would give the newcomer too much leverage. Some indicated that they would try to quash the project by promising to deliver similar capability themselves. Mr. Kapor found that, in any case, he was years away from having a product and was running through $300,000 a month. So, in December 1988, he says, "we took the plan out and we shot it. We got it up at six in the morning, blindfolded it and shot it."

The company fell into chaos for three months. Employees started arriving late and leaving early. Some drifted away as their work disappeared. Others were asked to leave. Mr. Kapor went to the venture capitalists for more money. Wags started calling the company OFF Technology.

Even though the company shrank 50%, three projects took shape. The first, called On Location, was handed over to two young programmers in April 1989. This followed conventional wisdom that, for good communication, software should be written by teams no larger than four people—that nine women can't have one baby by being pregnant a month each.

The senior programmer was Roy Groth, now 27 years old, who spent his evenings and weekends playing trumpet in various bands. The other was Rob Tsuk (pronounced Chook), a husky 24-year-old. Also heavily involved was graphic designer Paul Moody, a 31-year-old car nut who kept a rearview mirror on his Macintosh so he could watch what was going on outside his office door. Mr. Miller, a 45-year-old who describes his style as management by walking around, was to supervise.

The basic idea behind the product was that people can store so much information on hard disks that the disks, like file cabinets, can become so crammed with stuff that it is hard to remember what anything was called or where it is. Products that search for files are slow. So, Messrs. Kapor and Miller decided there's room for a product for the Macintosh such as On Location, which would keep an index of what's where. The index would take up 1% to 2% of the hard disk but, they said, would find files 10 to 15 times faster than other products used by the four million Macintoshes operating world-wide.

The Work Technique

The basic approach was to build, try out and then fix repeated prototypes, with each a bit closer to the final product. That paid off when a mockup was shown to three industry gurus. One of them, Bobby Orbach, until recently a senior executive at 47th Street Computer, a New York retailer, said the product must be able to find any word in any file, not just the file names as originally planned. That proved to be a crucial piece of advice.

Messrs. Groth and Tsuk started churning out the code, writing in a language with few verbs and awash in punctuation such as: printf("%3.0f %6.1f/n"fahr,celsius);. They appeared to be making progress toward a shipment date of early November. Mr. Kapor turned to marketing and hired Conall Ryan, a 32-year-old who once worked for him at Lotus.

Mr. Moody started what the team called the product's choreography, figuring out how the user would use the product and anticipating all the errors he might make. It's a daunting task. Mr. Moody went through more than 100 versions of how the program should look on a monitor.

The office became intense, with programmers on all three projects sometimes working in bursts and then falling asleep in their offices, sometimes working well into the night at home. Spirits were high; the ping-pong games turned fierce. Mr. Ryan instituted a Friday-afternoon party, whose start was signaled by blasting music over the intercom and then by the sound of beer glug-glugging into a glass.

By early September, Mr. Miller said the product's features were essentially complete, and Mr. Kapor said he would be surprised if it wasn't finished by November. But then everything started going wrong. Features that were supposed to take a day to produce took three or four.

An Indexing Problem

The biggest, potentially fatal problem concerned the product's ability to index automatically. A tiny piece of the software was supposed to be always active in the main memory, watching to see when a file is created or changed, so it could call in more of the software when the computer is idle and update the index. But the Macintosh operating system tries to kill off pieces of software like that. There appeared to be no solution.

The group pored over lengthy printouts, called dumps, that contain a sort of map of what's going on in the computer's main memory. The dumps consist of groupings of letters and numbers that, if they weren't arranged in eight-character strings, would look as though someone had rested his elbows on a keyboard for an hour. To the initiated, they reveal an artful way to hide from the operating system by hiding *inside* it. It is a dangerous game of hide and seek. Mr. Tsuk later spent several days debugging this bit of software, and it kept crashing the system right up until the end.

In September, Mr. Ryan started what he called Real Dinners for Real People: He brought in half a dozen Macintosh users, fed them lasagna, and got their reactions to the latest prototype of On Location. This proved to be a smart move because it gave the team extensive feedback much earlier than usual. Most software is like a digital watch—there are features that nobody needs, and it's tough to figure out which does what to whom. But feedback helped Mr. Kapor keep banging away at two truths in software design: Simplicity is paramount, and less is often more.

At the first Real Dinner, Mr. Groth recalls, the Real People looked at the installation procedure and said, "You must be kidding." He laughed. "So, we said, 'You're right. We were kidding.'" Several more tries, and dinners, were needed to get it right. In the process, the team discarded a plan to let people keep their own indexes of all the files on all the hard disks on a network. It was hard to write the code and impossible for users to figure it out.

Slipping Schedule

But the schedule kept slipping further and further. As the shipment date headed toward the end of last year, Mr. Kapor worried that ON would miss the Christmas selling season. "It's like a Russian doll," Mr. Ryan says. "Every time we finally crack open one problem, we find there's another one inside."

The company also was running out of money again. So, Mr. Kapor had to go back to the venture capitalists, a move that would raise total financing to $9 million with no product to show for it. Mr. Kapor made a get-tough speech at a weekly staff meeting in September. "I'm not going to bail this out if it fails," he said. "We're playing with live ammo."

Two weeks later, Mr. Kapor got excited because he had an idea about future products that he described as being as good an idea as the one that led him to fame with Lotus 1-2-3. But it required cancellation of the two products beyond On Location. Five more programmers left.

The lone survivor from one of the projects was 27-year-old Nancy Benovich. She was asked to write the software to do so-called fuzzy searches, so that if someone wants all the files that contain the word "love," he will also get "loves," "loving" and "loved." Messrs. Kapor and Miller believed that her role would be discrete enough not to cause a problem. It did.

Ms. Benovich and Mr. Tsuk wound up writing codes that overlapped ever so slightly but bollixed up matters for days. In certain circumstances, their codes could clear a bit of memory twice, a nasty development that usually made the system crash—and so as to leave the basic problem hard to locate. However, debugging tools have improved so much that, once the type of problem was recognized, the team sent some software over telephone wires, attached its sensors to On Location, and quickly pinpointed the problem.

Debugging Woes

As it became clear that Christmas was out, shipments were postponed until January, and the developers breathed a sigh of relief. But even as most of the features were completed, development slowed as the bug-fixing process kicked into gear.

Bug-fixing is actually much simpler on the Macintosh than on IBM-compatible PCs. There are only a few types of Macintoshes, all made by Apple Computer Inc. In contrast, there are hundreds of IBM-compatible computers, all slightly different and all able to trip up the software in mysterious ways. Nevertheless, thousands of Macintosh applications are on the market, and the team had to make sure that its software didn't foul up any of them.

Candace Clampitt, 33, who ran the bug-fixing process, had three people banging on machines all day and had tests run automatically through the night. Mr. Tsuk sometimes spent whole days trying to duplicate, and then resolve, problems reported by people inside ON or by outside test users. At one point, he made a typing error and wiped out three computers, which had to be painstakingly resurrected. Mr. Groth put a "Do Not Disturb" sign on his door and forged ahead.

As the hours got longer, Mr. Groth got carried away when writing messages that alert the user to options or problems. Instead of the computer screen showing a box that read "Cancel" when someone has the option of killing a file, he had the box say, "Make My Day." But, as Messrs. Groth and Tsuk worked through the holidays, they seemed to be getting close. Shipment was set for mid-February.

Mr. Ryan, meanwhile, was winding up the marketing end. The list price had been set at $129.95, with the actual retail price at $75 to $85. The hope had been that users could be persuaded that On Location was in a different class than other software and thus should cost more. But the Real Dinners made it clear that wouldn't work. So Mr. Ryan told Lillian Rosen to get below $8 the unit cost of duplicating the disks and putting them in the boxes. She succeeded: Each unit would cost ON $7.47.

Squeezing Down

Mr. Kapor moved everyone into half the office space on the floor and prepared to rent out the other half. When Ms. Benovich completed her task on On Location, she was told there was no more work for her and was asked to leave. "It's one of those tough business decisions you have to make," Mr. Miller said. ON was no longer a think tank.

When announcement day, January 22, finally arrived, Mr. Kapor charmed a group of about 30 reporters at a press conference in the cafeteria. Afterward, as the programmers ran off to change out of their suits and ties, a reflective Mr. Kapor expressed some mixed feelings. "Software planning, at its best, is a mess," he said. "And this wasn't its best."

Everyone acknowledges being far too optimistic on timing. Mr. Kapor also says some problems could have been solved by tighter management, to keep Messrs. Groth and Tsuk from spending too much time polishing their code and from fixing bugs before they knew that the solutions wouldn't create more problems later.

The prototyping, though helping with the design, may have hampered the scheduling. Jeff Gibbons, a 37-year-old senior programmer, says it is relatively easy to know how long it will take to add a feature, but hard to know how long it will take to turn a feature from bug-ridden code into a finished version.

Nevertheless, Mr. Kapor declares himself pleased with the design process. And early reviews support him. "On Location winds up being a pretty incredible product from a design standpoint," says Stewart Alsop, the editor of PC Letter, an industry newsletter. The only complaints have been that the company didn't deliver on its initial vision and used a whole lot of brain power to attack a narrow problem. "It's as though William Faulkner wrote a really nice cookbook," says Richard Shaffer, the editor of Technologic Computer Letter.

The shipment date slipped to late February, but that seemed a small problem. At a PC conference in late January, Mr. Kapor made a tough speech about the sorry state of software design and generated interest in forming a group to figure out ways to attack the problem.

A Nasty Surprise

But Mr. Kapor had a nasty surprise awaiting him when he returned. On Location was slipping again. This time, no one even pretended to know how far behind the product really was. The marketing people told Mr. Kapor that they couldn't operate without a firm schedule and that they no longer had any confidence in the development group's ability to provide one.

Mr. Kapor had some long, hard sessions with Mr. Miller, who stormed out once but then returned. Mr. Kapor decided to become his Siamese twin in managing the project. They gathered the team together and produced an excruciatingly detailed accounting of all the work still to be done. They decided they could finish in a bit more than a month, but only by stopping work on the second project and devoting three more programmers to On Location.

"This is a mess," Mr. Kapor said. "A month's delay isn't that bad, but it's sort of, 'Do I really need this?'"

Office tensions heated up again, but the process stayed remarkably close to the new schedule. The product—the 30th version circulated internally—finally went to manufacturing.

Even that wasn't the end of the turmoil. Two weeks later, Mr. Miller quit, and Messrs. Groth and Tsuk agreed to leave. Mr. Kapor says there was less here than meets the eye—Mr. Miller may work on another project that Mr. Kapor would back, and Messrs. Groth and Tsuk were leaving because of personality conflicts that developed during the final days. Still, the departures left the young company with still-another set of challenges.

Mr. Kapor, reflective again, says, "I view this as character-building." The former transcendental-meditation teacher adds, "I'm moving closer to spiritual enlightenment. I'm not 10,000 miles away. I'm 9,999 miles away."

He, and all the others, vow to do better with their next project. But there's another software axiom that usually proves true. Called Hofstadter's law, it's circular: It says software development always takes longer than you think, even when you take into account Hofstadter's law.

2.2.2 THE PROJECT FROM HELL

by Jean Stanford

It Happened One Day

I thought I'd go in, do my job as an internal technology consultant and go home. Instead, I got involved with the Project from Hell.

My former boss, Joe, asked me to join a group of people analyzing the way my company was building software. Things had gotten out of hand on a $500 million project. Even with staff working more than 60 hours a week, late deliveries and mismatched components were the norm.

Why me? Well, my department is part of the technical staff for corporate headquarters. We're supposed to help the divisions put in place best-of-breed practices for systems development. Joe also came to me because I wasn't part of his developer group. I didn't have a vested interest. I couldn't be fired or promoted by anyone I'd be auditing.

What follows is the true account of my travails trying to get to the bottom of our development problems. It's not a pretty story.

Why is it every time I ask about what's going on in software development, I hear sunny-day stories from a bunch of information systems managers who are used to fooling the HQ pests? They'll tell me there are a few little glitches in the process, but those are under control, and everything is fine. I suppose I can't blame them; I've done that a few times myself. Joe's got 25 years of experience in IS, and I trust his intuition that something's terribly wrong. How can I find out what's really going on?

Went to see Joe. This project is huge! We're talking a real-time technical application worth more than $500 million. It has hundreds of programmers writing hundreds of thousands of lines of code in several languages, such as Ada and C, for multiple platforms, including Unix, VM, MVS and DOS. The project's cost-justification included building in code reuse, so I know the software development process will be complicated beyond anything I've ever seen.

This article was originally published in Computerworld, September 4, 1995. Copyright 1995 by Computerworld, Inc., Framingham, MA 01701.

I'm really worried. There are too many players and processes for me to assess on my own. It's going to take weeks just to learn the org chart. Besides, lots of these folks don't even work for Joe, so they'll welcome me like a visitor from the IRS.

I just read a cool book called *The Wisdom of Teams* by Jon R. Katzenbach and Douglas K. Smith (Harvard Business School Press, 1993) about how to form multidisciplinary teams. I'd like to form such a team to do the audit. The idea is to gather a bunch of techies who are actually doing the work and ask them how the thing is going. Bet it would be revealing—certainly more revealing than talking to project managers who bring me their blue-sky charts and tell me how things are *supposed* to work.

By forming a team of low-level technical staff from the various IS groups, I can find out what the critical issues are at the grassroots level. Then I can convert what we find out into higher-level process recommendations.

Joe was a bit taken aback this morning when I offered up the idea of using teams. It made him nervous because, after all, for the past 25 years he's only talked to managers about how things were going. Getting the scoop from the trenches isn't the traditional way to do an audit—and Joe is the most traditional of men. But after a while, he warmed up to the idea (I guess when you're desperate, you do unusual things). Later in the afternoon we went around to the user department managers to recruit nominees for our audit team.

Well, the software development managers hated the idea. They told us to drop dead (pretty much what I expected).

The development managers say they aren't interested in creating more work for their overburdened staffs. Everyone already has worked incredible overtime on this project. The customer keeps changing requirements. Get this: It now wants to move pieces of the project from a mainframe to a client/server platform.

Joe and I tried to convince our developers that if we smooth out the process, it will mean less work in the long run.

At least Joe's on my side.

I can't believe it, but I'm finding some pockets of support. One systems engineer is going to join the audit team because her manager wants to know what we're up to—kind of like having a spy in our midst.

Three people are coming from the test group. These guys are all for the idea because they're getting hurt by the shape of the software they're getting to test. The manager of the test department told me in no uncertain terms that the software developers better get their act together.

The rest of the team is coming from the technical staff of the build department and the systems configuration management (CM) department. The CM guys deal with the overall structure of the system such as hardware components and specifications. Specs have been changing so rapidly, they want to get a handle on what is coming at them. The software guys keep saying, "Trust us. We're working as hard as we can. We'll explain things when we're done." Which, of course, never happens.

There are 20 people on the team.

We've just had our second two-hour meeting. I thought we would all work together to do a top-down map of how the process works. Then we could analyze the process and make it more efficient.

Not on your life. These guys don't want to spend time doing a process map—even though that's what all the process improvement books say to do. They say they're too busy, and they don't care about the overall process anyway. Now what?

Today's meeting was a little better. The data dictionary support group, which is responsible for standardizing data elements across the application, walked through its process for handling bug reports.

The presentation generated a lot of discussion. People actually said they had a better feel for the issues in handling the data dictionary and a little more sympathy for the poor guys trying to manage the big beast. We agreed to meet for two hours next week to discuss how bug reports are managed in the test tools department.

We got into the bug-fixing process for reused code today. What a rat's nest! If the programmers don't have a way to record exactly which bug they fixed when they check in the code, we can't tell if the reused code is up to date or not.

We got into this area because of a "hot button." One of the guys had spent all weekend testing something that turned out to have a bug that others had known about.

Programmers are reusing code that isn't quite ready for prime time. They are just copying source code and making their own changes to those copies. So when someone finds a bug in Copy A, he has to notify the people who have Copy B and make sure they make the fix. Multiply that by hundreds of reused files, and you have—well, you have a mess. You also have a lot of coordinating to do. The source code management process needs to be spiffed up.

If we get a better source code management tool and get the software developers to use it, it will save a lot of time. Instead of calling each person you think might have copied the code, we could put a public notice on our Unix-based groupware software that something had been checked in with a certain bug fix. Then everyone who needed the fix could copy the file.

We spoke with some programmers about checking in the files each time they make a change and recording the bug report number. Get this: That's already what they're supposed to do, but they've been circumventing the whole bug report process. They proudly demonstrated a clever tool they had written that faked out the central repository and let them avoid checking for bugs with each change.

They were supposed to be checking in files as they completed each change. Instead, they kept all their working files in their home directories. Once every three months, their ingenious little tool swept their directories and checked everything en masse for the whole subsystem. If that wiped out some fixes, well tough. They met their schedules, and that's all that mattered because that's what they were measured on. No wonder the test schedule is trashed. The test guys are getting a totally unstable system every time. The testers are ready to bomb the lab, and I can hardly blame them.

It's time to tell IS management what we've found—that the change control processes (such as bug reporting) need a lot of work, the software build process is out of control (surprise) and that they will miss customer delivery dates if there aren't changes. We're not talking about missing dates by months but by five years or more—no joke. We need process fixes, new people and organizational structure as soon as possible.

This isn't going to be a happy meeting. I'll do the briefings because I'm from HQ, and they can't fire me. None of the people on my team want to come. I don't blame them.

The managers thanked me for my report and said they would handle it from here. Why do I think it fell in the bit bucket? I gave a copy of the report to my manager, just in case.

A month has gone by. My friends tell me the process is as screwed up as ever. My manager is going to mention it at the next program review. Bet he'll get more of the same IS management show biz.

It all hit the fan today. The last delivery fell completely apart. The subsystems that had worked together before the release suddenly didn't talk to one another. Reports were wrong. Functions that worked before were now broken. And systems performance degraded, too. (Click on an icon and you could go out and get a cup of coffee while you waited for a response.) Worse yet, the customer's test people were in the lab to see it. Talk about irate! Uh, oh.

My bug report process maps are coming in handy. I've been appointed to an emergency team to fix the process so the customer regains some confidence. Funny, this time the software people are working with us.

There have been a lot of changes in the past six months based on our team's suggestions. A new person is in place—her official title is Configuration Management Process Owner—who will be responsible for every aspect of configuration, from requirements tracking to hardware and operating system configuration to the actual configuration of each release and delivery. This is the first time we've had someone in charge of the development picture from end to end.

There was a lot of moaning and groaning, but now IS audits every step, and developers have to check in code for each bug report change made. To everyone's surprise, overtime has gone down. Working with a more stable base is making everyone's job easier. The software installs better, and it is running more predictably.

I can't believe I'm writing this, but I'm off to do another audit in which I'll apply the same techniques. Into the next fire!

2.3 TECHNOLOGY NEW TO THE ORGANIZATION

In this section we find the biggest surprise in this book. New technology, often touted as the cure to software's problems, is frequently not the solution to, but the cause of, some of those problems. That finding is manifested in this book in two ways—it was mentioned prominently in the research findings we discussed earlier in the book, and it shows up here in this section through the number of runaways we found that fit into this category.

It is a fascinating finding. For years—perhaps decades—software engineering people have been saying that weaknesses in management, not in technology, are the prime cause of software project failures. And, in the research study we presented earlier, we saw that until recently that was apparently true. But in recent years—the survey finds the increase in technical failures happening between 1989 and 1995—the situation has changed.

What happened during those years that might have caused or accelerated this change? Probably the most relevant reason would be the increase in the appearance of highly-touted new technologies (Fourth Generation Languages (4GLs), CASE tools, object-orientation, client/server, expert systems, business megapackages, etc.) that originated or accelerated during that period. When each of these technologies was identified as a "breakthrough" in the journals read by corporate management, it was difficult for most software practitioners to resist the downward-focused pressure to use them. The wise practitioner tried out the new technology on a small, pilot project. But money for pilot studies is all too rare, and unfortunately the result is that these new technologies are all too often tried out on full-fledged, major projects. It is those kinds of projects, and the failures that ensued, that form the basis for this section of the book.

Before we get to the stories themselves, there is another important issue to deal with. Does the fault lie with the technology, or the people using it? The answer, as you might expect, is not clear. In nearly all of the following stories, outside "experts" were working on, and often leading, the project—thus minimizing the chance that people were the problem.

In any case, advocates for the technologies often blame the people; in turn, the practitioners themselves blame the technology. The correct answer, as is often true of answers to complex questions, probably lies somewhere in between. In the stories that follow, the technologies in question were used on projects where:

- They did not scale up (it is important that the limitations of new technologies—and they all have them—are well understood before they are used on a major project).

- They are a solution to the wrong problem (just because a technology is new does not mean it is appropriate for any problem you may be trying to solve).

- They did not have the required functional capability (in one of our stories below, the new technology could not address one facet of the user's problem. Not now, not ever!).

In other words, the mix of inexperienced people using immature technologies is a dangerous one. In the stories that follow, the mix sent one company into bankruptcy, and caused the others to throw out all or part of the new and return to the old after spending huge amounts of money attempting to use the new.

The lessons learned on these projects are nicely presented in this collection of pithy quotes:

- "If you've got enough cinder blocks [untried technologies] in a rowboat, it's going to sink," even if not one of them alone would cause a failure.

- "Elegant solutions based on new technology often seem great in theory, but are difficult and expensive to learn and deploy."

- "The DMV's operation fell apart . . . because of their prescribed remedy rather than the problem they had diagnosed."

- "If there appears to be more buzzword than substance, turn off the money spigot . . ."

Wise advice, painfully learned. And now, on to the technology-caused failure stories.

2.3.1   WHEN THINGS GO WRONG

by William M. Bulkeley

In 1994, when FoxMeyer Drug Co. was showing off plans for a $65 million computerized system to manage critical operations, then-Chief Information Officer Robert R. Brown told the trade publication *Computerworld*: "We are betting our company on this."

They lost.

In August, FoxMeyer, which had $5.1 billion in sales last year, filed for bankruptcy-court protection from creditors. The drug wholesaler was overwhelmed by huge expenditures for new computers, software and the consultants who were supposed to make it all work, and by the ruinous snafus that ensued.

In October, McKesson Corp., FoxMeyer Drug's largest rival, agreed to pay $80 million in cash for the company, the main unit of FoxMeyer Health Corp., which wasn't included in the bankruptcy filing. The parent's stock had crashed to around $3 a share from a December high of $26.

Sweeping automation, when it works, can bring about greater efficiencies and reap big savings for a company. But the dark side of computerizing organizations is that often it doesn't work. "Fundamentally," says Wade Hyde, a spokesman for FoxMeyer Health, "the computer-integration problems we had were a significant factor leading to the bankruptcy filing."

Few companies are crippled by technology problems as FoxMeyer was. But most big operations have painful scars. Standish Group International Inc., a Dennis, Mass., research firm, found in a 1994 study that 31% of all corporate software-development projects are canceled before they are completed, and 51% cost two to three times budgeted amounts and take three times as long as expected.

Occasionally, giant headaches like the Denver airport's automated baggage-handling system or International Business Machines Corp.'s media information system for the Atlanta Olympics come to light.

But companies brush most failures under the rug because of corporate embarrassment and the need to maintain civil relations with software vendors and consultants who may be their only hope of cleaning up the mess. "You have to grin and bear it and go forward with the supplier," says John Logan, a consultant with Aberdeen Group, a market-research firm in Boston.

Cautionary Tale

FoxMeyer's fate shows why chief information officers lie awake nights and serves as a warning to chief executives who expect too much from silicon and software. "This is a good example of seeing technology as a savior and finding out that it can be a black hole of expenditures and resources," says Lawrence Marsh, who follows FoxMeyer for Wheat First Butcher Singer in Richmond, Va.

FoxMeyer, the nation's fourth-largest drug wholesaler, expected technology to cut costs, speed up inventory turnover and provide a way to serve its customers by giving them better information about their ordering patterns. "They featured computerizing as a highlight of increasing their efficiency," says Christina Valauri, formerly an analyst for PaineWebber Inc. who followed the company. "That was a major focus."

Touting technology as the way to compete with larger rivals and be one of the survivors in the rapidly consolidating drug-wholesaling business, management decided to push the technological envelope, and do it fast. It ordered a companywide software system to replace FoxMeyer's aging Unisys Corp. mainframe, which could track inventory only daily—not minute by minute—as deliveries came and went.

In 1995, Thomas Anderson, then FoxMeyer Health's president and chief operating officer, who championed the technology drive, promised that the three-year project would "enable us to accelerate sales growth without proportional increases in head count and operating expense, automating functions that now are manually driven and improving the quality of our service."

Insiders say top management was so overoptimistic about computerization that it recklessly underbid contracts, expecting electronic efficiencies to lower costs enough to make the deals profitable.

FoxMeyer, based in Carrollton, Texas, declines to comment on any contracts.

The company spent $4.8 million for a modern client-server computer system from Hewlett-Packard Co. and nearly as much on software from SAP AG, a German company that is a leader in information systems. It spent tens of millions for high-priced advice from Andersen Consulting, one of the nation's biggest computer-systems-integration firms. And it spent $18 million building a 340,000-square-foot warehouse in a rural Ohio town, where computerized robots fill orders from Midwestern hospitals and pharmacies.

But the warehouse opened months late. Auditors later determined that incorrect orders it sent out cost the company a whopping $15.5 million in unrecovered excess shipments in just a few weeks. The companywide system, which was supposed to cut costs by $40 million a year, was completed late and saved less than half that amount. For a company in a low-margin business with a heavy debt burden, the shortfalls were overwhelming.

Problems and Delays

A major problem FoxMeyer found with the SAP software, known as R/3, was that it wasn't powerful enough to handle the vast number of orders the company gets daily. Every day, FoxMeyer fills orders from thousands of pharmacies, each of which orders hundreds of items, totaling up to 500,000 items a day. FoxMeyer says SAP can handle only a few thousand items a day.

The SAP software had never been used by a company that processed such large amounts of orders, and there wasn't any way to test in advance. "We ran some simulations," says Douglas Schwinn, FoxMeyer's current senior vice president and chief information officer, "but not with the level of data we have in an operating environment."

An SAP spokeswoman says the German company "did end up having people go on site to perfect some of the interfaces between SAP and (existing) legacy systems. That did cause some delays, which isn't unexpected given the fact that legacy systems are notoriously hard to interface with."

FoxMeyer had wanted the new client-server system to replace the old mainframe completely. But today, the Unisys mainframe continues to handle order processing, inventory control and invoicing for most of FoxMeyer.

"They wanted to leapfrog the competition because they saw a risk in the market," says Kenneth Woltz, a Chicago-based consultant who advised FoxMeyer. But "there is a high risk associated with a relatively new product and processing high volumes in a client-server environment. A more prudent thing to do would have been to stretch the program out a little longer."

People who worked on the project recall that in 1993, FoxMeyer's information-systems department was working to pick a new system. But before it could send out requests for proposals to software firms, computer salespeople from Digital Equipment Corp. reached Fox-Meyer's top management. Digital persuaded company officials to look at SAP software, which was sweeping the U.S. manufacturing community. Digital, like other computer makers, often plays up software that runs well on its computers.

A Digital spokesman says the company continues to recommend SAP software to its customers. He says the company isn't familiar with the FoxMeyer situation since it ultimately lost the sale to Hewlett-Packard.

SAP had been growing more popular with computer salespeople because it works well with client-server setups that can replace aging mainframes, and it integrates new computers with multiple facets of corporate operations. "SAP at the time was relatively new," says Mr. Woltz, the consultant who had recommended going slow. "It's a very difficult system to implement." Worse, it had never been used to manage a large wholesale distributor. SAP was originally designed for manufacturers, and lacked many features for the wholesale distribution business.

Hard Sell on Software

But it had built strong adherents. Consultants loved it because it was immensely comprehensive, covering every area of a business, while assuring that high-paid software engineers from the consulting firm would be needed to make it work. "There's a lot of people jumping on the bandwagon," says Mr. Woltz. "It's a consultant's dream."

And many corporate-information staffers are eager to work on SAP because the experience makes them more employable. "If you're a $45,000-a-year systems guy and you get experience with SAP, you could get $70,000 on your next job," says Mr. Woltz.

The FoxMeyer executives were convinced. "We were given an assignment to find any gaps in the SAP system," recalls one FoxMeyer information-systems manager. But systems people found they were encouraged to minimize problems. "It wasn't appropriate to criticize SAP," the manager says. Adds a consultant who worked on the project: "Every time we showed something that didn't work, they'd say 'Is this a deal-breaker?' Well, no one was a deal-breaker. But if you put enough cinder blocks in a rowboat, it's going to sink."

FoxMeyer was committed to SAP as the core of its system. After careful examination, it decided on using Hewlett-Packard servers instead of Digital Equipment's. And in January 1994, FoxMeyer started work on what it called the Delta Information Systems project. The company used Hewlett-Packard's software experts to implement much of the system. It also hired Andersen Consulting, which brought in some 70 analysts and programmers.

But business pressures were changing the demands on the system. In May 1993, Phar-Mor Inc., a Midwestern pharmacy chain that accounted for more than 15% of FoxMeyer's business, filed for bankruptcy-court protection in the midst of an accounting scandal. It soon became clear that much of the business was gone forever, crimping FoxMeyer's growth prospects. In its desperate search for more business, FoxMeyer targeted University HealthSystem Consortium, a national network of major teaching hospitals. Even though the scattered hospitals necessitated opening six new warehouses in the West, FoxMeyer bid aggressively, betting that computerized efficiencies would make the deal profitable.

Promising Contract

The company signed a five-year deal with University HealthSystem in July 1994, with deliveries scheduled to start in early 1995. It predicted the contract would generate $4 billion to $5 billion in revenue over the life of the contract.

FoxMeyer crowed about the pact in a press release, and its stock rose. But in the computer room, the programmers groaned. To meet the contract deadline, they would have to get parts of the SAP financial software running three months sooner than planned. "Being an (information-systems) person, I would never plan on moving implementation up by 90 days," says one programmer who worked on the project.

FoxMeyer says it did start filling hospital orders on schedule. University HealthSystem declines to comment on the contract. But FoxMeyer says data errors occurred that meant it wasn't keeping accurate records of sales histories for customers' information, even though correct bills were being sent out. To save time in development, programmers had skipped testing some parts of the system where the software hadn't been customized. "We might have caught the data errors if we had," the programmer says.

Executives also later conceded that sales executives had shaved their bid on the contract by assuming FoxMeyer would quickly realize Delta's projected $40 million in annual savings. "When contracts leave you no room for error, that's not the time to experiment with advanced systems and new contracts," says a systems manager who worked on the project.

Mr. Schwinn, FoxMeyer's chief information officer, says the new contract increased the difficulties of the already-ambitious plan. The old Unisys mainframe needed an uninterrupted four-hour period to do the customer invoices, and time-zone problems took away two hours when the West Coast warehouses opened. So FoxMeyer had to use SAP software to manage each of the Western warehouses while using the old mainframe for the rest of the country, eliminating some anticipated efficiencies.

In addition, because of the time pressures, FoxMeyer wasn't able to re-engineer its related business practices to make the software more efficient. "Your focus becomes 'I need to get this open,' not 'I need this to cut costs,' " says Mr. Schwinn. "You don't do as much process re-engineering."

For example, the new software was designed to forecast inventory needs by closely tracking purchase rates for each product. But because of the new University HealthSystem contract, FoxMeyer had to rush to buy additional goods before it could analyze its inventory turnover, and it took several extra months before that capability began to pay off, Mr. Schwinn says.

Today, he says, the system is saving the company money, although not as much as hoped because of the additional complications of the University HealthSystem contract. "The $40 million estimate was reasonable if we'd had a steady-state business," Mr. Schwinn says, but "the contract as bid was reaching. . . . The whole $40 million wasn't going to be there in the time frame even if everything had gone perfectly."

Trouble in the Heartland

The most visible automation disaster, though, was the new computerized warehouse in Washington Court House, Ohio. While most drug wholesalers use automated pickers and conveyors for about one-third of its items, FoxMeyer planned to have 80% of all items picked automatically. That required state-of-the-art computerized pickers and far more conveyor lines than any other plant.

The operation is working well today as the most automated in the country, FoxMeyer says. But the system, developed by Pinnacle Automation Inc., St. Louis, was so bug-ridden at first that even after extra months of testing, the software kept shutting down key parts of the system such as carousels and conveyors, forcing troops of temporary workers to try to put orders together on the right trucks.

Scheduled to open in May 1995, the warehouse finally started delivering goods in August, Mr. Schwinn says. Though systems weren't ready, FoxMeyer had to start using the plant because the Cincinnati and Cleveland warehouses it replaced were "degrading, with people leaving." Experienced workers at the older warehouses had departed in droves, knowing their jobs were soon to be eliminated.

Bruce Pence, an attorney for the Teamsters local that represented workers in Cincinnati, says, "It doesn't take a genius to figure out you can't give good service if you lose experienced people and replace them with temps."

At Washington Court House, "the underlying software of the picking machines would fail in the middle of the process, so we'd have to stop and restart in the middle of intense picking hours," from 8 p.m. to 3 a.m., says Mr. Schwinn. Sometimes scanners that read bar codes on boxes and direct them to the right trucks would stop reading. Boxes would pile up in a holding area waiting for warehouse workers to put them on the right trucks. And shipments would have to be recorded manually and entered into the computer later, leading to many errors. "When a scanner fails during a shipping event, it's pretty significant," says Mr. Schwinn.

Or, the pickers or conveyors would shut down while an order was being filled. The first six boxes, accompanied by an invoice for a full order, might get onto a truck, but the rest of the order might be delayed to a later truck. The next day, when clerks at the drugstore checked the invoices, they would call FoxMeyer and complain about missing items. FoxMeyer's customer service representatives, who weren't on the warehouse floor, would order the warehouse to ship out missing items, without realizing they were already on later trucks.

Predictably, many customers didn't report when they finally received both the original order and the makeup delivery.

"Paperwork for the order wouldn't come through for 90 days," Mr. Schwinn says. "The enormity of the duplicate orders wasn't clear until we did an inventory." He adds: "The customer-service organization was trying to do the best they could with customers and I think they overreached to a significant degree."

Taking a Hit

Christopher Cole, executive vice president of Pinnacle Automation, says, "We had problems, and results didn't ramp up as quickly as we would have liked." However, he says, many of FoxMeyer's problems can be traced to the complexity of integrating the corporate-information system, and "what we did was relatively small. Automation shouldn't take a black eye here."

The financial effects of the warehouse's problems became fully apparent in July, when FoxMeyer announced it was taking a $34 million charge for its fiscal fourth quarter ended March 31 to cover uncollectible costs on customer orders and inventory problems.

But hints that the entire computerization project wasn't going as smoothly as planned had been seen as early as February, when the board removed Mr. Anderson, the executive who had championed the automation initiative, citing the delays in the warehouse and in realizing the savings from the Delta project.

Today the entire system is working well. FoxMeyer is almost done writing an invoicing system of its own to run on the Hewlett-Packard computers and replace the mainframe. And the Ohio warehouse is handling more volume than any other at FoxMeyer. But the delays and overconfidence spawned by the technology were too much for the company to endure.

"In hindsight, I'd stand up in front of the board of directors and say, 'Don't spend that money. There are cheaper ways to do it,' " says Mr. Schwinn, the chief information officer. "There are better ways to do it that aren't quite as technologically advanced."

2.3.2 INTELLIGENT ELECTRONICS LEARNS THE PITFALLS OF NEW TECHNOLOGY

by David Baum

We all know client/server and distributed processing are the rage these days. Everyone is scrambling to redesign aging legacy systems and adopt workstation-based technologies. Or so it seems. The press is brimming with success stories featuring the latest client/server tools and object-oriented languages. IQ Pro was even featured in the 1995 InfoWorld 100, where Intelligent Electronics Inc. (IE) was dubbed one of the 10 most innovative implementers of client/server technology. (See Sept. 18, 1995, page 53.) But instead of using IQ Pro, IE decided to build on its existing system.

You don't often hear when projects go awry, when companies fail to count the costs, or when even the best-laid development plans don't reach production mode. IE, a computer distributor in Exton, Pa., found this out the hard way while developing a new client/server system for its nationwide network of 2,200 resellers. IE buys computer hardware, software, and peripherals from companies such as Apple Computer Inc., Hewlett-Packard Co., IBM, and Compaq Computer Corp. It stores the components in warehouses and distributes them to resellers, often adding value by creating custom-configured systems.

"In the early days of client/server, many companies were misled by the apparent cost reductions on the hardware side," says Brian Cunningham, chief information officer at IE. "A mainframe hosting a bunch of dumb terminals was more expensive than intelligent clients and downsized servers. We now know that the real cost of deploying client/server applications lies with the intangibles, such as training, systems management, distributed data management, and technical support."

For years, IE has depended on a homegrown application for order processing and order management called the Intelligent Reseller Information System (IRIS). Based on an HP-3000 host computer, it featured a session-based architecture and character-mode user inter-

---

This article was originally published in Info World, January 29, 1996.

face that resellers found difficult to use. Because the majority of IE's orders were taken on-line via dial-up connections, moving to client/ server would give resellers more control, they reasoned.

Clean Break

So began an ambitious client/server development project to simplify the order-entry process, add capabilities for automatic order tracking, and tie the ordering process more directly to the reseller's own internal business systems. The new client/server system was dubbed IQ Pro, and, like many projects of its type, it was publicized far and wide.

"Initially, we thought client/server was the right architecture for IQ Pro due to its ability to divide computing tasks among multiple locations—in this case, multiple reseller sites," Cunningham recalls. "We also thought object-oriented technology would be the best way to achieve automatic order tracking. Instead of requiring a dedicated connection, as the old system did, an object-oriented application could send and receive messages asynchronously, allowing resellers to write orders off-line and be automatically notified of an order's status as it moves in the system."

Culture Shock

Developers were putting the finishing touches on the first production release of IQ Pro when Cunningham and other company officers began to have second thoughts about the new architecture.

"Once we took a hard look at the ramifications of what we were attempting and started putting out feelers to our user base, we realized it made better sense to capitalize on the systems we had in place," Cunningham says.

There were three primary reasons for putting on the brakes. The first was the complexity of the new technologies they were using, based on the Smalltalk language.

"It was difficult enough to become proficient with object-oriented techniques. On top of that, maintaining such a highly skilled staff was a challenge. These skills aren't readily available in the open market," Cunningham says.

The second reason for questioning the efficacy of IQ Pro was the deployment costs for resellers, especially the training requirements and hefty equipment purchase requirements because more CPU power would be required on their end to make the applications work.

But what really tipped the scales against IQ Pro was work IE's resellers had already done.

"Our resellers have invested a lot of time and effort into learning IRIS," Cunningham explains. "We have 2,000 customers out there who are accustomed to a certain type of system. We're talking about our primary revenue base. At your peril rock that boat!"

Gradual Migration

Working closely with Bonnie Lawson, manager of support services at IE, Cunningham and his IS team began to evaluate alternative ways to accomplish many of the same benefits promised by IQ Pro using their existing, host-based system. They set the goal of making a series of incremental improvements to IRIS that would be easier to develop and require less upheaval among their reseller base.

Soon they devised a gradual migration plan that would deliver essentially the same functionality promised by IQ Pro for a lot less effort. The key differentiator between IQ Pro and the new versions of IRIS they envisioned falls into the realm of application partitioning. IQ Pro sought to off-load many local processing tasks to the reseller sites, thereby offering greater autonomy and more hooks into the resellers' own business systems. But that meant a powerful workstation on the reseller side, on-site knowledge of client/server, and in some cases a local server as well.

IRIS 3.2 and IRIS 5.0, by contrast, offer the same aesthetic benefits via an ADP terminal emulator that allows resellers to connect graphical desktop clients to IE's HP-3000 host at headquarters. Users can work with a Windows, DOS, or Macintosh-based interface written in Visual FoxPro. But the main processing and database management functions remain on the host.

IRIS 3.2, released in December 1995, offers numerous enhancements requested by resellers during the past five years. IRIS 5.0, now undergoing beta testing, is backward compatible with IRIS 3.2 and also supports Windows 95 and a TCP/IP connection to a H/P-9000 Unix server.

"The primary advantage is that it is the same basic system resellers are already familiar with," Lawson says. "Users will be given a choice regarding if or when to upgrade. Instead of the clean break with the past that IQ Pro would have required, the new versions of IRIS are all backward compatible with the earlier ones."

The old IRIS system was synchronous and session based, requiring a dial-up connection from resellers. Newer versions offer a frame relay connection option and, eventually, a TCP/IP Internet connection.

For both IRIS 3.2 and IRIS 5.0, the user interface has been completely reworked, revamped, and renovated. IRIS 5.0 sports a Windows 95 look and feel, but it too will be supplanted by a classy new interface designed with Microsoft Corp.'s Visual Basic.

Client/Server or Not?

"People can debate endlessly what true client/server really means," Cunningham says. "But the role of IS remains the same: delivering effective systems that get the job done."

"We've taken a different path to get to approximately the same place," Cunningham continues. "If we were starting a new company and building our information systems from scratch, it might be feasible to architect a robust, 100 percent client/server operation. But to build a cohesive application infrastructure invariably implies some type of legacy system in the mix."

Cunningham won't reveal just how much money was spent or how many development hours were consumed before IE pulled the plug on IQ Pro.

"We were able to rebuild IRIS with the remaining IQ Pro budget," Cunningham says.

The moral of the story? Elegant solutions based on new technology often seem great in theory but are difficult to learn and expensive to deploy.

"Client/server has tremendous potential to change the way our information systems are constructed, but don't try to change too much too fast," Cunningham advises. "Any time you put in something brand-new, there is risk associated with it—new architecture, new code, new platforms. There are so many unknown factors, so many intangibles that are difficult to foresee.

"In the end, it was really quite simple," Cunningham says. "We listened to our users."

2.3.3   ANATOMY OF A 4GL DISASTER

by David Kull

The team developing the New Jersey Division of Motor Vehicles' new computer system still had time to avoid disaster in December 1984. It had been working on the system for more than a year, using Ideal, the fourth-generation language from Applied Data Research Inc. (ADR), Princeton, NJ, as the primary programming language. The delivery deadline was seven months away, but a recent system test had revealed unacceptably slow response times. At a development team meeting on December 4, Ranjit Advani, a partner from Price Waterhouse & Co., the New York-based Big Eight accounting firm and consultancy producing the system, noted that no one had ever used Ideal to build a comparable system. Project manager Robert Kline, then DMV's deputy director, concluded that, at this late date, the project was "still a guinea pig." But the group was not able to swerve away from its reliance on the untried language. Instead, the project team sped onward and the completed system crashed as if it had run into a wall.

The resulting backlogs left thousands of the state's 7 million motorists to drive with invalid registrations or licenses through no fault of their own. Hundreds of thousands of others encountered errors and delays in their dealings with the division. Overtime pay for employees trying to clean up the backlogs totaled hundreds of thousands of dollars. Six months after the scheduled delivery date, the new system, with parts rewritten in Cobol, the more established business-applications programming language, still was not up and running.

The New Jersey DMV's fourth-generation development project is a classic story of failure in the adoption of new technology. It's a story of an organization and individuals abandoning established management and data processing practices and, it appears, common sense, in a rush to collect on the promise of the new generation of program-

This article was originally published in Computer Decisions, *February 11, 1986. Permission to reprint requested; no response received (*Computer Decisions *has ceased publication).*

ming languages. It's a unique story, however, only in its visibility. Details rarely surface from other organizations' fumbles with early fourth-generation projects. But angry citizens at DMV offices across New Jersey bore evidence of the fiasco and the media carried the story across the country. Moreover, a state legislative committee hearing cast a spotlight on every act that contributed to the debacle.

A review of testimony and evidence presented to the committee and interviews with the principals and outside experts provides a rare look into a project run amok. The story—of expert advice and internal controls ignored, of system tests improperly designed or not performed at all, of suspiciously cozy relationships between consultants and their employers, of developers locked into hopeless methods by budgetary constraints, and of a new system crashing after its working predecessor had been shut down—holds lessons for all organizations.

What went wrong? Almost all participants now agree that the project team's primary mistake was the misuse of Ideal. It and other fourth-generation programming languages offer big programmer-productivity benefits over older languages. When misused, however, fourth-generation languages produce programs that overtax computer resources. The DMV system was to have more than 1,000 terminals generating tens of thousands of transactions per day against a database containing information on 7 million licensed drivers, 6 million registered vehicles, and 20 million title documents. The language could not develop such a large, online system able to respond fast enough to user requests. Ideal was also incapable of creating batch programs that ran fast enough to complete a nightly database update by morning.

The more difficult question is, how could such a mistake have been made? According to outside experts, testing before and during development should have determined the tool's inadequacy for the job. That the mistake was not discovered—or, if discovered, not corrected—until the system crashed on takeoff represents a management rather than a technical failure. And the failure must be laid to the organization, rather than to individuals. Again according to outside experts, organizational controls, including checks and balances between competing interests, should have caught the errors made by individuals in time to correct them.

In the summer of 1983, the DMV was contemplating ways of implementing a master plan for upgrading its record-processing systems. The plan had been developed for $88,000 by Price Waterhouse under the state's previous, Democratic, administration and enjoyed bipartisan support under the new Republican regime. All parties agreed that the system needed upgrading; in the words of Clifford Snedeker, then DMV director, the question was "not what to do, but how to do it." Snedeker and Robert Kline, his deputy, held strong opinions about the how.

In a June 1983 memo—written by Kline, signed by Snedeker—to Governor Thomas Kean's office, the pair made clear that they believed implementation could not be done in-house by the DMV's data processing support group, the Division of Systems and Communications (SAC), and should be done by Price Waterhouse. They based their argument on what they claimed was a crucial need for speedy completion of the project. "SAC personnel are either carry-over appointees or civil service employees," Kline wrote. "The secure environment . . . provides little incentive for employees to extend themselves." SAC did not have enough qualified personnel to implement the plan on time, the memo said, and its "greatest weakness is project management and control." In favor of outside implementation, Kline wrote that Price Waterhouse had the resources to get the job done quickly. He added that "Price Waterhouse has much to lose, and much to gain by completing the project on schedule. . . . Price Waterhouse's greatest strength is project management and control."

SAC officials disagreed and were surprised to find themselves in competition with Price Waterhouse. They felt capable of implementing the plan and had assumed they would—with help from outside consultants, including management support from Price Waterhouse. At this time, Price Waterhouse, working under a separate $700,000 contract, was already well into developing requirements and specifications for the system. Implementers would follow these detailed descriptions of what the system should do when they designed the actual system.

In the summer of 1983, DMV management gave SAC three days to come up with a proposal for completing a comprehensive system that fulfilled the master plan by the summer of 1985. Their hurried proposal called for $2 million for additional personnel and outside help and $3 million for hardware to do the job. According to Robert Meybohm, at that time SAC's deputy director, the master plan called for integration of separate applications for driver licensing and automobile registration and titling, for more frequent batch updating of those applications, and for online updating of parts of them. It also called for development of several new applications to automate tasks being done manually.

SAC's implementation plan would have had the division's own personnel modify the established applications, with which they were already familiar, to meet the new requirements. New hires and contract developers under SAC management would build the system's new portions using Cobol. "We would have touched all the bases from the master plan," Meybohm says. Meanwhile, over the previous year, Price Waterhouse had developed a separate proposal to implement the master plan itself with a totally new system—a "turnkey" system for $6.5 million, with another $8.5 million needed for additional hardware.

Besides offering an alternative to the Price Waterhouse plan, SAC officials argued against giving the job to Price Waterhouse because they believed the consulting firm did not have the necessary expertise. The Big Eight in general, they contended, do well in analyzing a business and developing system requirements, but are inexperienced in actually implementing systems. "You don't go to those people for that kind of help," says Donald Bianco, then SAC's director. Besides, SAC contended, turnkey systems are inherently risky because their developers walk away shortly after delivery, leaving ongoing maintenance to others, who have had little or no say in design issues affecting the system's maintainability. Snedeker and Kline, however, discounted SAC's advice—as they would do throughout the project. In their memo to the governor's office, Snedeker and Kline expressed their support for the Price Waterhouse proposal over SAC's.

SAC officials, who of course had an interest in retaining the project, were not the only ones with reservations about the wisdom of giving the job to Price Waterhouse. Awarding the contract to Price Waterhouse would require a waiver of the state's bidding procedures. Before approving the waiver, the governor's office sought the opinion of Science Management Corp. (SMC), a consultancy based in Basking Ridge, NJ, that was working on a plan to reorganize the state's executive branch. SMC had extensive experience in systems implementation and an intimate knowledge of the state's data processing services.

According to Douglas Davidson, executive vice president of the computer services group, SMC recommended against granting Price Waterhouse a blanket contract for the entire project. It recommended instead that the state break the project into smaller tasks, and that the state's data processing services maintain ultimate responsibility for all of them. It did advise that the state grant a waiver allowing Price Waterhouse to *participate* in the first phase of the project.

In arguing for Price Waterhouse, Snedeker and Kline contended that the consultancy was best suited to get the system up quickly because it had written the requirements and specifications and, therefore, would not have to spend time learning them. Davidson says, however, that as a general rule for government projects, the firm that writes the requirements and specifications should not actually implement the system.

The federal government prohibits that arrangement in its computer projects. Splitting the two development phases builds checks into the process. The implementer can objectively judge the work of the specifier. And because the specifier knows it won't implement the system, it's not likely to build in expensive but unnecessary features. "The public sector needs these kinds of checks and balances to protect the taxpayer," Davidson says. New Jersey's state treasurer, in fact, has since issued a regulation prohibiting an outside firm that writes a system's specifications from implementing them.

SMC passed its advice to the governor's office in the summer of 1983. And SAC's Donald Bianco sent SMC's memo summarizing it over Kline's and Snedeker's heads to Irwin Kimmelman, New Jersey's attorney general, whose purview included the DMV. Nevertheless, the state approved a blanket bid waiver for Price Waterhouse and Kimmelman signed the $6.5 million contract in November 1983. Kline, a lawyer with no previous data processing experience, was named project manager. It would take him more than a year to realize that he, in fact, had assumed command of a project exploring uncharted fourth-generation territory.

It may be impossible to determine why the DMV and Kimmelman disregarded the opinion of both in-house and outside experts and gave the whole job to Price Waterhouse. Snedeker and Kline point to time pressure as partial justification for their decision. The state legislature had mandated implementation of a system to collect automobile insurance surcharges from unsafe drivers by January 1984—giving the DMV less than a year. Snedeker and Kline contended that the system and the comprehensive overhaul of other division operations were inextricably linked. That surcharge system, however, did not require use of Ideal or ADR's Datacom/DB database management system, which would be used to integrate the comprehensive system. Since Price Waterhouse had the surcharge system running on schedule while the comprehensive system was still relatively early in development, Snedeker and Kline's rush seems unjustified.

The reason may have been a true sense of foreboding about the DMV's systems. In their June 1983 memo to the governor's office, Snedeker and Kline wrote that, if the comprehensive systems overhaul were not completed by the summer of 1985, "the division's operations will begin to fall apart." When Price Waterhouse's new system was brought online in the summer of 1985, however, the old system was performing as well as it had for the previous five years. According to state data processing sources, there were no pressing technical or operational reasons to abandon the old system until the new one proved adequate for the job. Another theory holds that the rush was meant to complete the system before the next election—in the fall of 1985. The old DMV systems were operational, but they were hardly models of efficiency. Putting the DMV in order would have been an obvious accomplishment for the administration. Still another theory holds that Snedeker and Kline were exaggerating the crisis to spur action, a common bureaucratic ploy. In any case, the new system went online according to schedule, and the DMV's operation fell apart just when Snedeker and Kline predicted it would—but because of their prescribed remedy rather than the problem they had diagnosed.

Price Waterhouse may also have done exceedingly well in selling the idea that it was the answer to the DMV's problems. Its zeal in maintaining favor with state Republicans shortly after being awarded the contract was considered excessive by state Democrats. Assemblyman Thomas Foy, who served on the legislative committee that investigated the project, says that Price Waterhouse's political contributions at the time, whether or not legal, "raise the unseemly specter of contracts being for sale."

William Driscoll, the Price Waterhouse partner who sold the DMV the proposal for the turnkey system, described the firm's contributions in two internal memos. The first was written in August 1983, after the firm had been awarded the contract, but before it was signed. Driscoll wrote that after consulting with Kline—"a masterful strategist . . . during the process which resulted in our sole-source contract"—it seemed a good idea to buy three tables at the Governor's Ball, a fund-raiser for Kean. The tables cost $5,000 each.

In another internal memo a year later, in September 1984, faced with another invitation to the Governor's Ball, Driscoll wrote that purchasing three more $5,000 tables might "perhaps buy some insurance on the DMV job." Actually, only the third table can be considered insurance. The first $10,000 for the governor kept Price Waterhouse only even with the top givers from the other Big Eight firms.

Whether or not Price Waterhouse needed insurance, by September 1984—10 months before the project deadline—the DMV project's wheels were beginning to wobble. A few months later, at the December 4 meeting with Robert Kline and other development team members, Driscoll reported on "problems with Ideal" and said that the project might run hundreds of thousands of dollars over budget. Driscoll began sketching alternative development plans, but the project team was unable to back far enough away from its reliance on Ideal.

Not that there had been no earlier warnings about the use of Ideal. Price Waterhouse's November 1983 contract specified the use of ADR's Ideal, which had been introduced about eight months earlier, as the primary programming language. According to the contract, Price Waterhouse had evaluated Ideal and determined it was suited to the job. Today, the firm will not discuss how it performed its evaluation—or any other aspect of the project. However, for SAC's Donald Bianco, evaluation wasn't even necessary. "It's simple," he says now. "You just don't use an immature, untested language for this kind of complex project." He not only passed that judgment to Kline and Price Waterhouse's development team leaders, Ranjit Advani and William Driscoll, at the beginning of the project but, through Meybohm, provided the results of SAC's own evaluation of Ideal as supporting evidence.

Meybohm says he was Ideal's earliest, most enthusiastic proponent within the state, hoping it would help increase the productivity of a programming staff that had not grown in a decade. He still favors Ideal and fourth-generation languages in general—when used by the right pros for the right jobs. SAC had already acquired ADR's Datacom/DB database management system and was satisfied with its performance on programs written in Cobol. When Ideal became available for use with Datacom/DB, Meybohm evaluated it for possible use in development projects other than the large DMV project. He concluded that the language was too "immature" for immediate adoption.

Meybohm identified three primary deficiencies. First, a simple test of Ideal's operating efficiency led him to believe it would not be able to handle development of large, online systems. For the test, he wrote programs for a simple database transaction—a data read, add-to-account, and data write—in both Cobol and Ideal. Cobol ran three times as fast as Ideal. "Since the program was about as simple as could be," Meybohm says, "I knew Ideal's performance would only get worse in more complex applications."

Second, Ideal did not offer index processing, a performance-related feature available with Cobol under Datacom/DB that had influenced SAC's decision to acquire that database management system in the first place. Index processing allows an application to store some data in the database index, rather than the database itself. If a police officer stopped a motorist and did a license check, for example, the system would look first in the index in order to locate the driver's record in the database. If crucial information, such as whether or not the license had been suspended, were included in the index, it could quickly be transmitted to the officer without a database read, saving processing—and the police officer's—time.

Third, Ideal did not allow computer-to-computer interfacing. This was crucial for the DMV's system because it would require communications between the SAC computer and 59 computers located in various law enforcement agencies and municipalities around the state. "Price Waterhouse never seemed to grasp this issue," Meybohm says. "It didn't seem to realize the system would not run on a dedicated DMV machine."

Whether or not Price Waterhouse grasped Bianco and Meybohm's reservations, it noted them and chose to move ahead with Ideal. In a memo to Kline in March 1984—16 months from the project deadline—William Driscoll wrote, "the uncertainties associated with the use of Ideal represent an acceptable risk." A change in "database software" at this time would cause a three-to-six-month delay, he wrote. Noting that SAC and Price Waterhouse were taking "separate paths" regarding Ideal's use, he pointed to a need for continued cooperation between the two groups, as well as strengthened "management commitment." "We should all be aware of this now," Driscoll wrote, "and not lose sight of it in the future when the road gets rougher."

Indeed, potholes gaped not too far ahead, and Price Waterhouse clearly hoped to pave them with ADR's enhancements to Ideal. It clung to this hope even though the project team complained bitterly about the level of support it received from the vendor even before Ideal was installed. In an April 1984 letter to John Bennett, ADR's chairman, DMV's Snedeker claimed that "the support (for Datacom/DB) necessary from ADR is slow and difficult to obtain." A few days later, Norman Statland, Price Waterhouse's national EDP director wrote Martin Goetz, then ADR senior vice president, now president, about the vendor's inability "to help resolve the problems quickly" or "to give an indication as to when and in what release these will be resolved." He added that the project team was currently evaluating Ideal in a test environment.

ADR's responsibility for Price Waterhouse's use of Ideal is a matter of some dispute. Price Waterhouse claims ADR should have warned about Ideal's limitations. ADR says it did. A Price Waterhouse attorney, preferring not to entertain questions on the issue, hinted that the disagreement may be settled in court.

Regardless of the specific facts of the matter, two general principles apply to a pioneering software project. No software arrives in the marketplace bug-free and in final working form. Many problems surface only after extended use. The vendor provides fixes and adds functions and features—enhancements—when its developers complete them. This "maturing" process proceeds unpredictably. Prudent users, therefore, don't count on capabilities that are not in hand. In a progress report to Robert Kline a year before the project deadline, Ranjit Advani indicated Price Waterhouse was doing just that. "We believe that satisfactory resolution of ADR-related technical problems would remove a major issue threatening timely completion of the project," Advani wrote.

Users should approach any vendor's claims with some skepticism. Says Shaku Atre, an expert in database management systems and fourth-generation languages: "No vendor will tell you its product can't do your job."

On the other hand, ADR had little to gain by watching a customer use Ideal to build a disaster. In May 1984, shortly after Price Waterhouse and DMV officials wrote to ADR's officers, the vendor assigned a technical liaison to the project, and the development team gave him a copy of its database design. From that point, ADR certainly was well aware of Price Waterhouse's plans. However, there is no evidence that ADR sounded an alarm about the inadvisability of using Ideal to carry them out until five months later. In a progress report to Kline, Advani wrote, "In late October and early November of 1984, ADR informed SAC and PW technical staff of two potential problems associated with the use of Ideal. These are: Slow response times . . . [and] limitation on the number of active online users. . . . ADR representatives are not able to identify the threshold of this limitation. . . . However, they have repeatedly cautioned us against adding a large number of online users under Ideal in a single step." By that time, Advani noted, about 70 percent of the project's coding had been completed in Ideal.

Full system tests at the same time also revealed trouble ahead. On several days in October, November, and December, after the DMV offices closed for business, testers brought up the system on a dedicated development computer and began entering transactions from terminals, attempting to simulate actual usage. Meybohm, who by then had left SAC for another state post, observed Price Waterhouse's tests. The system's functions worked as planned, he says, but fewer than 10 percent of transactions executed in less than 10 seconds. SAC guidelines for its other systems called for five-second response times at most, he says. In his judgment, the test results were unsatisfactory, particularly since the tests ran on a dedicated machine. In use, the DMV system would contend for computer resources with other agencies' applications. It would, in fact, represent only about 20 percent of the hardware's load. "The tests should have run like greased lightning," Meybohm says. "Instead, results weren't near what would be needed."

The programs for the batch updates could have been tested separately merely by running them with files of test data. According to Meybohm, the development team knew by September 1984 that the batch programs written in Ideal would not run fast enough to get the work done in the available time. Any action taken as a result of this knowledge was insufficient since failure of these programs caused much of the havoc when the system was turned on the following summer.

Price Waterhouse also might have used analytical modeling to estimate how the finished system would operate. Modeling is frequently used to assess the operating characteristics of systems under development. There is no evidence that Price Waterhouse employed it in this case.

The system tests and Price Waterhouse's concern about what ADR had told developers in October brought the project to a watershed. Price Waterhouse had assumed a risk when it embarked on the project with Ideal. At this point, the developers realized the bet was in jeopardy. There was still time, however, to cut their and the state's losses. According to one data processing professional familiar with Ideal but not involved in this case, the implementation plan should have provided for fallback and recovery procedures for the types of problems the project was encountering. "I can't imagine that they went as far as they did before throwing up their hands and getting help," he says. "Either they didn't have a good plan, or they ignored it."

Robert Kline discovered two things at the December meeting with the Price Waterhouse development team: that the DMV project was a "guinea pig" and that Price Waterhouse was temporizing in a search for a backup plan. The primary alternative sketched by Driscoll and detailed in a later memo by Advani called for limiting online terminals to 200—rather than the more than 1,000 called for in the specifications—until "after a resolution of the technical problems," as well as the delay of delivery of two "noncore" modules and the recoding of parts of the system in Cobol. Price Waterhouse also asked for an additional $600,000, primarily to hire extra programmers. "This extra effort totaling 4,500 to 6,000 hours is being expended (by Price Waterhouse) as a result of technical problems with ADR software, a factor clearly beyond our control," wrote Advani. "It was not anticipated as part of our planned system development activity and was not included in our project estimates."

Kline agreed to the alternative but left open acceptance of the system pending the lifting of the 200-terminal limitation. He also refused the request for the additional funds. Even under these revised ground rules, the project was destined to fail. Portions of the system were brought online in stages between January and July of 1985. The system screeched to a halt shortly after completion. Log-on sometimes took an hour. Response times lagged up to three minutes. Nightly batch updates required days.

Why was the old, working system turned off before the new one was turned on? Parallel operation of the two systems would have allowed for failure of the new system without wreaking havoc on DMV's operations. According to a source in the state's data processing service, the computer resources on hand were not able to handle parallel operation. Price Waterhouse, the source says, did not try to obtain the hardware necessary for this type of implementation. "We in the state wouldn't have gone that route," the source says. "But Price Waterhouse was in the driver's seat."

In retrospect, it may seem difficult to understand how the project team could have missed or proceeded in spite of the danger signs. Large projects almost always take on lives of their own, however, and participants—concentrating on their particular goals—lose sight of the big picture. Organizations can avoid this problem by providing for ongoing project review by a detached, objective observer. This quality assurance must be provided by personnel with the technological expertise to recognize missteps, and the standing to enforce judgments that may run counter to the individual interests of team members.

According to an outside observer with extensive experience with large development projects, the DMV system failure, to a large extent, was caused by the failure of Price Waterhouse's quality-control procedures. "It's easy to imagine a meeting of the Price Waterhouse team in the press of battle," he says. "The technical people argue strongly that the plan isn't going to work and the people responsible for the bottom line argue that it has to work." An objective reviewer would have prevented the wrong side—in this case, the profit-and-loss faction—from winning the argument. The reviewer would have needed some clout in the organization, however. According to this source, "It takes a loud voice to rise above the thundering herd and say, 'Hold on, slow down.'"

Price Waterhouse's profit-and-loss faction was operating under intense pressure, however, because it was locked into a fixed-cost contract. The state was to pay Price Waterhouse $6.5 million for the system, no matter how much it cost to produce. And Price Waterhouse was bound to produce on time or pay damages beginning at $10,000 per month after the July 1985 deadline, escalating to $50,000 per month in September. Any extra expenses that Price Waterhouse incurred where it couldn't use Ideal would be deducted from its profits and might even add up to a loss. When Ideal's inappropriateness for the job became apparent in the system tests 10 months before deadline, and the DMV refused to redefine the contract, the Price Waterhouse team had two choices: take their lumps immediately, or push on with the language and hope for the best.

A development team not constrained by a fixed-cost contract or otherwise held to a strict budget would have enjoyed more options.

Large development projects frequently encounter legitimate, unexpected cost overruns. Rational compromises in such situations—perhaps a sharing of the extra expenses by developer and client for contract jobs or a budget revision for in-house projects—allow for happy endings to these situations. Selection of Ideal for the DMV project might have been a good bet if there had been a reasonable way of recovering when the tool didn't work exactly as planned. As it was, Price Waterhouse hoped for the best, and the worst occurred.

When it became obvious that the system was a nonperformer, Price Waterhouse did accept its lumps—but after lawyers for the firm and the staff wrestled briefly with the technical issues. In its initial move, state attorneys demanded that the entire system be converted from Ideal to Cobol. Price Waterhouse said it would be happy to provide line-by-line conversion—for $25 per programmer hour. It estimated the job at 25,000 to 30,000 hours. Price Waterhouse ultimately committed to "remedy the system . . . within the terms and conditions of our existing contract . . . at our expense." It acknowledged that under the commitment, it was "prepared" to replace Ideal with Cobol. As it turned out, total conversion was not necessary.

According to Joseph Farrell, ADR's director of research and development, 800 program modules for the DMV system had been written in Ideal. Only six or eight modules, those used for the nightly batch updates, had to be rewritten in Cobol, he says, in order to eliminate the huge DMV backlog. The finished system, Farrell says, "may be the biggest production application database, fourth-generation system that has ever been built."

According to sources within SAC, more than eight modules will have been rewritten from Ideal to Cobol before the system is done. SAC and the state's other data processing agencies have been consolidated under one division, the Office of Technology and Information Systems (OTIS), headed by Donald Bianco. Bruce Jones, deputy administrator of OTIS, is charged with picking up the pieces of the Price Waterhouse project. According to Jones, besides the batch programs, about 50 online programs that handle about 85 percent of the system's volume have been rewritten. And the repair requires more than a simple line-by-line conversion. Some of the programs have had to be redesigned to achieve the best functionality and performance after the change in languages.

Many observers, including participants in the DMV project, worry that other developers will view Price Waterhouse's failure with Ideal as an indictment of the product or fourth-generation programming languages in general. Many organizations have achieved successes with the newer languages, including Ideal. Washington Metro, the public transit agency in Washington, for example, used Ideal and other ADR tools to put together in six months an application for managing bus maintenance using only a senior analyst and junior programmer. According to the agency's MIS director, J. Michael Murray, the application cost $320,000, including about $200,000 to buy the tools, which are also being used for ongoing development projects. A comparable application for railroad car maintenance written in Cobol took two years and cost $500,000, he adds.

The key to using fourth-generation tools, Murray says, is to use them for the right jobs. The application written in Ideal, for example, comfortably supports about 25 terminals and handles between 1,500 and 3,000 transactions per day. But, says Murray, "I'd never use Ideal for batch processing or for heavy transaction processing."

Shaku Atre also warns against trying to do too much with fourth-generation languages. As a rule, she says, fourth-generation languages advertised as being appropriate for production processing run about one-third as fast as Cobol. For example, she describes a database of about 1 million records accessed by about 500 terminals. Applications written for that database in Cobol to run on IBM's IMS database management system should handle about 20 transactions per second. Those written in a fourth-generation language will handle six or seven transactions per second. If more than one database contends for a computer's resources, she adds, the processing will be even slower.

Robert Meybohm, who warned against Price Waterhouse's use of Ideal for the DMV system, speaks highly of fourth-generation languages but warns against their misuse. "They are the only way data processing will be able to deliver the service users are demanding at a reasonable cost," he says. "But as with any powerful tools, if you put them in the hands of amateurs, someone is going to get hurt."

2.3.4   WESTPAC BANK: THE ANATOMY OF A RUNAWAY

by Robert L. Glass

"Bob, there's something important brewing at Westpac Banking Corporation in Australia."

The voice on the telephone was a friend, tipping me off to one of those "best of practice" stories I'm always seeking for *The Software Practitioner*. The date was late 1989. I didn't know it at the time, but this was to be the first chapter in a boom-and-bust, best-to-worst story; a computing project that failed and did serious damage to the enterprise that sponsored it.

Not knowing how it would all come out, I followed up on the tip, and wrote a letter to Westpac, asking if they'd like to share with SP readers an article describing what they were doing. In the return mail, I received from Steve Allworth, a Vice President at Westpac, a handsome brochure describing what Westpac was doing. It was titled "CS90—Westpac Banking Corporation's Core Systems Redevelopment" (CS90 was trademarked), and it looked like a lot of energy and pride had been poured into creating it. I wondered at the time if as much energy and pride had been poured into the system itself.

On Feb. 12, 1990 I wrote to Allworth again, asking for "a programmer's realistic view of what you have done . . . most of all, it [must] be honest in its claims—nothing even close to resembling a sales pitch, and preferably [containing] some negative learning experiences sprinkled in among the positive ones." Allworth never replied to my letter, and I have not heard from him again.

Why did I emphasize "realistic" and "honest" and "negative among positive" in my letter? It may seem like wonderful hindsight now, but in fact there were some interesting and troubling clues in the brochure Allworth sent me. Given that this project became a monumental failure, one that drained $150 million from Westpac's coffers without leaving behind much to show for it, there could be some interesting lessons for the future here.

This article was originally published in the Software Practitioner, November 1992. Used with permission.

That brochure is still in my desk. Let's get it out, and thumb through it. Here is a key page. It's multicolored, and its title is "CS90 Methodology." The page is split in half, with "generic" concepts on the left, and "specific" ones on the right. Straddling that line is something called the "CS90 engine." Feeding into this engine are "reusable building blocks" (from the land of the "generics") and "business procedures" (from the "specifics"). Out the other end, in the land of the "specifics," come application programs. The text beneath the engine says that it "selects, makes specific and assembles copies of building blocks into applications." I would reproduce the figure here in *The Software Practitioner*, but down at the bottom right corner of the page it says "Westpac Banking Corp., Copyright 1989."

Creeping Buzzwordism

Right away, the approach sounds simplistic. Fire up the engine, feed in reusable building blocks, and out come programs? That's well beyond the state of the practice. And, for that matter, the state of the art.

There is more on this colorful brochure page. Where did those reusable building blocks come from? They evolved from "business objects," which were in turn derived from something called "supertypes." "Supertype classification schemes," says the figure, "bring all subjects of interest to the business into a formal structure."

I think it was here that I began really forming doubts about CS90. There's a strong buzzword flavor to this page. We've already seen an "engine," "reuse," "object-orientation," and "formal approaches." None of these things necessarily characterize a project doomed to failure, of course, but the buzzword-to-reality ratio is getting dangerously high.

The task of building CS90, the next page of the brochure tells us, is to

- "extend the reusability inherent in the information and system architectures"

- "build the software engines to manage the reusable components"

- "configure the necessary application systems from these components using knowledge engineering techniques."

It all sounds so straightforward, doesn't it? But there is another warning sign here—in the midst of this further explanation, yet another buzzword has crept in—"knowledge engineering." The buzzword to reality ratio grows even larger.

The brochure isn't just buzzwords and braggadocio, however. Let's turn a few more pages. The rationale for why reuse would work is especially appealing. Here are some compelling words: "A review of Westpac's portfolio of existing systems, many nearly 30 years old, identified a large amount of functional redundancy across these systems. Many times, the same function had been implemented over and over again in different systems. Further, it was found that, over the years, some 1800 transaction codes had been allocated across the various product systems—but that in reality there were nothing like this number of unique transactions. These 1800 transactions were reduced through further analysis to less than 50 generic types." I wondered, as I originally read that page, if that perhaps didn't apply to most enterprise information systems worldwide. And certainly it was easy to accept that it applied to Westpac.

But let's look further. Here, several pages later, the buzzwords reappear. "A new approach was required. A significant contribution came from Westpac's knowledge engineers who introduced the object oriented design approach which further refined the representation techniques for reusable objects. This clarified the principle of inheritance . . . [and] helped tie together the high level supertypes through requirements to the lower level design and implementation objects." The buzzword quotient is reaching alarming heights.

Was Westpac alone in this project? No, the brochure tells us on the next page. "Westpac had contracted IBM's System Integration Division (SID) to provide skills in large project management. From the world of system engineering in aerospace, SID introduced the idea of the state-machine model in which operations can be viewed as functions applied to a defined set of data items." The good news is that they weren't going it alone; the bad news is, with the help came a whole new cluster of buzzwords.

Let's keep going to the end. Here, on the final brochure pages, some degree of reality returns, at least enough to make you wonder which would win out in the end, creeping buzzwordism or practical thinking. That CS90 Engine, as it turned out, wasn't all smoke and mirrors. At the next level of detail, we learn here, it has

◆ a systems development facility, wherein information systems staff create reusable building blocks

◆ a product development facility, wherein product managers and "relationship managers" oversee the creation of applications

◆ a transaction processing facility, wherein customers and staff generate management information

◆ and a decision support facility, which delivers the management information to the customers and staff

Pretty high level, without much technical content, and yet at least there was another level of detail present.

The Runaway

The clock ticked on, and months went by, and to be honest I forgot about Westpac and CS90. I would have welcomed an article from Steve Allworth or one of his people, but it isn't unusual in this business to find that a potential author's initial enthusiasm dwindles under the pressure of project work.

It was December 16, 1991, before I heard about Westpac and CS90 again. The circumstances, as this article has hinted all along, were not pleasant. There, in *InformationWeek* (one of the better news magazines in our business), was a story titled "Reining in Runaway Systems." As an old storyteller of computing failure tales, I naturally started to read it. And there, in the very first line of the story, were Westpac and CS90.

"Westpac Banking Corp. had high hopes for Core System 90 (CS90)," began the article. "In 1988, when Westpac launched the $85 million, five-year, soup-to-nuts project, CS90 was slated to redefine the role of information technology at the Sydney, Australia based bank giant. The plan was to create a showcase of decentralized data systems, allowing branch managers to spin out new financial products rapidly using CASE (computer-aided software engineering) tools and expert systems." (Sounds like a few more buzz words got thrown in before the whole thing collapsed!)

"But," said the article, getting to the bottom line, "those hopes have been dashed. Last month, more than three years after CS90 was begun, Westpac reluctantly ponied up to the worst: The project is out of control. CS90 has already drained nearly $150 million from Westpac's coffers—and the bank has virtually nothing to show for it. What's more, CS90's scheduled 1993 completion date is now just a pipe dream."

The article goes on. "Frustrated, Westpac is cutting its losses. IBM, the lead systems integrator and software developer, is off the project."

What went wrong? The article sought insight from some of *InformationWeek's* ghost gurus, who provide anonymous opinions on technical matters of interest. "CS90 was doomed to fail because it combined an ambitious business agenda with technology that didn't exist," they quote one such expert as saying. "CS90 was hammered," said another, "by IBM's inability to deliver critical technologies it had promised, notably the data repository components of its AD/Cycle initiative."

Based on our trip through that brochure at the beginning of this article, it's not at all hard to believe the first guru. That stuff about CASE and the repository, although certainly a major problem for IBM, is a little harder to tie into this story, since the original Westpac description said nothing about CASE—and had enough other buzzwords to contend with that one might suspect CASE couldn't help OR hurt it in the long run.

The Tombstone

More time passed after that *InformationWeek* piece. It was early 1992 before I heard anything more about Westpac and CS90. And then, in another news brief in the "Executive Summary" section of *InformationWeek*, appeared the CS90 tombstone (but, as it turned out, not the final word on the story): "Westpac banking, Australia's largest bank, will eliminate 500 jobs from its development technology area, saving $37 million a year. The action follows the termination of a runaway systems project that cost $150 million—nearly twice the original estimate when the project started in 1988." Now this project, a technical disaster for some time, was beginning to take on human overtones—500 jobs lost. But, when you stop to think about it, did assigning 500 people to a project like this ever make sense, from the very beginning?

I said, in the previous paragraph, that the CS90 tombstone wasn't, in fact, the end of the story. What was?

It appeared in an Australian newsletter published in the U.S. for Australian expatriates who want to keep up with the news from home. One June 1, 1992, *The Southern Cross* reported:

"WESTPAC REPORTS RECORD $1.66B LOSS FOR SIX MONTHS TO MARCH"

"Westpac reported a stunning interim loss of $1.66 billion, the first loss in 175 years of operation and the biggest ever by the big four Australian banks." The article went on, "Were it not for a tax credit of $712 million, Westpac's reported loss for the six months would have been above $2 billion."

Here, outside the computing literature, the reasons for the bank's problems went well beyond the CS90 debacle. "Analysts blamed the bank's poor position on a decision four years ago to go for rapid growth in property loans."

Perhaps. But I can't help but think, as I ruminate over the troubles of Westpac, that $150 million wasted on CS90 is certainly a significant, if not overwhelming, portion of that $2 billion loss.

What lessons can we learn from all of this? That it's hard to pull off dramatically scoped systems and software projects? That major computing failures are beginning to affect the enterprise's bottom lines in noticeably unpleasant ways? That, as someone wiser than I once said, "if it sounds too good to be true, it probably is"?!

The lesson I choose to learn, however, is a little narrower and a little simpler than all of the above. When some crazy-sounding new proposal comes along, watch the buzzword quotient. If there appears to be more buzzword than substance to the proposal, turn off the money spigot. And don't let it flow again until those buzzwords are converted, perhaps in pilot studies with small (read "inexpensive") teams of key players, into something real, something with technical credibility.

If that doesn't happen, just think of it this way. Better to stay with your old, non-buzzword technology, than to appear on the pages of the news media. With your name paired in a headline with the word "Runaway."

2.4 INADEQUATE/NO PROJECT MANAGEMENT
METHODOLOGY

It is clear from the preceding war stories in this chapter that no run-away project gets that way because a single problem occurred. There may be technical snafus, or poor planning, or shaky requirements, but there are lots of other things going wrong as well.

One of the most prominent of those "lots of other things" is mis-begotten project management. After all, with suitable management it is often possible to avoid many technical snafus, improve planning, and stabilize requirements. The historic software engineering belief that poor management is the cause of most software project failures is solidly founded.

Remember that we are using the categories defined in the run-aways' research described in Chapter 1 as the organizing template for this chapter? There is something peculiar about the title of this section derived from that research. Note, above, that the word "methodology" is coupled with the word "management."

Those two words form an odd couple. Management, for all the knowledge and skills required of those in charge of software projects, is and will probably always be an art. There is no blueprint, or recipe, or methodology that can convert a poor manager into a good one. So although we use the term methodology that the re-searchers specified, we are a little uncomfortable with the implications of that word.

Be that as it may, in the three war stories in this section the dom-inant failure cause is poor management. What do we mean, "poor management"? Check out these quotes from the stories that follow.

Regarding the IRS Tax Systems Modernization effort:

◆ "It was planned badly, contracted badly, and built badly."

◆ A congressional watchdog committee recommended that they "Hire more technically proficient managers, develop real metrics for IS performance, and enforce standard interfaces on key applications."

◆ IRS problems "are rooted in deep cultural, political, and organizational problems."

◆ "The IRS has had three commissioners in five years and two deputy commissioners without technical backgrounds."

Regarding the California DMV database project:

◆ "No one was questioning how long the project was taking, how much it was costing, what were the benefits to be derived, or when it would be completed."

◆ "The DMV painted itself into a corner, unable to develop a migration path . . ."

Regarding the Bank of America MasterNet System:

◆ "MasterNet provides an excellent example of how not to manage risk."

◆ "Modular design, limited functionality, and full-load testing were all disregarded."

◆ "BofA also failed to keep a semblance of continuity in its management."

The fact that there are only three war stories in this section is something of a surprise, given all that we and others have said about management being the prime problem in runaways. But, as we noted above, poor management is an underlying problem in nearly all of the war stories in this book.

And now for a visit to the IRS, followed by a trip to California for the DMV and Bank of America.

2.4.1   IRS PROJECT FAILURES COST TAXPAYERS $50B ANNUALLY

by Gary H. Anthes

It may be the most expensive systems development fiasco in history. Delays in overhauling the federal tax systems are costing the U.S. Treasury as much as $50 billion per year, a *Computerworld* investigation has found.

That figure represents what the federal government *could be* collecting in additional taxes if the Internal Revenue Service had succeeded in its decade-long attempt to modernize its 1960s-era computer systems.

Now trying for the third time to revamp its tax collection systems, the IRS spends hundreds of millions of dollars annually on the effort. But critics say much of that money is wasted through mismanagement and primitive development practices. And IRS officials concede many of those points.

Yet direct expenditures on the IRS' $8 billion Tax Systems Modernization program pale beside a less-noticed cost: the revenue that might have been.

The IRS admits that the lack of progress in developing new automated compliance tools stands in the way of its goal to boost tax collections from 87% of amounts due today to 90% by 2001. At current collection levels, that 3% is worth about $50 billion per year, or more than $500 per U.S. household.

"The opportunity costs of not doing tax systems modernization are huge," said Lynda Willis, director of tax policy and administration issues at the U.S. General Accounting Office in Washington. "System improvements are necessary for getting to that 90%."

"I've seen abuse of the tax system that would turn your stomach," said Hank Philcox, former chief information officer at the IRS. "You wouldn't believe what some people get away with, and information technology can offset a lot of that unfairness."

This article was originally published in Computerworld, October 14, 1996. Copyright 1996 by Computerworld, Inc., Framingham, MA 01701.

But it doesn't—at least not yet. The IRS has 8,500 people in information systems management and development, and 2,000 of them are assigned to tax systems modernization. A recent estimate by a committee of the National Research Council in Washington said there are 10 outside contractors working on the Tax Systems Modernization (TSM) program for every IRS employee on the project.

"The IRS has spent $4 billion on TSM so far and has basically nothing to show for it," said Rep. Jim Lightfoot (R-Iowa), chairman of the House committee that approves IRS funding. He is one of the IRS' most vocal critics.

Although the IRS has made some progress in recent years in improving its computer systems (see story, below), critics have trained a harsh spotlight on some troubled development activities at the agency.

According to government and private groups that have reviewed the IRS' systems work over the years, the agency's biggest problems center on several key areas. They say the agency has done the following:

- Failed to do much-needed business process redesign before it began its systems development.

- Neglected to develop an overall systems architecture or development blueprint.

- Employed primitive and, at times, "chaotic" software development methodologies.

- Failed to manage information systems as investments.

- Neglected information security.

"We recognize that our software development capabilities, as well as those of our contractors, must be improved," said IRS Commissioner Margaret Richardson. "We have taken steps in that direction."

To appease its critics, the IRS has made several major adjustments in its approach to the massive modernization program, which is a collection of about 50 projects. The agency last year overhauled its TSM plans, scaling back some activities and postponing others.

Cutting Back

"Perhaps we took on too much, and we cannot afford to do all this at once," acknowledged Marilyn Soulsburg, a TSM executive at the IRS. She said the agency has decided to outsource more of the program and to cut back individual development efforts to no more than two-year projects.

But outsourcing won't be a "silver bullet," said Rona Stillman, chief scientist for computers and communications at the GAO. Her agency has written dozens of reports criticizing TSM management. "They'll do no better with outsourcing than they have with in-house development unless they can institute some discipline," she said.

Some earlier outsourced work, such as the $1.3 billion Document Processing System (DPS), has produced dubious results so far. Intended to scan and capture data from incoming tax forms, the DPS was conceived in 1988 as a cornerstone of the IRS' strategy for automating manual and paper-intensive processes. It was also considered essential to meeting TSM's quality and cost goals.

But after having spent nearly $300 million on the DPS, the IRS last week officially pulled the plug on the project. It blamed the cancellation on "revised priorities and budget realities."

"They are now looking at very basic things—such as what forms to scan and what data to capture—after spending hundreds of millions of dollars (on DPS)." Stillman said. "Why are they asking requirements questions so late in the game?"

Cybermess with CyberFile

Stillman also pointed to the IRS' CyberFile project for electronic filing of returns. CyberFile was contracted out last year, but it collapsed last month under mismanagement after costing $17 million.

"It was planned badly, contracted badly and built badly," she said.

In a letter to the House Governmental Affairs Committee, Stillman outlined 49 lapses in security alone in the CyberFile project. They included a hole in a data center wall large enough to walk through and passwords shared by employees and posted in public places.

"The bottom line is none of our recommendations have been implemented—none." Stillman said. "Why? There is no organizational will. It's a matter of discipline, and nowhere have they exerted discipline."

In a written reply to that charge, the IRS told *Computerworld* it is "committed to implementing a more rigorous, disciplined approach to designing, developing and managing" IS investments. Next year will be "a transition year for TSM" in that regard, the agency said.

And while Congress rails, the GAO scolds and the IRS flounders, taxes go uncollected, shifting the tax burden to those who do pay their fair share.

When asked at a recent congressional oversight hearing how the agency can improve the collection of taxes, IRS Commissioner Richardson said, "Implementing the technology modernization program is vital."

Richardson said productivity increases from TSM will "translate directly into additional tax collections in the bank."

The TSM initiatives aimed specifically at increasing tax collections include the following:

◆ The Compliance Research Information System, which includes a sample database on which the IRS can model the effects of alternate compliance strategies. It is projected to increase tax collections $2.9 billion per year.

◆ The Corporate Accounts Processing System, which is the central taxpayer account database and processing system at the heart of TSM. It will let the IRS perform extensive compliance checks, such as income and withholding validations, before fraudulent refunds are made. Today, those compliance checks are usually done after the fact.

◆ New statistical tools, which will be used to spot suspicious returns and evaluate the effectiveness of compliance techniques.

The IRS has already shown that modest system improvements can boost tax collections considerably. With new and improved "computer filters," the IRS last year spotted and rejected 4.1 million suspicious electronic returns. That is up fourfold from the previous year.

The people who filed those returns were notified of the problems, which included an invalid Social Security number. But an audit later discovered that 29% of the rejected electronic returns were refiled on paper—with exactly the same errors—and resulted in refunds being paid. But there is no data available on how much money was lost in fraudulent refunds.

And better computer checking of 1 million suspicious paper returns, coupled with more vigorous follow-up by IRS examiners, yielded $800 million in added revenue and reduced refunds last year.

Despite those bright spots in an otherwise gloomy record, Willis said recent changes in TSM plans cast doubts on the IRS' ability to increase overall compliance from the current 87% to 90%, the 3% difference that would put $50 billion more a year into federal coffers.

For example, the agency has postponed indefinitely its Taxpayer Compliance Measurement Program, the primary program for getting taxpayer compliance data. It also put on hold until after 2000 the ability to do up-front matching of tax returns and information returns such as W-2 and 1099 forms. Repeated requests by *Computerworld* to find out why these programs were delayed went unanswered by the IRS.

IRS: TOUGH TO GET ANY RESPECT

by Gary H. Anthes

The IRS has agreed with much of the criticism leveled at it over the years, but the agency claims it hasn't gotten the credit it deserves for having made substantial improvements to its systems.

"All this criticism is leveled by people who can't recognize a huge amount of progress," said Hank Philcox, former chief information officer at the IRS and now CIO at DynCorp in Reston, Va. "We wasted $2.5 billion? No, we built an infrastructure. To say we made no progress ignores where we started from."

Philcox said that when he assumed responsibility for TSM in 1986, the IRS' computer systems were on the verge of collapse. Underpowered mainframes and inefficient software took five days to do "weekend" file updates. The 1985 tax-filing season was an information systems and public relations disaster as tax refunds to 85 million individuals suffered long delays.

Essentially no data was available online, so IRS workers relied on tons of paper documents and computer printouts. Updates to the master file—on some 3,000 magnetic tapes—were propagated to regional centers by flying tapes across the country.

As a result of the 1985 fiasco, the IRS established three key systems priorities: boost computer power and optimize existing software, connect IRS centers with a high-speed data network and automate the manual processes of case workers by getting key tax information online. By the early 1990s, Philcox said, automation plus the network had reduced processing delays and manual effort so much that the IRS was able to eliminate 4,500 clerical positions.

Philcox said the new Integrated Collection System, scheduled for full implementation in 1998, has improved by 30% the productivity of case workers where it is installed. But final rollout of that system—and other worthwhile systems in the development pipeline—

---

depends on the IRS' future budget for the Tax Systems Modernization program, said Mark Cox, director of the IRS' southwest district.

The budget and plans for this latest collection system are under review by the IRS. Cox said the IRS has accomplished much over the past five years. "I don't think it's a totally negative story at all," he said. "I keep hearing people externally saying we haven't gotten the message, but folks internally have gotten the message on what needs to be done, and they are trying real hard."

The agency has also been listening lately to the siren song of outsourcing. Declaring that its expertise is in taxes, not systems, it has been parceling out more pieces of TSM.

Philcox agreed with the GAO's call for the IRS to do business process reengineering, but he said the IRS' decision to automate only existing processes was the correct one at the time. "Our strategy all along was to get the near-term improvements and to ensure a return on investment as we went along," he said. "And we did that."

LEARNING LESSONS FROM IRS'S BIGGEST MISTAKES

by Joseph Maglitta

The serious and costly delays in the Internal Revenue Service's Tax Systems Modernization program are rooted in deep cultural, political and organizational problems within that agency, many observers agree.

Yet even so, experienced information systems executives, megaproject managers, and consultants, say the decadelong project has much to teach other organizations tackling major technology projects.

Some of those lessons are painfully obvious: The keys to success remain strong leadership, technical competence and clearly stated goals and targets. Other nuggets of advice include the following:

- **Avoid big bangs.** "The words 'IT' and 'megaprojects' do not belong in the same sentence," said Gopal K. Kapur, president of the Center for Project Management in San Ramon, Calif. He and others advise "chunking" projects into small, stand-alone modules that deliver value in themselves. "You need to ask, 'If the project were halted today, would we be able to use what we delivered?' If the answer is no, go back," said John Hammitt, former chief information officer at United Technologies Corp. and now a vice president at Giga Information Group in Cambridge, Mass.

- **Pin down committed leadership.** At the IRS, critics say the lack of clear project champions has been a big problem.

The IRS has had three commissioners in five years and two deputy commissioners without technical backgrounds, said Robert P. Clagett. A 30-year AT&T Corp. veteran, Clagett headed the now-defunct Committee on Continued Review of the Tax Systems Modernization from 1990 to 1995. "The [IRS] said, 'It's an improvement and upgrade. We don't have to get involved.'"

This article was originally published in Computerworld, October 14, 1996. Copyright 1996 by Computerworld, Inc., Framingham, MA 01701.

Kapur advises project leaders to make a list of 10 to 15 responsibilities for executives. Ask how many hours per month they can devote to the project and whether they really have the time

◆ **Use small time frames.** "I will not commit to any deliverable that requires more than 12 months," said Christopher P. Higgins, a vice president at BankAmerica Corp. in San Francisco. "By then, the technology has changed and the business has changed."

The key, he added, isn't skimping on the project's requirements. Sponsors may chafe, but don't hesitate to take three to six months to get a clear, detailed plan and business case.

◆ **Make sure you have the talent to do the work.** The IRS and other organizations balk at admitting when a job is beyond them. It has a "congenital disability" when it comes to attracting and retaining qualified systems management talent, "especially at the executive levels," said Paul A. Strassmann, former CIO of the U.S. Department of Defense and now a consultant in New Canaan, Conn.

◆ **Use your best people to manage subcontractors.** Critics say a big problem at the IRS is that major contractors, notably TRW, Inc., often are far sharper technically than the government employees who manage them. As a result, some charge, it is easy for the IRS to get buffaloed.

A simple remedy: Assign your sharpest managers to manage outsourcers.

"You see at a place like Xerox that spends $3 billion on outsourcing [that] the key senior managers are as strong and competent as those from the [Electronic Data Systems Corp.] organization," Hammitt said.

◆ **Set your customer service sights high.** Another major mistake the IRS made was comparing its tax service and systems with those in other countries, according to Grover Norquist, president of Americans for Tax Reform, a Washington-based lobbying group and member of the National Commission on IRS Restructuring.

Service-minded organizations should always aim much higher, he said. "Instead of comparing how you do with the French tax system, for example, you should be looking at American Express, Citibank, and other leading customer-friendly firms," Norquist said.

◆ **Start fresh if necessary.** Don't be afraid to kill a runaway project, said Michael Hammer, president of Hammer and Company in Cambridge, Mass.

"Burn it down and start again," he said. "By not doing that, you make the project worse."

2.4.2   AGENCY'S DRIVE TO NOWHERE

by Chuck Appleby

Runaway computer projects at public agencies are political time bombs waiting to explode. And when they involve upward of $44 million in expenses with no return, as is the case at California's Department of Motor Vehicles (DMV), everyone starts looking for someone to blame.

According to an internal investigation released by the DMV on May 24, the agency's technical staff and the state's information technology management must shoulder the bulk of responsibility for the disastrous six-year project. "No one was questioning how long the project was taking, how much it was costing, what were the benefits to be derived [or] when it would be completed," the report says.

The original goal was to develop a relational database to register the state's 31 million drivers and 38 million cars. DMV director Frank Zolin pulled the plug on the entire project late last year when he found it would take another $100 million, on top of the $44 million already spent, and another four years to make it work.

A DMV spokesman says the agency had simply adopted untested relational database technology that could not handle the transaction demand from more than 40,000 users, with peaks of 30 transactions per second and 1 million per day.

The project was supposed to convert the state's 28-year-old DMV database from an IBM ES/9000 mainframe platform to 24 Tandem Computers Cyclone machines running the Non-Stop Cyclone SQL relational database. But unspecified software problems kept the project stalled. In 1988, the DMV signed consultants Ernst & Young to develop applications for the platform, but that $5 million effort was abandoned, reportedly by mutual consent, after $3 million had been spent in less than a year.

"The fundamental problem is that the DMV focused on hardware and not on software," says Jeff Lohrmann, a consultant with San

This article was originally published in InformationWeek, June 13, 1994. Copyright 1994 by CMP Publications, Inc., 600 Community Drive, Manhasset, NY 11030. Reprinted with permission.

Francisco's Strategic Partners, a technology planning firm. As a result, Lohrmann says, the DMV painted itself into a corner, unable to develop a migration path for relational technology. A Tandem spokesman denies that the technology it supplied was at fault.

Conflict of Interest?

One person at the center of the controversy is Office of Information Technology director Steve Kolodney, who oversaw the state's IT concerns when the original contract was awarded to Tandem, took a leave from his post to work as a consultant for Tandem in 1989, and then returned to his old state job one year later to oversee the project again. State Assemblyman Richard Katz, chairman of the transportation committee, charges there was a serious conflict of interest in Kolodney's actions.

Kolodney denies this and asserts he contracted the state's Fair Political Practices Commission for its approval before taking the consulting job.

Both Kolodney and Tandem also deny Kolodney played any role in the vendor winning the contract for the project. They insist the DMV chose Tandem over IBM's DB2 in a rigorous and highly touted evaluation process that also tested offerings from Software AG and Teradata.

"The role of my office is to review and approve business proposals that are conceptual in nature," Kolodney asserts. California agencies then conduct their own IT evaluation and development, including selection of vendors. "My only involvement was to approve DMV's business proposal to go out and explore relational technologies to modernize what was then a 1960s database," he says.

As the series of quite public investigations and finger pointing intensifies, the California DMV, and its millions of customers, are forced to rely on the department's strained IBM mainframes while the newer $44 million system sits full of updated but unusable data.

2.4.3 BANK OF AMERICA'S MASTERNET SYSTEM: A CASE STUDY IN RISK ASSESSMENT

by Jeffrey G. Szilagyi

Abstract

In 1982, Bank of America initiated the development of the Master-Net trust accounting system. After $78 million in losses on the project, the bank announced in 1988 that its trust business was being given to a subsidiary because it could no longer handle the operational requirements. MasterNet quickly became known within the information system industry as a classic case of a system that had fallen far short of expectations. The failure was particularly difficult for Bank of America with its rich history of technological successes.

While information system successes have received substantial trade press and academic coverage, system failures have drawn significantly less attention. Only recently has academia started examining the causes of information system development failure. Clemons has developed a five risk framework for assessing the total risk of a project in an attempt to understand the possible sources of failure. This thesis will examine the MasterNet project using Clemons' five risk framework as a basis of analysis. This analysis will demonstrate that Bank of America did very little to manage the total project risk spanning the five dimensions. Consequently, the project was a likely candidate for failure.

III. Bank of America's Master Net Story

This section will provide brief coverage of Bank of America's 1970s history and then proceed through the 1980s with a closer examination of the MasterNet story.

This article originally was a Master's Thesis. Used with permission of the author. Master's Thesis Supervisor: Chris F. Kemerer.

Sections I and II of this thesis are not included here in the interests of length.

A. Tom Clausen's Reign of Neglect

On January 1, 1970, Tom Clausen took the reins as Bank of America's president. At the time, Bank of America tended a stable and profitable retail business that served two and a half million customers.[18] The decentralized retail business proved very easy to run for the bank's corporate management because an effective set of controls had been established. Thus Clausen's two predecessors—S. Clark Beise and Rudolph Peterson—both looked to diversify and nurture new business. As a result, BofA's corporate finance and international lending grew during these years to become significant enterprises. The move toward making large loans to large corporations worked against A.P. Giannini's philosophy that emphasized the "common man," but the new business seemed appropriate for a company that had been successful in traditional commercial banking areas.

Clausen took what Beise and Peterson started and pushed the expansion of large corporate and international lending. This policy fostered several negative effects. First, the overseas operation grew so quickly that the resultant organization was disorganized and lacked the necessary controls for prudent lending. BofA sent inexperienced managers into new countries who, without an understanding of local conditions, made poor credit decisions. Second, Clausen, in his push for a consistent 10% yearly growth in profits, pressured credit officers into extending lower quality loans. These two conditions significantly weakened BofA's loan portfolio. Third, the retail operation was ignored and neglected. While other banks expanded and modernized their retail operations, BofA spent few resources on the retail side, instead choosing to commit to the new corporate and international lending efforts.[19]

The economic downturn of the late 1970s and early 1980s strained BofA's weak loan portfolio enough to slice into profits. The first quarter of 1981 brought BofA's announcement of the first decrease in profits in fourteen years. Clausen had taken steps to ensure steady and predictable profit increases through the 1980s, quite often using accounting manipulations to adjust earnings. These manipulations were stock-

---

18. Gary Hector, *Breaking the Bank*, p.67.
19. Gary Hector, *Breaking the Bank*, p. 98.

piled as weapons against poor quarters, but by the early 1980s, the stockpile was exhausted.[20] In 1981, Sam Armacost took over as president of Bank of America while Clausen moved on to become head of the World Bank. At the time, BofA's loan portfolio was falling apart, the bank was large and bureaucratic at the corporate level, and internal systems were strained under increasing pressure.

Armacost understood the need for stronger operational systems and planned a technological spending program in an attempt to push BofA back into the lead. The phrase that he liked to use was "leap-frogging into the 1990s." One area that Armacost emphasized was the trust department because it was mired in a 1965 vintage batch processing system. In 1982, Armacost named Clyde R. Claus executive vice president in charge of the trust department. Claus was given the orders to either fix the outdated department or close the business. BofA's internal staff had attempted to develop a modern system in 1981, but failed after spending $6 million and a full year's time.[21]

The complete trust business encompassed three broad areas:

1. Corporate Trust—the bank acts as registrar and transfer agent for stock and bond issues.

2. Employee Benefits—the bank holds and manages assets of private retirement plans.

3. Personal Trust—the bank helps manage the money for wealthy individuals and estates.

The employee benefits area is subdivided into master trust and master custodial accounts. Also, the corporate trust and employee benefit areas are sometimes referred to together as institutional trusts. The size of the accounts can be as small as a few thousand dollars for individuals, up to billions of dollars for pension funds. Corporate trust is a relatively simple activity requiring minimal resources. Employee benefits and personal trust are more complicated because they involve investments in real estate, stocks, bonds, commodities, and other legitimate financial investments. Master

---

20. Hector, pp. 93–95.
21. Douglas Frantz, "Computer: Bank Slips in Bid to Leap into 1990s Technology," *Los Angeles Times*, February 7, 1988, p. 1.

trust clients are mostly corporate pension plans that fall within the stricter regulatory reporting requirements of the Employees Retirement Income Security Act of 1975 and related laws. Master custodials provide the same services as the master trusts but management is retained by the client.

Master trust and custodials provide such trust services as securities lending, portfolio analysis, performance measurement, benefits disbursement, and record keeping. For both types, the operation is difficult because of the complexity involved in tracking each account given the varied needs of each client and because of the complexity and dynamics of the government regulations. Consequently, the trust department must provide extensive records of transactions, current positions, and statements of explanation for all actions taken. BofA's $38 billion of institutional trust assets was split about in half between corporate trusts and employee benefit trusts.

Claus quickly discovered that the bank's trust department was necessary to maintain solid client relationships. Quite often, a client that maintains a large corporate account keeps a trust account for convenience. After the system development failure in 1981, Claus was reluctant to turn to his internal staff and proceeded to search for an outside vendor to contract the project.

The trust industry held its annual convention in the fall of 1982. At that time, two key data processing executives under Claus met Stephen Katz of Premier Systems. Katz had recently formed Premier after leaving SEI Corp., an organization that he and Alfred West began. SEI sold a software system based on concepts in Katz's MBA's thesis to about 300 banks through the 1970s, and Katz was entering the same business with Premier.[22] At the convention, Katz met with some BofA officials and began to hammer out a deal for Premier to develop a trust accounting system for BofA.

BofA and Katz then proceeded in 1983 to create a consortium of banks in order to share the development costs and risks while participating in the development.[23] The consortium of banks agreed to

22. Douglas Frantz, "Computer: Bank Slips in Bid to Leap into 1990s Technology," *Los Angeles Times*, February 7, 1988, p. 1.
23. Tom Anderson, "MasterNet—A Technical Postscript—Part I," *The Financial Systems Journal*, Vol. 1, No. 1 (April 1988), p. 7.

advance money to Premier to develop a state of the art trust accounting system. The other banks—Seattle-First National, United Virginia, and Philadelphia National—were all using an SEI system at the time. Seattle-First National was a subsidiary of Seafirst Corp. BankAmerica, BofA's parent holding company, acquired Seafirst early in 1983 when Seafirst began to falter with losses in its substantial holdings of energy loans. Thus, Seattle-First National became a subsidiary of Bank-America and a sister bank of BofA, although BofA remained a significant part of the total business.

B. Development of the MasterNet System

Katz and Premier researched the project until March of 1984, when Claus presented Premier's proposal to BofA's management committee. The system, called MasterNet, was to consist of a large trust accounting system, called TrustPlus, plus eight smaller systems that augmented the core system. Each system would be developed or purchased and integrated to provide the full complement of trust automation and would be accessible to remote clients on a real-time basis.[24] BofA's ultimate goal was to sell the trust accounting services of the system to small and mid-size banks.[25] MasterNet's initial budget was 420 million and the completion date was set at December 31, 1984.

Katz's design engineers at Premier were to work with BofA's systems engineering and trust department to develop MasterNet. The design and implementation of the computer system followed a reasonably standard plan. A committee of all departments affected by the new system, including those from the consortium banks, met monthly to define requirements. BofA's data-processing staff met weekly with Premier's designers to discuss progress and needs. Also, expert users were assigned from all banks to become involved with the design process and provide continuity from design to implementation. Data processing executives felt that the degree of camaraderie and cooperation were exceptional throughout the design process.[26]

---

24. Anderson, p. 7.
25. David A. Ludlum, "$80M MIS Disaster," *ComputerWorld*, February 1, 1988, p. 10.
26. Tom Anderson, "MasterNet—A Technical Postscript—Part I," *The Financial Systems Journal*, Vol. 1, No. 1 (April 1988), p. 7.

Also, BofA took significant steps to ease conversion to the new system. A comprehensive training program was implemented that assigned user/trainers to develop courses including videotape, classroom, and hands-on terminals. The material was so well-designed that BofA earned a $1.5 million grant from a California state program that rewards companies for committing resources to employee retraining.[27] Later, these knowledgeable trainers served as code testers and certifiers.[28]

Though the initial December 31, 1984 deadline passed, Claus was not worried because of the progress in the system's development. Meanwhile, BofA was restructuring the organization of the bank under the guidance of Armacost's personally hired management consultant, Ichak Adizes. Armacost dreamed of a united team of executives supporting his vision of the bank and hired Adizes to orchestrate the effort. One outcome of Adizes' work was the formation of BASE—BankAmerica Systems Engineering—a consolidation of the assortment of systems engineering departments at BofA.

BASE was headed by Max Hopper of American Airlines' SABRE fame and would be responsible for the management, development, and application of technology. BASE also spearheaded a $5 billion, five year technological spending program that the bank announced at the same time.[29] Clausen's neglect of systems during his reign allowed a collection of over sixty networks to develop worldwide at BofA. Although the systems were reliable, the whole situation needed consolidation in order to allow orderly expansion and improvement.[30] Organizing BASE was a first step toward this goal by bringing together the various groups responsible for the bank's domestic and international computer and telecommunications opera-

27. Tom Anderson, "The MasterNet Story—Part II," *The Financial Systems Journal*, Vol. 1, No. 2 (August 1988), p. 6.
28. Tom Anderson, "The MasterNet Story—Part II," *The Financial Systems Journal*, Vol. 1, No. 2 (August 1988), p. 6.
29. Jonathan B. Levine, "Bank of American Rushes into the Information Age," *Business Week*, April 15, 1985, p. 110.
30. Van Collie and Shimon-Craig, "Bank of America Launches a Comeback," *Computers in Banking*, Vol. 6, No. 5 (May, 1989), p. 71.

tions. BofA expected that BASE would not only improve operations but sharpen the bank's competitive edge as well.

As a result of the formation of BASE, Claus lost authority over his portion of the systems engineering department. He also lost the securities clearing operation due to other restructuring activities. Consequently, he found it increasingly difficult to get these two groups and his trust department to work together. Despite this, MasterNet development continued through 1985 and into 1986 until March when Claus thought that the system was ready to be publicly announced. In May, BofA staged a lavish two-day demonstration of the system. Many of the bank's most important corporate clients attended the $75,000 party that touted the "industry's most sophisticated technology for handling trust accounts.[31] Claus was positive about the presentation and felt that clients were impressed by the system's advanced technology. Claus apparently believed that the system was ready for production use, while other executives felt the show was staged merely to appease anxious customers.

During 1986, Claus' department began to prepare for the conversion to MasterNet. The first step called for the movement of the $38 billion worth of institutional trust customers first. The smaller consumer division accounts would be converted later. The department made repeated attempts in late 1986, but were continually stopped by technical problems. The most glaring problems included poor response time and days-long system crashes. Despite the problems, Claus' department pressed on, putting in long hours in continuous attempts to get the system up and running. The enormity of the conversion task made it particularly difficult. Every single client asset had to be classified into one of the approximately 128 asset types. Personal notes kept by trust employees had to be gathered, reviewed, updated, and loaded into the system, entirely separate from the financial data.[32]

Meanwhile, Bank of America as a whole was having significant problems. 1985 and 1986 brought the bank losses of $337 million

31. Douglas Frantz, "Computer: Bank Slips in Bid to Leap into 1990s Technology," *Los Angeles Times*, February 7, 1988, p. 1.

32. Tom Anderson, "The MasterNet Story—Part II," *The Financial Systems Journal*, Vol. 1, No. 2 (August 1988), p. 7.

and $518 million respectively.[33] Since Armacost had become president, problem loans had been uncovered at an increasing rate. Also, news of the bank's losses and bad loans fueled rumors that BofA was in danger of failing. These rumors caused confusion in California where consumers began to close their accounts, causing a loss of more than $2 billion out of $44 billion of domestic deposits.[34,35] These problems forced BofA's board of directors to oust Armacost and replace him and his vision of technology with the returning Tom Clausen. In October of 1986, Clausen regained control and immediately began cutting costs and selling assets in an effort to restore profitability.

C. MasterNet's Failure and Postmortem

In early 1987, the system stability had improved enough to consider a serious conversion effort. A date of March 2 was set as the conversion deadline. As the systems engineering staff of sixteen rushed to complete the preparations, half of the group was pulled off of the project. In an effort to offset losses, BofA sold its consumer trust business to Wells Fargo for $100 million. The proceeds could be booked in the first quarter if the deal was closed by March 31, so the half of the staff that was pulled was assigned to transfer the accounts to the SEI-based Wells Fargo system.

The remaining staff worked continuously up to March 2 and all of the institutional accounts were transferred by the deadline. Six days later, the first of over a dozen Prime disk drives failed. The staff spent a weekend downloading back-up data and the rest of the month dealing with the remaining failures. It turned out that the faults inherent in the Prime disk drives didn't show up in the first months of testing.[36] Eventually, 21 of the 24 disk drives were replaced.[37]

33. *BankAmerica Corporation 1986 Annual Report.*
34. Gary Hector, *Breaking the Bank*, p. 306.
35. *Bank America Corporation 1986 Annual Report.*
36. Douglas Frantz, "Computer: Bank Slips in Bid to Leap into 1990s Technology," *Los Angeles Times*, February 7, 1988, p. 1.
37. Tom Anderson, "The MasterNet Story—Part II," *The Financial Systems Journal*, Vol. 1, No. 2 (August 1988), p. 8.

BofA decided in April of 1986 to move BASE to Concord, a suburb about half an hour east of San Francisco, in an attempt to tap the synergies of a large group of technologists and hopefully create better programs faster. It was an opportunity for the bank to replace antiquated technology with cutting edge technology and consolidate sixteen separate groups spread across San Francisco. The new technology center was also intended to attract recent college graduates.[38]

Several key employees quit and morale sank as the pressure and stress of the last few months combined with the move announcement pushed them over the edge. Similar difficulties had arisen in the securities clearing operation based in Los Angeles the previous month. This group was responsible for the tracking and reconciliation of the purchase or sale of stocks or other securities. In March, BofA announced that this group was to be moved to San Francisco. The reaction here, similar to that of the data-processing group, was employee dissatisfaction and defection. The bank eventually put the decision on hold for three months, but the damage to morale had been done. In order to fill the gap in Los Angeles, high-paid consultants were brought in to complete the work.

Meanwhile, improvements to MasterNet were being made and many of the problems of the previous year were cleared up. Unfortunately, new problems surfaced—for example, two new types of system halts were discovered in spring. Also, because the processors were fully utilized an additional two units were added to the current three. The hardware and software problems created an operational backlog that delayed processes such as monthly statement generation. Some accounts received monthly statements as much as two months late. Also, the backlog made it difficult for the trust department to maintain current data. In an effort to keep updated, fund managers were forced to get current information on portfolios directly from investment managers instead of through MasterNet. Many began to consider switching to other organizations to handle their trust business.[39]

---

38. Paul E. Schindler Jr., "Bank of America Consolidating Data Processing into One Site," *Information Week*, August 26, 1985, pp. 36–37.
39. Michael A. Robinson, "BankAmerica Fires Two Over MasterNet Problems," *American Banker*, October 22, 1987, p. 3.

In July of 1987, BofA announced that it was reserving $23 million related to losses due to MasterNet problems.[40,41] This reserve covered costs related to the hiring of consultants and accountants needed to clean up the damage, expected loss of fees, compensation claims for securities delivered late, and potential losses due to transaction discrepancies.[42,43] While BofA publicly assured others that the problems would be solved, it was quietly seeking a buyer for the institutional trust business. In October of 1987, both Claus and Mertes resigned in wake of the problems. The bank immediately assembled a seven member team to handle the MasterNet problem. Michael Simmons, formerly in charge of computers and telecommunications at Fidelity Investments in Boston, was hired in July of 1988 to replace Mertes as head of BASE.[44] The stock market crash of late October exacerbated the problems with the transaction processing and statement generation portion of the system.

Software industry sources said none of the other banks involved in MasterNet had become as deeply enmeshed with MasterNet as BofA. Philadelphia National Bank dropped out of the consortium two years before. United Virginia Bank used MasterNet only for its custodial trust business, which is less complicated than master trust services, and Seattle-First National appeared to have delayed adopting MasterNet in its employee benefits business.[45]

In January of 1988, BofA announced that an additional $35 million would be added to the current $23 million reserve for MasterNet malfunctions.[46] In comparison, BofA earned $60 million in the fourth

40. Michael A. Robinson, "BankAmerica Operating Profit Is First in Five Quarters," *American Banker*, October 23, 1987, p. 3.
41. Michael A. Robinson, "BankAmerica Fires Two Over MasterNet Problems," *American Banker*, October 22, 1987, p. 3.
42. Michael A. Robinson, "BankAmerica Is Computing More Trouble," *American Banker*, July 16, 1987, p. 1.
43. Michael A. Robinson, "BankAmerica Slips to 3rd Largest in US," *American Banker*, July 24, 1987, p. 1.
44. Kathy Chin Leong, "Simmons to Shoulder BankAmerica's Burdens," *ComputerWorld*, July 18, 1988, p. 2.
45. Michael A. Robinson, "BankAmerica is Computing More Trouble," *American Banker*, July 16, 1987, p. 1.
46. "Inside Lines—Break the Bank," *ComputerWorld*, January 25, 1988, p. 102.

quarter of 1987. Business began to evaporate as clients pulled their accounts from BofA. The number of accounts dropped from 800 to about 700 and total institutional assets declined to $34 billion from $38 billion. A few days after this first announcement, BofA announced that 95% of its institutional trust services clients would be shifted to BankAmerica's Seattle-First National subsidiary.[47] The remaining 29 clients, representing BofA's largest and most complex accounts, would be given outright to State Street Bank and Trust Co.[48]

In May of 1988, BofA completed the conversion of its trust account processing to a service bureau system running at the SEI data center while Seattle-First National handled day-to-day trust operations for its sister subsidiary. Thus, four years after the start of the project, not only was the system a major failure, but the whole trust business was lost. A total of $80 million was spent on the "stillborn" system and BofA received substantial press coverage of the debacle. The *L.A. Times* said in a front page story that BofA slipped in its "bid to leap into 1990s technology,"[49] while *ComputerWorld*, an information systems trade newspaper, called MasterNet an "$80 Million MIS Disaster."[50] These words were especially harsh given BofA's technological leadership throughout most of its history.

At a time when BofA was struggling to regain profitability, the bad press helped convince the world that BofA really did have significant internal problems. At the same time, BofA was also getting press coverage for its loan losses and attempts to stay afloat as one of the largest banks in the country.[51,52] MasterNet is now considered a classic example of an information technology failure.

47. Michael A. Robinson, "BankAmerica Scraps Faulty Trust System," *American Banker*, January 22, 1988, p. 1.
48. Dennis P. O'Connell, "BofA loses 29 Big Trust Clients," *American Banker*, February 1, 1988, p. 3.
49. Douglas Frantz, "Computer: Bank Slips in Bid to Leap into 1990s Technology," *Los Angeles Times*, February 7, 1988, p. 1.
50. David A. Ludlum, "$80M MIS Disaster," *ComputerWorld*, February 1, 1988, p. 1.
51. "Problems Still," ed. Thomas Jaffe, *Forbes*, May 30, 1988, p. 330.
52. "BankAmerica Tries to Tighten Its Grip," *The Economist*, March 21, 1987, p. 24.

IV. A Risk Assessment of MasterNet

This section will assess the risks that Bank of America was exposed to with the MasterNet project. First, Kemerer and Sosa's work and Clemons' follow-up work in the area of risk management will be reviewed. Then, the MasterNet project will be analyzed using Clemons' five-point risk assessment structure.

A. Review of Previous Works

In their 1991 paper "Systems Development Risks in Strategic Information Systems," Kemerer and Sosa examine strategic information systems (SISs) that have fallen short of expectations. In contrast, current writings use such well-known successes as American Hospital Supply's ASAP order entry system as encouragement for the use of SISs. Kemerer and Sosa chose to examine failed SISs in an attempt to identify the barriers that prevent successful SIS development. Their thesis states that "there exist significant systems development challenges that present risks or even barriers to some organizations' attempts to use IT strategically, and that executives and systems developers who are considering an SIS development must plan carefully to avoid these pitfalls and increase the likelihood of a successful SIS."[53]

Kemerer and Sosa illustrated their position by collecting a broad array of SIS failures and categorizing the types of problems that plagued them. These problems were divided into the three phases of the systems development life-cycle model: definition, implementation, and maintenance. Kemerer and Sosa then developed a matrix that corresponds the particular pitfalls with the firm's relative position along three dimensions: monetary resources, technological sophistication, and organizational flexibility. The purpose of the matrix is to allow firms to identify their most likely pitfalls according to the characteristics of their organization and then adjust their plans to balance risks as they desire.

Clemons' 1991 paper "Evaluation of Strategic Investments in Information Technology" took the evaluation process one step further

---

53. C. F. Kemerer and G. L. Sosa, "Systems Development Risks in Strategic Information Systems," *Information and Software Technology*, Vol. 33, No. 3 (April 1991), p. 212.

and developed seven lessons that can be applied to the evaluation of a firm's investment decision in SISs. Clemons' third lesson—it is necessary to balance many forms of risk—lists five basic components of risk which must be managed and traded off depending on the firm's comfort level.[54] These five risks are classified as financial, technical, project, functional, and systemic.

B. The Five-Risk Analysis

This section is devoted to assessing the MasterNet project along Clemons' five-risk framework. Five subsections follow, each devoted to a particular risk.

1. Financial Risk

The first of Clemons' five risks is financial risk. Clemons defines excessive financial risk as unacceptable financial exposure or costs that are out of line with expected benefits. The examination of Master-Net's financial risk will concentrate mainly on Bank of America's weak overall financial condition and the significant downside financial exposure of MasterNet.

During the MasterNet project period, BofA's finances can best be described as weak. In the early 1980s, Bank of America experienced a severe downturn in its financial condition. In 1982, BankAmerica (the parent holding company whose most substantial holding is BofA) posted a $457 million profit on $4.2 billion of revenues. This is a mere 2.2% increase from the year before. At this time, the discovery of bad loans was accelerating and its true exposure to bad credit was just being realized. BankAmerica posted even lower profits in 1983 and 1984, until it posted a $337 million loss in 1985. The organization bottomed out in 1987 with close to a $1 billion loss.[55]

Mentioned earlier, the bank set out on an aggressive $5 billion, five year systems spending plan in 1985. With revenues of $5.3 billion in the same year, Armacost and Hopper planned on spending

---

54. Eric K. Clemons, "Evaluation of Strategic Investments in Information Technology," *Communications of the ACM*, Vol. 34, No. 1 (January 1991), pp. 30–31.
55. *BankAmerica Corporation 1986 Annual Report.*

nearly 20% of revenues on systems maintenance and improvement alone.[56] The $1 billion per year figure is over 25% higher than the spending in 1984 of $780 million.[57] This spending was concentrated in BASE, a group consisting of less than 10% of the bank's employees. Relative to $5 billion, the $20 million spent on MasterNet is a .4% portion.

While Armacost committed huge sums to technology, he was also slashing costs in other parts of the bank in an attempt to streamline. Armacost withdrew services, closed about 200 branches since 1981, and jettisoned entire lines of business including the FinanceAmerica subsidiary, a national consumer loan network.[58] Armacost was taking BofA in an entirely new direction, shifting expenses away from the bloated retail business and corporate bureaucracy into systems spending.

Other banks in the master trust industry were also spending significant money on their systems. From 1983 to 1987, First Pennsylvania Bank spent $8 million to develop a new master trust system.[59] The bank had $31 billion in managed master trust and custodial assets as of mid-1987.[60] Also, Banker's Trust planned on spending $10 million in the late 1980s to update its master trust capabilities.[61] It had $118 billion in master trust and custodial assets as the third largest master trust bank in the country.[62] Banker's had a 1977 vintage system that worked efficiently—the money was budgeted for incremental improvements, such as the ability to handle more sophisticated securities.

---

56. *BankAmerica Corporation 1986 Annual Report.*

57. Jonathan B. Levine, "Bank of America Rushes Into the Information Age," *Business Week*, April 15, 1985, p. 112.

58. Jonathan B. Levine and Dorinda Elliot, "BofA Is Becoming the Incredible Shrinking Bank," *Business Week*, January 27, 1986, p. 78.

59. Trudy Ring, "The Cost of Competing," *Pensions & Investment Age*, September 7, 1987, p. 35.

60. Hank Berkowitz, "Master Trust—Assets Hit $1.32 Trillion," *Pensions & Investment Age*, September 7, 1987, p. 36.

61. Ring, p. 35.

62. Berkowitz, p. 36.

While the basic MasterNet project was budgeted for $20 million, the potential loss due to system failure could be higher due to other, auxiliary factors. These potential factors include:

♦ *Completion of Work*—A system failure such as MasterNet's forces the bank to perform the intended services in an ad hoc manner, usually via manual labor. For example, in 1983, BofA's Investment Securities Division (BISD) installed a new computer system to handle the volume of transactions flooding the operation. The new system was started up while the old system was shut down. Unfortunately, the new system worked improperly, misrecording thousands of transactions. Teams of auditors were brought in to sort through every transaction by hand. In this case, a $20 million reserve was set up to cover losses and audit expenses.[63]

♦ *Inaccurate Transaction Recording*—When a bank cannot accurately record transactions, it must resort to "blind settling"—the practice of accepting the transaction terms that the counter-party recorded. If the comparison of BofA's records and the counter-party's records indicate a discrepancy, then the counter-party is normally not paid until verification. When blind settling, the counter-party is automatically paid and the exception is verified manually. BofA had such a huge backlog of exceptions that it would be impossible to retrieve all overpayments due to the extreme delay.[64]

♦ *Inaccurate Asset Tracking*—The MasterNet system was designed to track the asset position of its accounts. Since BofA managed $38 billion institutional dollars, the exposure to mistakes was significant. The personal trust business was never transferred to the system, so it was not at risk.

♦ *Loss of Managed Assets*—Before the institutional trust business was given away, the total managed assets had slid from $38

63. "BofA's Hopper: Is BASE a Balloon?" *Data Communications*, May, 1985, p. 88.
64. Michael A. Robinson, "BankAmerica Is Computing More Trouble," *American Banker*, July 16, 1987, p. 1.

billion to $34 billion. This represents a 10% decrease and an approximate revenue loss of 10%.

◆ *Loss of the Business*—Obviously, the giveaway of the institutional business to Seattle-First National and State Street represents a total loss of all future cashflows. BofA was fortunate to sell the personal trust business and obtain compensation.

◆ *Loss of Peripheral Business*—The press coverage of the MasterNet project damaged BofA's reputation. While the effect on BofA's development of new business was unknown, the event certainly had a negative effect.

◆ *Litigation and Fines*—In the regulated trust business, banks can be fined by the government for not adhering to the regulations. Litigation costs include lawyers and court costs.

In retrospect, BofA spent an additional $58 million over the original $20 million in direct costs cleaning up the MasterNet mess.

The basic financial benefit of the MasterNet project is not so much the generation of new cashflows but the continuation of current cashflows. In 1987, BofA made nearly $100 million on its trust business despite the MasterNet problems.[65] MasterNet was primarily intended to be a "catch-up" project with the highest priority of continuing the old system's operation, albeit more efficiently. A secondary goal of the MasterNet system was to add enough functionality to attract new clients. This new business could consist of additional trust accounting or the sale of the trust accounting services. Management thought the real value of the project rested in the new technology. If by the end of the 1980s BofA had a 1965 vintage system, it is clear that the bank would have little strategic edge in this highly competitive arena.

Because of the risks involved, the bank did attempt to reduce the financial exposure. The consortium was formed primarily to reduce exposure by spreading costs among the group, but the inclusion of Seattle-First National made this diversification less effective. Seattle-First National, like BofA, was a subsidiary of BankAmerica (the parent holding company). Therefore, the financial risk was not really re-

---

65. Mary Tobin, "Shakeout in Trust," *United States Banker*, February, 1989, p. 38.

duced for BankAmerica, because the finances of its BofA and Seattle-First National subsidiaries are consolidated into its own financial statements. Keeping the banks involved with the project was another problem. In 1985, Philadelphia National Bank dropped out, leaving just three banks remaining.

Bank of America found it necessary to undertake the MasterNet project. In assessing BofA's financial risk with MasterNet, two items in particular must be considered. First, the overall financial health of the bank was weak and deteriorating. Second, the downside costs of failure were significant given that MasterNet handled billions of dollars of client assets.

2. Technical Risk[66]

Clemons defines the second risk, technical risk, as the possibility that the project just cannot be accomplished because the supporting technology is not available. This section will take a broad view of this definition and include not just the chosen technology, but the process of converting from the old to the new. In this context, technology refers to the basic processing platform, the surrounding telecommunications network, and the necessary software.

MasterNet was an aggressive attempt to provide a full complement of trust automation. Most of this functionality was directed at the master trust and custodial trust business, both of which are significantly more complicated than the corporate trust business. The core trust accounting system turned out to be the most difficult to implement. In fact, six of the eight subsystems were successfully implemented and used within the bank. MasterNet planned functionality was grand: an international network, full customer access, and on-line reporting.

Initial designs called for the use of a single eight megabyte, one MIP Prime processor. As database and functionality requirements grew through the development, the system grew to three sixteen megabyte, eight MIP Prime processors on the conversion date in March of 1987. This represents a 24-times increase in computing

---

66. Tom Anderson, "The MasterNet Story—Part II," *The Financial Systems Journal*, Vol. 1, No. 2 (August 1988), pp. 4–9.

power. Two of the processors were used as front-end devices, while a single processor connected to thirteen 600 megabyte disk drives served as the back-end. This configuration required development of various new components: a special data communications channel between CPUs, changes to Prime's PRIMOS operating system, changes to Premier's NEXUS database, and special RAM disk storage for paging. The development of these components stressed the design groups at BofA, Premier, and Prime. As the operational backlog grew through 1987, two more processors were added to expedite statement generation.

The decision to use Prime hardware was driven by Steven Katz of Premier. BofA succumbed to Katz despite the fact that BofA had been an IBM house since 1955. At the time, BofA had been using nearly 20 IBM or plug-compatible mainframes.[67] During the conversion in March of 1987, 21 of 24 Prime disk drives had to be replaced due to defects that didn't show up until after nine months of operation.

The MasterNet network connected 35 sites with up to 900 asynchronous terminals connected through 64 multiplexors. The sites were located primarily in California. The local lines were connected to five high speed data nodes that were spread around the state. The network was designed so that any one node could go down without destroying the integrity of the system. The multiplexors were state of the art and the bank had not previously used the high speed communication protocol chosen. Despite initial problems, the network design eventually stabilized and withstood stress and response time tests.

The software development effort was vast. Premier had over 100 programmers on its staff for MasterNet development. The end result of the project was a system with 3.5 million lines of code, a large amount by any standard. This huge amount of code caused substantial system paging as the number of users increased. Thus, the development team added the RAM disk storage to help improve paging rates.

The enormity of the system development task is approached in difficulty only by the conversion process. To simplify the process, BofA hired several conversion professionals to work with the devel-

67. Jeffry Beeler, "BankAmerica Inaugurates $5 Billion Overhaul of MIS," *ComputerWorld*, February 4, 1985, p. 8.

opers. These professionals handled the coordination of data gathering and translation. The pre-loading of static data (e.g., names, addresses, etc.) began years prior to conversion. As mentioned previously, some particularly difficult aspects of the conversion included the gathering, updating, and loading of personal notes and the alignment of existing asset positions with the approximately 130 asset types.

The development task was enormous and expensive. New hardware, software, and communications had to be developed and integrated. Almost all aspects of the project were developed from scratch—a tremendous challenge.

3. Project Risk

According to Clemons, project risk is the possibility that the firm cannot execute the task. He cites such possibilities as the project is too large or complex or the skills and expertise of the staff do not match the needs of the project. Project risk has the broadest reach and thus demands detail along many different dimensions. Therefore, this section will be broken into five subsections.

a. Management Philosophy and Vision

Armacost began his presidency with a commitment to improving Bank of America's systems. His phrase "leap-frogging into the 1990s" characterized his desire to improve and his acknowledgment of the bank's deficiencies. Armacost's creation of BASE and the $5 billion technological spending program exemplified his commitment. Armacost also wanted BASE to be the focal point of attention; therefore the announcement was well-publicized.[68] He also put Max Hopper in charge of BASE—Hopper was a high-profile systems manager who had fantastic success in developing American Airlines' SABRE reservation system. Armacost hoped that Hopper could bring his experience and success to BofA. Armacost had a vision for technological success, but because he was a banker with little information system experience, he didn't thoroughly understand the technical issues.

---

68. *Software Maintenance News*, Vol. 3, No. 7 (July 1985), p. 18.

As for other managers, Clyde Claus quickly recognized the trust department's need and immediately set out to develop an aggressive new system.[69] Max Hopper was a terrific visionary in the airline industry, having put in place one of the most successful strategic information systems in business history. Although he understood technology, his lack of in-depth banking knowledge slowed him. It is also not clear whether the position he held reserved any significant power to implement daring strategies.

BofA's early success with technology was driven by men like S. Clark Beise and A.R. Zipf. These two men alone were responsible for many of the innovations of the 1950s. They were both hands-on managers who understood technology and its limitations. They both also understood that technology was the key to future competitiveness, and that taking technical risks was necessary for long-term success.

When Tom Clausen took over in 1970, the technological vision became clouded. Under Clausen, innovation came to a virtual standstill and investment in computers and telecommunications was delayed.[70] His return in 1987 signaled a return to old times despite his increased awareness of the need for long-term system spending. Clausen's immediate concern was to get the bank back on its feet again and he took whatever short-term measures were necessary.

b. Consultants

Bank of America made significant use of consultants throughout the MasterNet project. In fact, the basic design of the system was given to Steven Katz of Premier Systems. In the 1950s, Bank of America established with the success of the ERMA project that consultant relationships can be very rewarding. The extraordinary cooperation and vision assured some level of success in that undertaking.

The selection of Katz was based mostly on his past accomplishments. As a partner with Alfred West, he successfully sold software systems to small banks through the 1970s. When Katz split off to

---

69. Douglas Frantz, "Computer: Bank Slips in Bid to Leap into 1990s Technology," *Los Angeles Times*, February 7, 1988, p. 1.
70. Gary Hector, *Breaking the Bank*, pp. 96–98.

form Premier, he took his experience with him and needed an opportunity to develop a new product. Sharing development costs allowed Katz to minimize Premier's start-up risk and guaranteed some customers for the new product. The relationship gave BofA an experienced hand in the trust business.

There are some indications that the relationships between Premier and BofA were not as cordial as they appeared at the upper levels. In their first meeting, Katz insisted on using Prime Computer while BofA wanted to stick with their more familiar IBM hardware. Katz had a long and solid relationship with Prime. Katz also asserted that he could deliver a product in less than two years. BofA representatives argued that that assertion was ridiculous. Some of the bank's personnel also found Katz difficult to deal with, especially on technical subjects. While staff were encouraged to learn aspects of other businesses on the ERMA project, Katz proclaimed "Don't give us the solutions. Just tell us the problems."[71] At lower levels of management and staff, it seemed as though relationships were cooperative and supportive.[72]

A major distinction can be drawn between ERMA and MasterNet in terms of consultant location. SRI was located within an hour's drive from BofA headquarters, while Premier was located in Pennsylvania. It was a goal of 1950s BofA management to find a local organization that could handle the work. Another distinction that can be drawn is the motivations of the consultants. SRI was an academic think-tank, interested in performing meaningful research. Premier was a young company that needed to establish some credible business. A contract with one of the largest banks in the country would give prestige to the Premier name as well as provide it with an infusion of capital.

---

71. Douglas Frantz, "Computer: Bank Slips in Bid to Leap into 1990s Technology," *Los Angeles Times*, February 7, 1988, p. 1.
72. Tom Anderson, "MasterNet—A Technical Postscript—Part I," *The Financial Systems Journal*, Vol. 1, No. 1 (April 1988), p. 7.

c. Management Capability and Continuity

In April of 1981, Sam Armacost became, at age forty-one, the youngest man to run the bank since A.P. Giannini's early days. Armacost was considered charming and personable, in direct contrast to the aloof Clausen.[73] Armacost had moved quickly through the bank's management hierarchy, never staying at a job for more than two years. He led a charmed career, having never been affected by an economic downturn, and was pushed to the top of BofA. Even he admitted in early 1981 that it might be too early for him to become president.[74]

Throughout the 1982–1988 period, Armacost was constantly occupied with some controversial events that put pressure on his tenure:

◆ Armacost completed the purchase of Charles Schwab in 1982 and troubled Seafirst Corp. in 1983.

◆ In 1984, the failure of Continental Illinois Corp. forced the Comptroller's office to clamp down on BofA and their problem loans. As government auditors from the Comptroller's office swarmed, Armacost remained defensive and protective of the bank's books, fearing loss of control.

◆ In early 1985, an Armacost attempt to cover up a $95 million mortgage scandal at a Los Angeles branch generated criticism from the press.[75]

◆ In 1985, Armacost began to have problems with the bank's board of directors that escalated through 1986.[76]

◆ Early in 1986, Sanford Weill, a successful securities businessman who built the brokerage arm of Shearson Lehman Brothers, offered to become the president of BofA and inject $1 billion of capital into the bank.[77] As a defense against the friendly bid,

---

73. Gary Hector, *Breaking the Bank*, p. 127.
74. Gary Hector, "More Than Mortgages Ails BankAmerica," *Fortune*, April 1, 1985, p. 50.
75. Gary Hector, *Breaking the Bank*, pp. 207-212.
76. Hector, pp. 259–261, 298–307.
77. Hector, pp. 265–268.

Armacost considered a merger with First Interstate Bancorp.[78] Weill subsequently withdrew his offer.

Meetings and sessions with Ichak Adizes consumed significant amounts of Armacost's and his executives' time. From late 1982 through early 1985, Adizes spent significant time with all of BofA's executives. Adizes' meetings no doubt helped communication among the top executives, but typically occupied up to 20% of their time. The process eventually hurt morale and drew insults from the lower ranks of managers.[79]

The unsettled picture at the top of BofA continued through 1986. Armacost was dismissed as president and replaced with Tom Clausen. Clausen's return continued the turmoil. Tom Cooper, appointed Chief Operating Officer by Armacost in February of 1986, did not get along with Clausen. Cooper was known as a dedicated cost-cutter and eschewed the luxuries of his office. Clausen, on the other hand, enjoyed the personal luxuries of his position, such as use of a limousine and company plane. As an executive, Clausen often consolidated his authority, and Cooper resigned in May of 1987 as his power was slowly being drained away.[80]

Closer to the trust business, Clausen had lost a portion of his authority with the formation of BASE. In late 1986, Hopper left BASE to return to American Airlines. In late 1987, Armacost launched an internal investigation of the MasterNet debacle. The report, by BofA senior vice president and director of litigation Winslow Christian, was not intended to lay blame on any individual but detail exactly what went wrong with the project's development. Shortly after the delivery of the report, both Clausen and Mertes resigned in October of 1987.[81]

Through the MasterNet period of 1982–88, BofA's management underwent the stress of a variety of events both internal and external to the bank. Upper management's preoccupation with these events

78. Hector, pp. 276–279.
79. Gary Hector, *Breaking the Bank*, pp. 179–186.
80. Hector, pp. 334–336.
81. Michael A. Robinson, "BankAmerica Fires Two over MasterNet Problems," *American Banker*, October 22, 1987, p. 3.

and the shuffling of executives resulted in a loss of continuity and control for the whole bank. Thus MasterNet, like many other projects and organizations in the bank, found itself without the guidance and direction of a strong upper management team.

d. Organizational Factors

Bank of America was concerned that it would be difficult to change a system that had been in place for twenty years. First, there are the problems associated with any move to a new system. Second, there are the problems related to the use of such drastically modern technology. The old system was based on batch processing, while the new system was real-time on-line reporting. To combat these problems, BofA created a comprehensive training program that eventually won grants from California's retraining program.

During this period, financial problems at the bank caused management to evaluate and make changes to the inner structure of the organization. Thus, the 1981–1988 period was a time of significant change and turmoil. The origination of BASE consolidated the bank's system engineering departments but removed some locality of authority. The movement of the BASE employees also put stress on the employees working on MasterNet. The stress of system problems had been growing for years, and the pressure to deliver to increasingly dissatisfied customers grew. Also, the poorly timed sale of the consumer trust department did not enhance employee's view of upper management's understanding of the MasterNet problem.

e. Other System Projects

As a large bank, Bank of America participated in many systems development projects. Directly related to the trust business and previously mentioned, the bank attempted to develop a new trust system in 1981 only to lose $6 million and a year's time. Other examples not related to the trust business exemplify the difficulty of systems development in the financial arena:

◆ The RISD failure detailed in the financial risk section put $20 million at risk in an area that performs functions similar to the trust business. Fortunately for BofA, the eventual losses turned out to be minor.

♦ In 1983, Hopper wanted to implement a system used by the airlines called TPF, or Transaction Processing Facility. TPF was a high-speed, expensive system built for massive volumes. Its high power was not necessary for 1983 volumes, but would be needed if optimistic projections were correct. Unfortunately, the projections were terribly inflated, and the investment in TPF was not immediately necessary.[82] Now, almost nine years later, the investment seems to be paying dividends, but only as the rest of BofA's systems have caught up. TPF currently handles BofA's bank card authorization inquiries and serves as a switching facility for the ATM system.[83]

♦ In late 1987, BofA dropped an effort to integrate a software package called TradePro into its securities clearing operation. The bank spent $5 million on the package and shipped personnel in from across the country. BASE was responsible for the development of the software.[84]

♦ Other failures in the 1984–85 period include a system that incorrectly sent statements to corporate clients and the collapse of a foreign exchange program that forced traders to use pencil and paper.[85]

The bank also had its share of successes:

♦ Despite a late start into the area, BofA initiated an intense effort to introduce ATMs into its California market in 1981. After spending over $100 million in a single year, the system was essentially complete and working correctly.[86]

82. Gary Hector, *Breaking the Bank*, pp. 173–175.
83. Van Collie and Shimon-Craig, "Bank of America Launches a Comeback," *Computers in Banking*, Vol. 6, No. 5 (May, 1989), p. 71.
84. Michael A. Robinson, "BankAmerica Confirms Latest Computer Snafu," *American Banker*, November 9, 1987, p.3.
85. Gary Hector, *Breaking the Bank*, p. 206.
86. Hector, p. 147.

◆ In 1984, BofA went on line with their point of sale system named Interlink. A successful real-time debit card service, BofA developed the product with three other west coast banks.[87]

◆ BofA developed a retail Customer Information File (CIF) system in 1988. The system integrates multiple databases to allow transparent access to account data. This system allows the cross-selling of products and services and the development of new products.[88] Renamed Customer On-Line Information Network (COIN), the system won an award for systems excellence from the Society for Information Management.[89]

◆ By 1989, BofA had seen success in its attempt to consolidate networks. The California Data Network (CDN) now connects the three major data centers in San Francisco, Los Angeles, and Concord with high-speed digital T1 communications lines. The new utility should've reduced costs by $5–10 million annually and provided faster response times.[90]

While BofA has had its share of failed projects, it has also had some significant successes. Clearly, BofA did have some systems expertise, but either did not appreciate the skills of the successful project managers or didn't have the organizational controls necessary to place these valuable people in strategic positions. Either way, BofA's past record provides substance to the charge of organizational weakness.

4. Functional Risk

Clemons defines functional risk as the possibility that the completed project either does not do what the user wants or users needs have changed enough to make the system useless. This section will detail

---

87. Van Collie and Shimon-Craig, "Bank of America Launches a Comeback," *Computers in Banking*, Vol. 6, No. 5 (May, 1989), p. 71.

88. Alan Alper, "Banks Seek Higher Yield from Info Systems Investment," *ComputerWorld*, August 15, 1988, p. 65.

89. Clint Wilder, "SIM Honors Hopper, Fadem," *ComputerWorld*, August 5, 1991, p. 88.

90. Van Collie and Shimon-Craig, "Bank of America Launches a Comeback," *Computers in Banking*, Vol. 6, No. 5 (May, 1989), p. 71.

the difficulty of operating a trust accounting business and how well MasterNet met this functionality.

The administration and accounting of a trust business is a difficult business due to the wide variety of assets, client needs, and government regulations. The master and custodial trust business in particular are tightly regulated and require extensive reporting. These various demands of the business forced banks to upgrade both hardware and software systems continually.[91]

The Employees Retirement Income Security Act (ERISA) of 1974 initiated the growth of the master trust industry. This act required the detailed reporting of trust activities for pension funds. Corporations looked to banks to handle this difficult responsibility. Additional changes and new regulations—such as the Tax Equity and Fiscal Responsibility Act of 1982 (TEFRA)—made adherence to the law even more difficult. A Trust Company Bank of Atlanta vice president stated "Every time Congress gets together, they make a change. And it's difficult to keep up with all the changing regulations."[92] To deal with the complexity, banks established programs to stay up-to-date with master trust technology, such as State Street's continuing professional education for master trust personnel begun in 1987. Custodial trusts have similar but less stringent requirements.

A good example of the growth of sophisticated financial instruments is the explosion of the mortgage-backed security market. These securities have floating interest rates, principal that can be pre-payed at any time, and monthly payments (as opposed to more typical semi-annual). These properties create variable monthly payments that are difficult to track and different from normal corporate bonds. In fact, there are several instances of funds having mortgage-backed problems with various trust accounting banks. For example, State Street lost an $8.6 billion Teamsters account because of mortgage-backed security problems.[93] Other securities that have gained favor

91. April W. Klimley, "Master Trust and Custodial Services," *Institutional Investor*, April 1988, p. S3.

92. Margaret Soares, "Banks Shy Away From High-Tech Master Trust Business Because of Regulations, Costs," *The Bond Buyer*, March 6, 1989, p. 11s.

93. Trudy Ring, "The Cost of Competing," *Pensions & Investment Age*, September 7, 1987, p. 35.

with clients are options, futures, and international securities, all of which are more complicated than more traditional stocks and bonds.

The high costs of maintaining sophisticated computer systems necessary to handle trust business scared many major players out of the market. Through the eighties, major banks including J.P. Morgan, Wells Fargo, First National Bank of Chicago, and Crocker National all left some portion of the business.[94] The business has also become highly competitive. This competition has sliced into profits and made the margin of comfort slimmer.[95]

MasterNet's functionality was additionally complex because it had to satisfy so many different groups. These groups included the four trust departments of the consortium banks and Premier personnel. One executive felt that the diversity of interests caused developers to accommodate all needs instead of limiting functionality.[96] Also, there is evidence that system functionality was not sufficiently tested. Both the bank's internal auditor and Ernst & Whinney, its outside auditor, felt that a conversion shouldn't take place because MasterNet was not adequately tested. An anonymous letter from a staff member sent to the trust department's internal newsletter pointed out that the system was not ready for use.[97]

The trust accounting business is a complex, technology-driven arena. Continual systems investment is necessary to keep up-to-date with current government regulation and financial innovation.[98] While BofA recognized the need for this investment, many environmental factors made the systems functionality quite complicated. The intrinsic complexity of the business was compounded by increasingly sophisticated financial instruments and the broad needs of many groups. In an attempt to satisfy everyone, the project be-

94. April W. Klimley, "Master Trust and Custodial Services," *Institutional Investor*, April, 1988, p. S3.
95. Klimley, p. S3.
96. Tom Anderson, "MasterNet—A Technical Postscript—Part I," *The Financial Systems Journal*, Vol. 1, No. 1 (April 1988), p. 8.
97. Michael A. Robinson, "BankAmerica Is Computing More Trouble," *American Banker*, July 16, 1987, p. 1.
98. Trudy Ring. "The Cost of Competing," *Pensions & Investment Age*, September 7, 1987, p. 35.

came bogged down in massive amounts of code that contributed to its downfall.

5. Systemic Risk

Systemic risk is different in that it implies successful implementation. Clemons says that systemic risk is the possibility that the system has such a large impact that it alters the environment and all assumptions about costs and benefits. By definition, this type of risk is entirely unpredictable. Therefore, very little can be done to combat it. For argument's sake, the design of MasterNet was unlikely to dominate the business. Features such as customer access were already implemented in other banks' trust systems, and some banks and companies were already selling these services. As for MasterNet's grand functionality, clients stress that accuracy and timeliness of reports are the most important factor in quality trust service, and that broad functionality is less critical.[99] Also, other banks in the business operated systems approaching the sophistication of MasterNet and had been since the technology was available.

C. Summary

Through this five-risk framework, it is apparent that BofA was not prepared to take on a project of such magnitude. Of the four controllable risks, BofA failed to sufficiently assess and manage all four:

♦ Financially, the bank was weak and getting weaker.

♦ The technical aspects presented a tremendous challenge even for the most sophisticated of organizations.

♦ The management and organization were not well suited at the time to handle a project of such magnitude.

♦ Functionally complex from the beginning, the project became more difficult due to greater user demands and market changes.

BofA made two critical mistakes in its handling of MasterNet. First, it did not realize the difficulty and scope of MasterNet and suf-

---

99. Carol Wiley, "Banks Key on Problem Solving," *Pensions & Investment Age*, August 22, 1988, p. 25.

ficiently assess its risks when it was proposed. Second, after the project rolled out of control, the bank failed to take the necessary steps to bring it under control. Only when MasterNet performed so poorly that it merited a $23 million loss coverage did management begin to take a closer look. The MasterNet debacle not only depicts poor project management unto itself, but is representative of the general state of affairs within the bank as a whole.

V. Lessons Learned

The MasterNet case makes obvious a lot of basic system management lessons. This section will briefly mention some of these lessons.

One of the most interesting contrasts between MasterNet and ERMA is the existence of visionaries. ERMA had two high-level managers, Beise and Zipf, who not only understood the technology, but were driven to include it in the operations of the bank. These men understood that technology was necessary for future competitiveness, and that the investment had to be made immediately. MasterNet had Armacost, who did have a vision of technology, but was both not well-versed technically and too busy with other problems to focus on the project. Clausen was motivated but did not have power within the organization to provide strong guidance.

The idea behind the visionary is more than strong guidance. The organization that sees upper management concerned and excited about its project will be motivated to perform to high standards. MasterNet staff members were generally shown little concern for their welfare—being split and moved.

Another important concept that becomes painfully obvious with MasterNet is continual investment. Through the 1970s, BofA neglected its systems development. It then expected to jump back in and immediately catch up with its competitors. This cannot be done for a variety of reasons. First, the resulting size and complexity of the new project far outreaches anything done before. Second, the necessary skills for success in the organization just aren't present. Lastly, a whole shift in the organization's attitude is necessary for the change to be successful. BofA attempted this huge jump without sufficiently preparing itself—it takes more than money to breed success.

The MasterNet project also violated some basic rules of large systems development. Modular design, limited functionality, and full-load testing were all disregarded. The project also failed miserably in converting smoothly. The staff should have recognized that the system could not keep up before the conversion attempt was made. BofA also failed to keep a semblance of continuity in its management. Many of the errors BofA made with respect to MasterNet are not specifically related to information systems but apply to all project management. The additional technical complexity of MasterNet only made the project management that much more complicated.

2.5 *INSUFFICIENT SENIOR STAFF*
ON THE TEAM

One of the best known books in the software field is *Software Engineering Economics*, by Barry Boehm. On the cover of that book there is a bar chart that presents the most important factors that affect software productivity. There are things like programming languages, and tools, and methods, and lots of other information. But head and shoulders above the rest in terms of its impact on productivity is the quality of the people and the team doing the work.

Boehm's book cover is the most prominent place where such bits of knowledge are found, but it is by no means the only place. Research studies over the years have found that individual software workers differ by factors of anywhere from 5:1 to 30:1 in their capabilities. Savvy software managers hire carefully and fire frequently in order to get and keep the best possible people: those 30:1 hotshots who can make the difference between a successful project and a failed one. It is no surprise that one of the important causes of runaway projects is the lack of appropriate people to do the job.

There are many ways of identifying those "appropriate people"; the research study from which we borrowed our categories used the term "senior staff." Certainly senior, experienced people bring enormous value to a project simply through that experience. Here, we choose to broaden the meaning of "senior staff" to all those whose capabilities are considerably stronger than the norm.

The link between the war stories that follow and the categorization we have given them is perhaps the most tenuous of all the sections in this book. That is, although a case can be made for "insufficient senior staff on the team" being the dominant cause of these projects becoming failures, the situation in each case is far more complicated than that. Things turned ugly in both of these war stories, and when accusations begin flying, truth is usually the first casualty. Those procuring the system tend to point to the people doing the work as the problem; the worker bees, in turn, point to the procurers.

However, in spite of the multiplicity of causes in these stories, there are some indications that senior staff was part of the problem.

Regarding the CONFIRM reservation system, the case is made fairly strongly in our war stories through such statements as these:

- "The AMR staff responsible for CONFIRM had proved to be 'inept.'"
- "AMR hired people off the street and proceeded without the right project manager running it."
- "About half of the people assigned to CONFIRM . . . were looking for new positions."
- "They have apparently deliberately concealed a number of important technical and performance problems."

Regarding the Adidas warehouse distribution system, the case is less clear, but there are some indications of people problems:

- "They're going through people like water . . . I'm told the situation is three [IS] people away from total meltdown."
- "Adidas had fired its lead integrator on the project."

Whatever the relevance of the people problems on these projects, the war stories, themselves, make fascinating telling. The ugliness of recrimination prior to and during the search for resolution is particularly awesome here. Because of the nature of these stories, we present two different views of the CONFIRM system debacle (recall that we presented two views of one previous war story in this book on the grounds that different people frequently see the same event in different ways). We have a nice collection of letters as well from various readers of one version of the story, agreeing or disagreeing violently with what it said. And finally, for the CONFIRM story, we have a short article giving us the final resolution of the issue. Verbal violence, we see in this ending, often fades away into a mere whisper.

2.5.1 MELTDOWN

by Marianne Kolbasuk McGee and Doug Bartholomew

Adidas America is hurting. Problems with an automated distribution system have brought its main U.S. warehouse almost to a standstill, with retailers getting few or no Adidas shoes so far this year. In January, the sporting goods company was able to fill only about one-fifth of roughly $50 million in orders—and that only with the help of direct shipments from overseas factories, according to people familiar with the situation.

The difficulties could continue for weeks or months. "It's been a fiasco," says Ron Gresko, owner of a chain of footwear stores in Pinebrook, N.J.

It was supposed to be state of the art. In August 1993, *Modern Materials Handling*, a distribution-industry trade magazine, gave its "Warehouse Of The Month" honor to Adidas, which was about to flip the switch on an automated distribution system at its Spartanburg, S.C., warehouse. But the project was plagued by constant problems and, at the start of this year, Adidas scrapped the first system's software and computer hardware in favor of a new architecture. Then things went from bad to worse.

Life has been one big headache for IS managers at Portland, Oregon-based Adidas. Many of the key players involved with the initial system's launch in 1993 already have left the company, and other IS staffers are heading for the exits, sources say. "They're going through people like water," says a former employee. "I'm told the situation is three (IS) people away from total meltdown."

The Adidas saga, like the continuing nightmare of Denver International Airport's baggage-handling system (see story elsewhere in this book), shows how easily efforts to automate the movement of goods can go terribly wrong. The pitfalls include dealing with small, sometimes unstable vendors, a lack of standards, and the complexity

---

of coordinating warehouse gear including tilting trays, conveyor belts, lifting equipment, and scanners.

Adidas hoped to overcome those obstacles when it upgraded the Spartanburg warehouse in 1993. The goal was to increase capacity, boost productivity, halve staff, and reduce the time needed to get orders out the door to 24 hours or less. The plan called for all bar-coded items to pass through a central tilt-tray sorter, which would drop the merchandise in various chutes bound for either stocking or shipment. Workers would pick up items based on instructions from arm-band-mounted wireless computers as well as from terminals aboard turret trucks or at the end of conveyor lines.

The problems stemmed not from the sorting equipment, but from the software used to run the system. The original software vendor, Integrated Software Logistics Engineering Inc. (Isle), in Norcross, Ga., marketed a system that ran under Unix. But Adidas decided to use fault-tolerant computers from Stratus Computer Inc. in Marlborough, Mass., running Stratus' proprietary operating system, because Adidas already was familiar with that platform. So Isle had to port its software to the Stratus platform, sources familiar with the project say. That created compatibility problems common with software ports. Those problems multiplied when Isle went out of business before the project was completed, leaving Adidas without adequate software documentation to fix bugs.

"Some of the software companies in this warehouse automation industry are embryonic," says Don Cooper, Southeast region sales manager at Symbol Technologies Inc. in Bohemia, N.Y., which did some work early on to develop the project's wireless terminals. "You've got to watch the weak ones, because it can be a disaster if you get one of them."

Meanwhile, Adidas had fired its lead integrator on the project. "Later, they begged us to come back but we didn't want any part of it, because it was already a train wreck," says a partner at the firm. A former Adidas IS official involved in the project adds, "Adidas shot itself in the foot by insisting to go online when the project was only 90% done."

The system ran, but not well. Eventually, Adidas decided to scrap the computer hardware and software—keeping the sorting equipment—and install an IBM RS/6000 server running warehouse management software from Exeter Systems in North Billerica, Mass. This is the system that has now brought the Spartanburg facility to its knees.

Adidas and Exeter refuse to discuss details of the warehouse situation. But Mary Ferreira, Exeter's director of marketing, concedes that Adidas is "going through some bad times." She adds that it's normal for a new warehousing system to require fine-tuning to get the various operations to work together properly.

A spokesman for Adidas America also downplays the problems. "We crossed over to a new computer system, and the system is slower than we expected. There always is a normal conversion process. Everything will return to normal by the end of the month."

Others have a different view. "They're killing us," says an official at a West Coast retailer of soccer equipment and other athletic gear. The retailer's sales of Adidas products normally make up half of its business, but are down about 90% because of the shortage.

Adidas has been bypassing the bottleneck in Spartanburg by shipping some shoes directly to large chains from overseas factories, and by manually distributing some goods from borrowed warehouse space, sources say. In a Feb. 12 memo Adidas sent to retailers apologizing for the delays, the company said it also would route some shoes through its Portland, Ore., warehouse, which mainly handles promotional accounts. The memo says Adidas and its retailers are "paying the price for what will be a state-of-the-art shipping facility by late spring."

Companies must be careful not to underestimate the amount of training required to move to a new warehouse system, says Ron Gable, managing partner of Systecon Logistics, a distribution division of Coopers & Lybrand in Atlanta: "These kinds of virtually instantaneous change-overs result in all kinds of chaos."

Others say the biggest problem may be the lack of importance Adidas placed on warehousing. "Warehousing is the stepchild when it comes to automation," says Richard Powers, an IT consultant on warehousing and manufacturing. "All other operations come first."

Unless that changes, other companies are likely to share the Adidas experience.

2.5.2 *WHEN PROFESSIONAL STANDARDS ARE LAX: THE CONFIRM FAILURE AND ITS LESSONS*

by Effy Oz

In 1988, a consortium comprised of Hilton Hotels Corporation, Marriott Corporation, and Budget Rent-A-Car Corporation subcontracted a large-scale project to AMR Information Services, Inc., a subsidiary of American Airlines Corporation. The consulting firm was to develop a new information system (IS) called CONFIRM, which was supposed to be a leading-edge comprehensive travel industry reservation program combining airline, rental car and hotel information. A new organization, Intrico, was especially established for running the new system. The consortium had grand plans to market the service to other companies, but major problems surfaced when Hilton tested the system. Due to malfunctions, Intrico announced an 18-month delay. The problems could not be resolved, however, and three-and-a-half years after the project had begun and a total of $125 million had been invested, the project was canceled.

In a letter to employees, Max Hopper, American Airlines Information Services chief, wrote: "Some people who have been part of CONFIRM management did not disclose the true status of the project in a timely manner. This has created more difficult problems—of both business ethics and finance—than would have existed if those people had come forward with accurate information. Honesty is an imperative in our business—it is an ethical and technical imperative." Apparently, the clients were misled into continuing to invest in an operation plagued with problems in database, decision-support, and integration technologies[7].

Undoubtedly, software developers, as experienced as they may be, may legitimately run into technical difficulties. The questions we, as IS professionals, should ask are: does a failure of this magnitude *have* to happen? If the developers realize they are facing technical problems, should they notify the client? How severe should the difficulties be to warrant alerting the client? If management does not share

This article was originally published in Communications of the ACM, October 1994. Used with permission.

information with the client, are the individual members of the project team expected to blow the whistle?

These questions should be addressed by professional codes of ethics and standards of conduct. The purpose of this article is to present the case and examine how IS codes of ethics address the issues raised. We will also try to draw practical lessons for providers of IS services and their clients.

Background

In 1987, a potential market caught the attention of AMR: centralized hotel reservations. As the company discovered, only 20% of hotel reservations were made through a centralized service, while in the airline business 80% of the reservations are made through a central system like AMR's SABRE. The company decided to take advantage of this situation in the form of a new, comprehensive system.

CONFIRM was the name given to an IS that was supposed to be the most advanced reservation system in the combined industry of travel, lodging, and car rental. The clients relied on the professionalism of the specialists who developed the highly successful airline reservation system SABRE. SABRE was a classic example of how an IS can gain strategic advantages for its user organization.

There are more than 85 hotel companies in North America. The major national hotel chains are Marriott, Hilton, Hyatt, Westin, and ITT Sheraton. The ease with which travelers can make reservations is vital to this industry. Over the past 16 years, each of these chains acquired a computer-based reservation system. The systems provide information to travel agents throughout the world. Some chains developed their own systems: others had vendors develop their systems. The systems varied in efficiency and effectiveness. For example, Marriott's MARSHA has been recognized as one of the best in the industry, while Hilton's NORTH dated from the early 1960s, and was inadequate and inefficient.

Like the major hotel chains, airlines, too, have acquired reservation systems. The most notable are SABRE and APOLLO. SABRE was developed by AMR, the parent of American Airlines Corporation; APOLLO was developed by United Airlines Corporation. The former has gained acclaim as the world's most successful airline reservation system. The system was installed in 1976 and has since been continually upgraded.

In 1986, AMR formed AMRIS, the information system's arm of the corporation. AMR's chairman hired Max Hopper to head AMRIS and offered him "a chance to combine running the SABRE business . . . and expanding it into other businesses, really leveraging it." AMRIS was to exploit its success with SABRE for business in other areas. But, unfortunately, the success of one system does not always guarantee the good fortune of a more advanced system. What follows is the chronicle of the events that led to the CONFIRM "disaster." The information is taken from media reports and the lawsuit filed by Marriott[15].

The CONFIRM Chronicles

On March 13, 1987, AMRIS representatives made a presentation to Marriott executives about a new reservation system they were preparing to develop. The system, named CONFIRM, would be superior to any existing reservation system in the industry. The representatives claimed it would be a state-of-the-art reservation system meeting all business needs of hotels and car-rental partners in the joint venture. According to the proposal, AMRIS, as a managing partner, would be in charge of the design and development of the system. The hotels would pay for this effort and would input the necessary data.

The partners, hotels and car-rental businesses, would use the system for their daily operations. In addition, they would join AMR in an effort to market customized versions of the system to other hotel and car-rental companies for profit. AMRIS was to operate the data processing center of the system.

From May through August of 1987, Marriott and other potential partners met with AMRIS executives to negotiate the deal. AMRIS people repeatedly assured the partners that CONFIRM would be superior to any current reservation system, while not more costly to use. They also promised that the project would be completed in time to outpace the competition in the hotel and car-rental industries.

On September 2, 1987, Marriott, a major partner in the venture, agreed to consider the AMRIS proposal although it already had an excellent system. The company's vice-president emphasized: "Marriott is pleased with its current reservation system . . . we have one of the best reservation systems in the industry in terms of both functionality and cost." Thus, he said his company would join the venture if "the joint venture can develop a reservation system that is functionally richer than the system we intend to operate [and that Marriott costs] will be less than the costs to operate our proposed system."

The first three partners to the joint venture were Marriott, Hilton, and Budget Rent-a-Car. In October 1987, they formed a consortium and named it Intrico. In late 1987 and early 1988, technical representatives from the four partners started to plan detailed performance capabilities of the new system. On May 24, 1988, AMRIS issued a press release announcing the commencement of the CONFIRM design process. In the meantime, the Intrico partners funneled large sums of money into the project. By September of 1988, Marriott alone spent more than $1.45 million on the preliminary design.

In September 1988, after a year of negotiations, Marriott, Hilton, and Budget signed a partnership agreement with AMRIS. According to the agreement, the objectives of the joint venture were:

◆ to design, develop, operate, and maintain a new "state-of-the-art" reservation-processing system to be marketed worldwide;

◆ to design and develop "interfaces" with airline computer reservation systems so consumers could make airline, hotel and car rental reservations through a single, computerized system;

◆ to market the reservations system and other communication services to customers for a profit; and

◆ to convert each of the partners' reservation systems to the newly-developed system.

AMRIS was designated "Managing Partner, Development" of CONFIRM. The agreement made the company responsible for all aspects of the design and development of the new system. The four partners undertook to pay AMRIS $55 million for the development. Each partner was to appoint a professional team that would be stationed in Dallas, at AMRIS headquarters, so that the partners would provide input as to what functions were needed, and also test and evaluate the system as it was developed.

The agreement stated two phases: the design phase and the development phase. The design phase was to take seven months, and the development phase was to be completed within 45 months after the agreement was signed. Thus, the deadline was the end of June 1992.

The contract provided that the total expenditure to develop CONFIRM would not exceed $55.7 million. AMRIS warranted that it had "no reason to believe" that the development costs would exceed this amount. The company also undertook to develop the system so that operation costs would be limited to $1.05 per reservation.

On December 30, 1988, AMRIS presented a "base design" of the system. Marriott claimed the functional specifications were not adequate. A 1992 internal audit by AMR's SABRE personnel stated that "these documents describe the expected functionality in general terms: they do not provide sufficient detail for a developer to understand what the user is expecting."

In March 1989, AMRIS declared the functional and technical specifications were complete. Late that month, the company circulated a preliminary development plan. The plan was unacceptable to the partners. The next six months were devoted to revision of the plan. During this time, AMRIS executives reassured the partners that the system would comply with all the requirements, and that it would be ready on time.

AMRIS completed the design phase in September 1989 and circulated a proposed development plan for the partners' review. At this time, the company increased the price of the project from $55.7 million to $72.6 million. It also stated that the cost per reservation would be $1.30 (instead of the original $1.05) in the first year of full operation, and decline to $0.72 and $0.40 in the fourth and fifth years, respectively.

According to the partnership contract, the three client-partners could withdraw when the development plan was presented. (A penalty of $1 million was involved.) The partners had to make the decision at this point. The per-reservation cost was crucial information in their decisionmaking.

On August 8 and August 15 of 1989, AMRIS representatives met with those of Marriott, Hilton, and Budget to review AMRIS' pro forma financial statements. Two years later, in August 1991, Marriott found that the statements were false. AMRIS understated the costs of personnel and other operating costs. The company also used numbers that overstated the total number of reservations. The actual processing cost per reservation was then estimated at $2.00.

Based on the 1989 statements, the client-partners decided not to exercise their option to withdraw. To Marriott, for instance, the value of the project declined by $1 million, but still promised a net present value of more than $3 million. In September 1989, the partners accepted the development plan. The deadline was revised from June 1992 to July 1992.

The contract outlined four major development phases: the business area analysis (BAA) to develop business models; the business system design (BSD) to enumerate detailed descriptions of the application systems; construction of the system's code (construction); and testing activities (testing).

On October 16, 1989, AMRIS assured the partners that the project was on time and on budget. However, in January 1990, the company missed the contractual deadline of completing the terminal-screen design. In February 1990, AMRIS missed the completion milestone of the BAA phase. Apparently, the developers redefined the unfinished work of this phase to become a part of the next phase.

In February 1990, AMRIS admitted it was more than 13 weeks behind schedule, but claimed it could catch up and recapture much of that lag. In March 1990, the company began a six-week "replanning" effort.

Millions of dollars kept flowing into the project. On May 15, 1990, AMRIS made a presentation to the partners saying the project was still on time and that the system would be ready by its deadline. At the same time, major players in the development effort were chastised for delays.

During the summer of 1990, both Budget and Marriott expressed concerns that the project was behind schedule and that its management was ineffective. While employees at the project office estimated CONFIRM would not be ready in time, they were instructed by management to change their revised dates so that they reflected the original project calendar. In August of that year, AMRIS declared the first phase complete, and entered the second major phase (BSD). When Marriott representatives asked to see some "deliverables" of the completed phase, the developers refused to show or explain their status. In October, the company admitted to the partners it was one year behind schedule. But company executives claimed they would still meet the deadline.

In February 1991, AMRIS presented a "Re-Plan" to replace the original development plan. According to the Re-Plan, only Hilton would be using the system by June 1992, and Marriott would not receive all the features it was promised before March 1993. Marriott later claimed that AMRIS executives knew they could not meet the new schedule. The hotel company said AMRIS forced employees to artificially change their timetable to reflect the new schedule, and that those who refused either were reassigned to other projects, resigned, or were fired. The Re-Plan attached a new price tag: $92 million, far above the original $55 million and the previously revised $72 million. The AMRIS president resigned in October 1991, and during the end of that year and the beginning of 1992 about 20 additional employees resigned.

AMRIS employees were dissatisfied with the way management handled the project. They believed their managers kept stating unrealistic schedules and lied about the project status. Many realized the "schedule" could not be met even with nine-hour workdays and work on weekends. By the summer of 1991, about half of the people assigned to CONFIRM (slightly more than 180 employees) were looking for new positions. A consultant was hired by AMRIS to evaluate the project. Dissatisfied with his findings, a vice-president "buried" the report and dismissed the consultant.

An evaluation by Marriott concluded that the developers could not complete the project. However, the hotel chain still gave them a chance: "As a partner, we hope that you will be able to perform as promised. However, as a user, we do not, based on experience to date, believe you can"[15]. AMR, the developer's parent company responded that CONFIRM's development was on target and that the system would be fully functional. AMRIS continued to bill Marriott at a rate of more than $1 million per month.

Finally, in April 1992, AMRIS admitted it was approximately two to six months behind schedule. Like Marriott management, Hilton management was still hopeful that "whatever has been broken can be fixed to meet the original schedule"[15]. But there was no basis for these hopes. That month, major problems surfaced when Hilton tried the system as CONFIRM's first beta-test user[7]. On April 29, 1992 the AMRIS chairperson wrote to the three partners:

> "Unfortunately, things have not gone as planned. Specifically: The individuals whom we gave responsibility for managing CONFIRM have proven to be inept. Additionally, they have apparently deliberately concealed a number of important technical and performance problems.[2] The technical staff, while skilled, has failed in the construction of the very demanding interfaces between the systems, and the extensive database, which will both be part of the completed CONFIRM system. The bottom line, gentlemen, is that in our best current judgment the system is 15 to 18 months from completion . . ."[15]

The company promised to repay 100% of the investment to any partner who wished to withdraw from the joint venture. A senior officer of AMRIS blamed employees for lying and the project management for concealing problems. The project, he said, was actually two years behind schedule.

On April 28, 1992, AMRIS fired eight top executives and replaced another fifteen employees. On May 1, 1992, the company's vice-chairperson circulated a letter to employees acknowledging that CONFIRM's "system interfaces and databases are inadequate to providing the necessary performance and system reliability." He explained:

> Our CONFIRM RS problem has many roots—one more serious than the others. Some people who have been part of CONFIRM RS management did not disclose the true status of the project in a timely manner. This has created more difficult problems—of both business ethics and

finance—than would have existed if those people had come forward with accurate information[15].

In July 1992, after three-and-a-half years, and after spending $125 million on the project, the Intrico consortium disbanded. Technically, the developers' main problem was to tie CONFIRM's transaction-processing facility-based central reservation system with its decision-support system. AMRIS's president admitted: "We found they were not integratable." Also, it was later discovered that the database was irrecoverable in the event of a crash.

Apparently, some of the failure is due to bad management practices of all the four partners in the Intrico consortium. The client-partner teams met with the developer's representatives just once a month. An AMRIS executive said: "You cannot manage a development effort of this magnitude by getting together once a month. Had they allowed the president of Intrico to function as CEO in a normal sense and empowered their senior reps [to] work together with common goals and objectives, it would have worked" [10].

AMR filed a countersuit against Marriott, Budget, and Hilton in September 1992. On May 14, 1993, AMR amended its suit to suggest that its partner-clients changed an approved plan to determine specifications for the common reservation system. Instead of a single system, AMR claims, the developers were encouraged to create three individual systems under CONFIRM. The company accused its clients of being "selfish" [11]. By January 1994, AMRIS had reached out-of-court settlements with all of its partners for undisclosed amounts. Some sources say the firm was facing damages suits of more than $500 million, and therefore agreed to pay about $160 million [18].

What can we learn from CONFIRM and similar cases? Experience shows that one or a combination of the following occurrences are the reasons for failure to develop a satisfactory IS:

1. Unforeseen and insurmountable technical difficulties;

2. Underestimation of cost and completion dates;

3. Failure of the developers to understand the system's requirements, or changing the requirements after the project started.

In its countersuit AMRIS claims the project failed because of the clients' demand to make changes long after the project started. What really happened and who is culpable in the CONFIRM case will probably never be determined. It may well be that all of the three reasons contributed to the failure. However, it seems that much of the damage in CONFIRM-like cases can be avoided with several simple principles.

Principles to Minimize the Damage in IS Development Failure

Principles for Managers of the Service Provider

1. In the business of software development, you always know when you start a project, but you never know when you will complete it. The consultant responsible for Bank of America's TrustPlus boasted he could complete the system by 1983. Attempts to salvage the system continued until 1988 [3]. When outlining the project schedule, be realistic and include an adequate "slack" time. Technical and other problems may occur. Problems often occur when a project involves interfacing two or more IS. Trying to entice the client with an unrealistically short schedule is not only unethical, but may eventually hurt your own effort.

2. When the phases must be sequential to assure quality, never start phase n before you resolve all of the problems of phase $n-1$, and avoid shortcuts. AMRIS left bugs to be resolved at a later time, while it went on with the next phase. Reports of other large-scale development failures point out similar practices. One former executive of Bank of America said: "There were still bugs, but the users felt they could run with it and work out the bugs as we went along" [3]. You should view the project plan as a part of the contract with your client, even if it is formally not. The client counts on you to manage the project to your best professional ability. Failure to do so betrays the client's trust.

3. Executives should not make any "calming" statements about the project status before they learn the facts. Making

uncorroborated statements is not only unethical to the client; it may also send wrong signals to employees.

4. Adopt a Code of Professional Standards and communicate it to your employees. The code should detail what an employee is to do when experiencing a persistent problem with a systems under development, to whom he or she should report the problem, and what steps he or she should take if immediate supervisors are not responsive to complaints. A clear policy ensures that both managers and their employees know what is expected of them, and fosters more ethical behavior.

5. Most important: being dishonest may hurt your client, but it may also hurt you and your company. The financial impact of lost business because of a failure due to lies may prove much greater than the lost income from a single mishap. If it is not the monetary gain that drives your judgment but the reluctance to admit professional weakness, think again. Failure to disclose the real status of the project to the client may exacerbate the damage. Unfortunately, honesty is not always in one's economic self-interest. Often, there is economic incentive to lying (e.g., when the transaction is a one-shot deal and if information of the incident does not spread [1]). But in this age of fast communication, especially in the IS industry, the news will travel fast. And your own employees may follow the bad example: they will lie to their superiors.

Principles for Employees

The first to observe technical problems are, usually, the employees: systems analysts and programmers. Employees have an obligation both to their employer and the client. When you realize there is a persistent problem, notify your supervisor. One wonders how long it took until the first employee stepped forward and did so in the CONFIRM case. However, some employees did complain about the technical problems—several of them paid for this with their jobs.

Principles for Clients

1. It seems that the three partner-clients kept loose vigil over AMRIS. This is surprising due to the fact that they had liaison teams that were supposed to keep track of the project progress. It is tempting to rely on a company that demonstrated success with another system. But this is not the same system. Previous success does not guarantee success with the system that is developed for you. Check the status of the project periodically. If you do not have qualified personnel, hire an independent consultant to do that for you.

2. In a suit filed by AMRIS against Marriott, Hilton and Budget Rent-a-Car, the plaintiff complained that the three client-partners in the Intrico partnership missed a deadline for providing a clear definition of system functionality [8]. Communicate to the developers exactly what your requirements from the new system are. You must realize that later modifications may result in a higher price and a later completion date.

3. Pay attention to alerting signals. When executives and other employees of the developer are either massively dismissed or voluntarily looking for new positions, ask questions. When the rats abandon the ship, it is probably sinking.

Conclusion

A word of caution before we conclude: as pointed out several times in this article, there is no conclusive data from which to draw hard conclusions about reasons for failure in systems development. Ideally, we would collect data on a large number of cases and find patterns. For obvious reasons, such data are extremely difficult to come by, if not impossible. However, it seems that the CONFIRM case contains many ingredients that are common in cases that have been reported in the media and trade journals.

An ancient proverb says: "You are a wise person if you do not make mistakes; you are a clever person if you make a mistake but do not repeat it; you are a stupid person if you make a mistake and repeat it." It may be hard to be wise the first time around, but let us not be stupid, either. As professionals, we are expected to learn from our own and our colleagues' mistakes.

The CONFIRM case draws attention because of the magnitude of resources expended. It is also a case of what seems to be the result of miscommunication at best or grand deception at worst. But there is reason to believe it is only one of many such cases. To minimize the probability of such mishaps, IS organizations have to adopt detailed codes of professional standards. The codes should outline to both managers and employees how to behave when projects do not proceed as expected.

Large development projects rarely proceed exactly as planned. This is true of IS development efforts as well. Management should be deeply involved in the progress of large-scale projects. If the professional team cannot overcome difficulties to comply with promised cost and timetable, it is the professionals' responsibility to duly report to management; then, it is management's responsibility to disclose the difficulties to the client and mutually outline a resolution.

Of course, there is no point in promoting a code of ethics and professional standards if executives do not demonstrate personal example. If not for reasons of moral obligation, at least for utilitarian principles, IS organizations should be honest with their clients. In the long run, honesty, indeed, is the best policy.

Acknowledgments

I thank Blake Ives for bringing this case to my attention. I am also indebted to my students Marsha Klopfer and Ken Horbatiuk for their assistance.

REFERENCES

1. Carson, T.L., and Wokutch, R.E. The moral status of bluffing and deception. In Robinson, W.L., Pritchard, M.S., and Ellin, J., Eds., *Profits and Professions*. Humana Press, Clifton, N.J., 1993, 141–155.

2. Donaldson, T.J., Accountability and the bureaucratization of corporations. In Robinson, W.L., Pritchard, M.S., and Ellin, J., Eds., *Profits and Professions*, Humana Press, Clifton, N.J., 1993, 215–224.

3. Frantz, D., B of A's plans for computer don't add up. *Los Angeles Times*, February 8, 1988. Reprinted in Dunlop, C., and Kling, R., Eds., *Computerization and Controversy: Value Conflicts and Social Choices*. Academic Press, Boston, Mass., 1991.

4. Friedman, M. The social responsibility of business is to increase profit. *The New York Times Magazine*. (Sept. 12, 1970).

5. Gladden, G.R. Stop the life cycle. I want to get off. *Softw. Eng. Not.* 7, 2 (1982), 35–39.

6. Halper, M. Outsourcer confirms demise of reservation coalition plan. *Computerworld 26*, 31 (Aug. 3, 1992), 1.

7. Halper, M. IS cover-up charged in system kill. *Computerworld 26*, 32 (Aug. 10, 1992), 1.

8. Halper, M. AMR sues partners over failed venture. *Computerworld 26*, 40 (Oct. 5, 1992), 1.

9. Halper, M. Marriott suit damns AMR role in CONFIRM. *Computerworld 26*, 41 (Oct. 12, 1992), 1.

10. Halper, M. Too many pilots. *Computerworld 26*, 41 (Oct. 12, 1992), 8.

11. Halper, M. AMR calls CONFIRM partners selfish. *Computerworld 27*, 21 (May 24, 1993), 4.

12. Jackall, R. *Moral Mazes: The World of Corporate Managers*. Oxford University Press, New York, 1988.

13. Johnson, D. *Computer Ethics*. Prentice Hall, Englewood Cliffs, N.J. 1985.

14. Mylott, T.R. III. Computer professional malpractice. *Santa Clara Computer and High Technology Law Journal*, 2 (1986), 239-270.

15. Suit: *Marriott v. AMR*, filed with the Circuit Court for Montgomery County, Maryland (Case No. 96336), September 26, 1992.

16. Oz, E., "Professional Standards for Information Systems Professionals: A Case for a Unified Code of Ethics," *MIS Quarterly 16*, 4 (Dec. 1992), 423-433.

17. Oz, E., *Ethics for the Information Age,* Wm. C. Brown, Dubuque, Iowa, 1994.

18. Zelner, W. Portrait of a project as a total disaster. *Business Week* (Jan. 17, 1994), 36.

THE COLLAPSE OF CONFIRM

by John P. McPartlin

Last April 29, AMR Corp. chairman Robert Crandall wrote to officials of the Marriott Corp., Hilton Hotels Corp., and Budget Rent A Car Corp. regarding the Confirm hotel and car rental computerized reservations system—a massive $125 million joint undertaking the four companies had agreed to fund and develop back in 1988. The letter, the contents of which Crandall and AMR now refute, was perhaps the most straightforward event to take place in connection with Confirm.

With great understatement, Crandall's missive explained that "unfortunately, things have not gone as planned." The AMR staff responsible for Confirm had proved to be "inept," he continued, and "have apparently deliberately concealed a number of important technical and performance problems."

The bottom line, he wrote, according to court documents filed by Marriott late last month, was that Confirm would not be ready in June, as expected, but instead was at least 15 to 18 months from completion. "In the event a partner is unwilling to continue," he concluded, "we are prepared to refund 100% of that partner's payments."

If the matter had ended there, it would have been a graceful conclusion for what otherwise had been a clumsy, inefficient, poorly managed project from the start. But it didn't.

On Second Thought . . .

One month later AMR, the parent company of American Airlines Inc., was singing a different tune. After taking a $109 million write-off to cover Confirm's costs, AMR reversed Crandall's original statements, claiming there never was a cover-up, nor had there even been an investigation of a possible cover-up. Eight Confirm managers— including the project's development leader—who had departed AMR the previous month were not fired but had merely resigned en masse. The spin doctors had begun their work.

This article was originally published in InformationWeek, October 19, 1992. Copyright 1992 by CMP Publications, Inc., 600 Community Drive, Manhasset, NY 11030. Reprinted with permission.

On Sept. 23, AMR filed suit against its erstwhile partners claiming that from the beginning it was Hilton, Budget, and Marriott that had impeded Confirm's progress by assigning personnel who "lacked adequate knowledge of the industry" and by failing to specify exactly what they wanted from the system.

But there are those who believe AMR's suit was a defensive measure filed in anticipation of the lawsuit against AMR initiated by Marriott Corp. two days later. Marriott's suit provides a detailed chronicle of Confirm's endless delays and cost overruns and asserts that AMR executives as far up the corporate ladder as Crandall and CIO and senior VP Max Hopper were involved in a concerted effort to conceal Confirm's countless problems from the rest of the consortium. Together with interviews of numerous sources associated with the project, a picture emerges of a strategic and potentially landmark IS project bungled by gross AMR mismanagement.

According to several sources present when AMR originally pitched the project back in 1987, it presented Confirm to hotel and car-rental companies as an opportunity to take advantage of the same systems development expertise that had made American Airlines' Sabre computerized reservations system the first and foremost service of its kind. Once Hilton, Budget, and Marriott signed on to Confirm, however, AMR began recruiting the development team from outside its organization. No one from Sabre was tapped for the job.

"The project was doomed to failure from the beginning," states James Yoakum, former head of IS at Marriott, who left in April 1990 to become senior VP of reservations and IT for Choice Hotels International Inc. "AMR hired people off the street and proceeded without the right project manager running it."

Yoakum, who says Marriott's decision to go along with Confirm was the main reason he left the company, maintains that even if Confirm could have been properly implemented, to make a profit the consortium would have needed an impossibly large number of customers. In addition, he says, AMR's position as both a partner and a service provider to the Confirm consortium created a serious conflict of interest that may have contributed to undermining the system.

From the start, sources say, the Confirm development team, led by John Mott, then president of the Travel Services unit of AMR Information Services Inc. (AMRIS), AMR's data processing and computer services subsidiary, was in way over its head. Development schedules were overly optimistic and relied on outmoded and unrelated technologies that were not up to the task (see story that follows). If employees spoke up about the problems, Marriott's suit alleges, they were quickly reassigned.

When time ran short, Confirm's managers quietly began eliminating functions from the system to speed up the process. The Marriott suit logs case after case where it expressed concern over Confirm's development and was in turn repeatedly assured by AMR executives that everything would be ready on time.

This past April, almost four years after the project began and only two months before the system was scheduled to go on line, Chuck Biebighauser, VP of operations at INTRICO, the Carrollton, Texas-based consortium established by the four companies to oversee Confirm's development and marketing, went to AMRIS president C.J. Atteridge and told him there were major flaws in a pilot project set to commence at Hilton in June. In response, Atteridge arranged for a team of 15 Sabre technical experts to audit the situation at Confirm. Their conclusion, announced a month later, was that the system was still 18 months away from completion. The jig was up.

Gone, But Why?

Shortly thereafter, the eight top AMRIS executives associated with Confirm, including Mott, were gone. Marriott's suit says they were fired for concealing information about the project. Mott insists he merely resigned and that there was no cover-up. He agrees with the assertions in AMR's lawsuit: that the indecisiveness of the three other partners impeded the progress of the system's development.

"Everyone was just too involved," he says. "They were investors in a great idea, they should have just sat back and let someone run it."

Mott characterizes the four years of Confirm's development as a "continuous debate" and asserts the partners really didn't know what they wanted in the first place.

Not so, says former Marriott CIO Yoakum. "Hilton and Budget worked for years before they signed up for Confirm and presented

AMRIS with a list of specs that literally stood six-feet high," he says. "That's a pretty darn good definition of knowing what you want."

AMR officials, including Crandall and Hopper, declined to be interviewed for this story.

In the end, Hilton, Budget, and Marriott shelled out more than $125 million on Confirm. For their trouble, the three companies are now significantly behind the curve in CRS technology.

For Hilton and Budget, the post-Confirm situation is even more bizarre. When they signed on in 1988, they also chose to outsource their mainframe data processing and reservations systems to AMRIS, planning simply to migrate to Confirm once it was completed. Now that Confirm is dead, the two companies are left fighting a legal battle with their former business partner, AMR, which is also their outsourcer.

Big Name In Hot Water?

As a direct or indirect result of the Confirm debacle, more than a dozen highly placed IS executives at AMR or its subsidiaries have left within the past 12 months, and there may be more departures to come. Rumors abound that Max Hopper, one of the best known and most highly respected IS executives in the world, may be on his way out. *InformationWeek* has learned that at least one highly placed IS executive at a large U.S. company has been contacted by an executive recruiter claiming to be seeking qualified candidates for Hopper's job at Crandall's behest.

"The press reports so far make it sound like Hopper was sent over to Confirm as a white knight to clean things up," says one former AMR executive who requested anonymity. "But let's face it, he should not have been outside the loop. He should have known what was going on."

Moreover, AMR may have yet to feel the full extent of Crandall's wrath. "When Crandall is unhappy about the performance of something, he is not reluctant to express his feelings about the situation," says Thomas Logman, an analyst at New York's Bear, Stearns & Co. Inc. "Is that a diplomatic enough way of putting it?"

Ironically, after all this some say AMR still may try to go ahead with Confirm by courting a new set of partners once the lawsuits are settled. "AMR, when they made their announcement, said they were 'suspending development,'" notes David Mellinger, VP of finance and the sole remaining employee at INTRICO. "They chose that word very carefully. I think they still hope they can overcome the technological problems and revive the project with other partners. That's AMR's logic."

With the Confirm debacle now headed for a nasty court battle, that seems like strange logic indeed.

How Confirm Worked—and Didn't

The technical snarls at Confirm were as debilitating as the political ones.

The system, comprising more than 3,000 programs, was to run on two IBM 3090 mainframes at AMRIS's data center. One would run IBM's MVS operating system, storing decision-support data such as pricing and customer information in DB2 databases and running programs generated using Texas Instruments Inc.'s Information Engineering Facility CASE tool. The other 3090 was to employ IBM's Transaction Processing Facility (TPF) operating system to process car and hotel reservations using programs written in the C language.

The two machines were supposed to communicate with the outside world through an AMRIS-developed program known as Transaction Management Function (TMF). It was meant to serve as both gateway and router to the various hotel and rental car airport reservations centers and would direct incoming data from each center to the appropriate mainframe. The two 3090s were to be connected to each other through a channel-to-channel bridge.

But when it came time to plug these two separately developed modules together, there was a hitch: They didn't communicate very well. The program sending information across the bridge in one processor could not coordinate with the program receiving the information in the other processor. And, in the event of a crash, it was discovered, Confirm's DB2 database would be recoverable only in pieces, not in its entirety. These problems were not insurmountable, sources say, but they would have required at least two years to fix.

—*J.P.M.*

EDITOR'S NOTE ON THESE CONFIRM
PROJECT STORIES

Time passed between the original publication (October 1992) of the Confirm collapse story that you have just read and a 1994 story presenting the resolution of that collapse. We present the resolution story after this note. The first Confirm story in this book, "When Professional Standards Are Lax," was also published in 1994, but focused primarily on the early events rather than the resolution.

During that interim period, the Confirm story by no means disappeared from the pages of the computing press. There were many letters to the editor of *InformationWeek* concerning the story and the project, some approving of the story and its conclusions, some not.

Sample comments of letter-writers reacting to the 1992 story include:

◆   From a representative of American Airlines: ". . . Flawed and distorted supermarket tabloid view of what happened." "A huge disservice to all the AMRIS employees assigned to Confirm." The letter makes the point that Confirm customers changed requirements and sought individual competitive advantage, even against their own Confirm partners. It also objected strenuously to statements that there was a cover-up.

◆   From a former employee of AMR Travel Services: "I am pleased to 'confirm' that your publication has captured the pertinent facts and reported them in an accurate and forthcoming manner." "The project had several fatal flaws, but the ones that did not get corrected were the arrogance and incompetence of the AMR Travel Services senior executives in charge of the project."

◆   From a disinterested party: "With regard to 'The Collapse of Confirm': Should it be Con Firm?"

◆   From another disinterested party: ". . . most enlightening." "I hope IW will maintain its crusade."

We have commented earlier in this book on the fact that multiple observers viewing an incident can see things quite differently. Obviously the letter-writers above fit that phenomenon!

And now, for the final chapter of the Confirm story.

BUMPY RIDE, SOFT LANDING

by John P. McPartlin

A lawsuit that began with a bang seems to be ending with a whimper, probably to the relief of AMR Corp. Only days before a potentially embarrassing trial was set to begin, AMR has reached out-of-court agreements with its three partners in the ill-fated Confirm hotel and rental car reservation system.

Thus ends AMR's two-year-old battle with its former business partners Hilton Hotels Corp., Budget Rent-A-Car Corp., and Marriott Corp. to assign blame for the collapse of the $125 million project. AMR is the holding company for American Airlines, which developed the Sabre reservation system.

In its original lawsuit, filed in October 1992, AMR claimed its partners continually changed the requirements for the system and demanded too many individual features to make Confirm financially feasible.

The partners then countersued AMR, claiming the holding company misled them about the level of expertise of its system developers and the final costs of the completed system. Confirm's costs rose rapidly from the original projections made when the project was first discussed in 1987.

Terms of the settlements are sealed, but all parties acknowledge that 11th-hour negotiations helped lead to a mutually acceptable conclusion. "The parties have settled their differences," says William Brewer, an attorney with Dallas-based Bickle and Brewer, who represents Budget in the dispute. AMR will reportedly pay some $160 million to the three companies, although details of the agreement preclude any discussion of the financial settlements.

AMR's Non-Airline Business Grounded?

A spokesman for Marriott says the hotel chain reached a deal with AMR late last month but made no announcement. It's unclear when

This article was originally published in InformationWeek, January 10, 1994. Copyright 1994 by CMP Publications, Inc., 600 Community Drive, Manhasset, NY 11030. Reprinted with permission.

Hilton settled. And Budget, the last holdout, came to an agreement with the company last week.

It's not known what effect the conclusion of the case will have on AMR, which has experienced severely rocky financial years due to the turbulence of the airline industry and several internecine price wars. The settlement may reflect badly on its ability to provide third-party systems development and integration work, a significant part of its strategy to expand non-airline businesses.

2.6 POOR PERFORMANCE BY SUPPLIERS OF HARDWARE/SOFTWARE

It is interesting to note, in the war stories that have preceded this section, that most of these runaways have occurred in spite of the best efforts of vendors, consultants, and service firms. In other words, these projects typically did not fail for a lack of (at least claimed) technical expertise. When the runaway projects sank, some of the best companies in the supplier community were on board!

That fact is something of a surprise. It is easy to imagine that runaway projects are staffed with inept people who are in over their heads on the projects in question, and stubbornly resistant to the idea of obtaining help. That, from our stories to date, does not seem to be the case.

In this section, we should focus on projects that in fact became runaways *because of* the participation of some of the suppliers. It is easy to see that a project sank with suppliers on board. It is less easy to be sure that they were at the helm, steering the ship in the direction of failure.

Because of that difficulty, we present no runaway stories in this section. There were simply no war stories in our collection that fit this slot sufficiently well that they could be included here. That does not mean that the suppliers helping these projects did not contribute to their demise; it simply means that, where there was plenty of blame to go around, there was not enough blame in these stories to cause suppliers to be called a dominant cause of failure.

2.7 OTHER—PERFORMANCE (EFFICIENCY) PROBLEMS

The research that provided us with our runaway failure categories found only six causes for failure—the six categories that preceded this one.

It is not surprising that such a categorization would be insufficient. We have invented the generic category "Other" to cover the fact that there are more than six causes of such failures.

What is surprising, however, is that our "Other" category turned out to represent only one additional type of failure. Several of the war stories above, and in particular the two stories that follow, were plagued by efficiency problems. The developed software system simply could not operate quickly enough to solve the user's needs on a timely basis. In the software engineering community, such problems are called "performance" problems.

This is a surprising finding because it resurrects an issue that most of us in the software business thought had been put firmly to rest several decades ago. In the early days of computing, it was not unusual to find a software developer spending half of his or her time to write a program, and the other half in making it operate faster. Machine time was valuable; machines were relatively slow (compared to today), and good programmers were those who could not only build software but optimize it.

All that died, we thought, with the advent of cheap and huge, powerful computers. It became common to say that programmers who spent time on optimization were wasting their time, and programmer trainees were taught to focus on the other aspects of quality, with very little time spent on efficiency.

Something has gone wrong with that belief. That change probably began with the popularity of interactive computing. No longer was one user waiting in the background for the results of some computer run. Now, through the magic of interactive computing, it was tens, or hundreds, or perhaps even thousands of users, simultaneously wanting to access the same software system. The services provided by the system may or may not have been complicated; however, it was the sheer volume of activity, perhaps more than the complexity of the activity, that began causing us to renew our attention to performance concerns.

We have characterized most of the runaway projects in this chapter as having been "huge." Huge, of course, can mean several different things. Usually in the computing business we take the term to mean a large and complex system. But huge can involve other factors. It can be a massive and complex database accessed by a collection of relatively simple systems. Or it can be a simple system, accessing a simple database, but with a huge number of users. Any one of these factors can cause performance to become a concern. But chief among them are factors involving interactions. The slowest thing computers do internally is to talk to external storage, such as collections of data. They are even slower when they talk to humans. When "huge" involves these interactions, performance may well become a problem.

Over the years we have learned many techniques for anticipating and warding off performance problems. Simulations can help make such problems visible well in advance, or they can identify some project goals or approaches that are simply infeasible. Management monitoring techniques can gather data during a project to see if initial performance targets are being met. When performance is found to be inadequate during an initial system test, timing analyses can be performed to identify the sluggish components, so that they can be rewritten with faster technology. It may be more complicated to build software that performs efficiently, but there are known techniques that may be applied to accomplish this. The number of failures in these war stories that are attributable, in the main or in part, to performance problems suggests that too many people are tackling time-critical problems for which they are not prepared.

It is interesting that, in the following two war stories, performance problems seem to be accompanied by reliability problems. Both runaway projects had mixtures of the two; in the MCC (Microelectronics & Computer Technology Corp.) CAD (Computer-Aided Design) project, the dominant problem was performance; however, in the NCR Warehouse Manager Project it was hard to tell which of the two was more problematic.

What did the principals in these projects have to say about the performance problems?

Regarding the MCC CAD project:

♦ ". . . scrapping four years of development work on a large-scale prototype because of performance problems that will require conversion of the Lisp-based system . . ."

♦ The system "didn't have the performance or stability we wanted."

♦ "Lisp hung us out to dry in performance . . . Lisp has a future, but it might not necessarily be in large systems."

(Note—Lisp is often (but not always) an interpretive language. Interpretive languages tend to run 10 to 100 times slower than alternative, compiled languages. This is a well-known problem with Lisp and other such languages; project principals should have known about that problem from the outset.)

Regarding the NCR Warehouse Manager system:

♦ "The system's response time would slow to a crawl."

♦ "Response time ranged from half a minute to several minutes, leaving . . . customers waiting in increasingly long lines."

Our final two runaway war stories follow.

2.7.1 *HOW AN NCR SYSTEM FOR INVENTORY TURNED INTO A VIRTUAL SABOTEUR*

by Milo Geyelin

To celebrate how his new computer would streamline his parts-supply business, Joe Hopper hoisted a circus-size tent, set up picnic tables and barbecued enough beef brisket to feed a small town.

In 10 years, Hopper Specialty Co. had grown from a small storefront into the biggest distributor of industrial hardware in northwest New Mexico, catering especially to oil and gas drillers. Now, in May of 1988, NCR Corp.'s highly touted Warehouse Manager computer package promised even better things to come.

When up and running, the computer system would track the thousands of items in a huge inventory, keep prices current, warn when items were running low, punch up invoices in seconds and even balance the monthly books—all at the touch of a few keystrokes. Particularly for drilling customers, who lose money every minute their equipment isn't working, anything that could get orders for parts filled faster would indeed be cause for celebration.

To mark the event, two NCR sales representatives were circulating at the party to extol Warehouse Manager. But unknown to Mr. Hopper, no one was celebrating back at NCR headquarters in Dayton, Ohio. Four months earlier, shortly after Mr. Hopper had placed his order, the $6 billion computer company had suspended sales of Warehouse Manager so its engineers could work out critical bugs.

And, coincidentally, two ominous internal reports on the product had arrived in Dayton the week of Mr. Hopper's fete. They revealed that the computer package had been inadequately tested and was performing unexpectedly badly in actual business settings.

Computerized Disasters

The reports from the field foreshadowed extraordinary problems Mr. Hopper would face as a product he had perceived as a miracle work-

This article was originally published in the Wall Street Journal, August 8, 1994. Reprinted by permission of the Wall Street Journal, © 1994, Dow Jones & Company, Inc. All rights reserved worldwide.

er emerged as a virtual saboteur. And he wasn't alone: Of the roughly 40 Warehouse Manager systems sold, at about $180,000 each, not one ended up working as promised. More than two dozen lawsuits, including one filed by Hopper, have resulted.

NCR, renamed AT&T Global Information Services after its 1991 acquisition by AT&T Corp., now concedes that Warehouse Manager was a disaster and stopped selling it several years ago. "With this particular piece of software, we did not do a good job," says spokesman Mark Siegel. "We did not service customers well." But few are aware of the debacle; the company has settled many of the suits under provisions binding the parties to secrecy.

In defending the cases still pending, the company denies responsibility and blames a flawed application program it licensed from a now-defunct software house called Taylor Management Systems Inc. Taylor's representatives, in Amarillo, Texas, blame NCR's operating system.

Meanwhile, customers such as Mr. Hopper still are digging out from the record-keeping mess Warehouse Manager created. Their nightmare illustrates both the risks in marrying one's company to a powerful new computer system and how limited the available remedies can be when things go wrong. All this, however, was far from Mr. Hopper's mind in 1987 when he began discussing with NCR how an automated system of computer controls could improve his business.

Software Incompatibility

He knew that several large computer vendors were selling packages aimed at inventory-intensive companies. What seemed to set Warehouse Manager apart was NCR's promise that all its crucial parts—the hardware, the various software components and all the countertop terminals—would be serviced by NCR under one roof. And salespeople were pitching it as a thoroughly debugged package that was running smoothly at more than 200 firms.

In fact, although the Warehouse Manager software package, developed by Taylor Management, was indeed a success at those 200 locations, it was working on an operating system made by Burroughs Corp. (now part of Unisys Corp.), not NCR. Through a licensing agreement, NCR had arranged to piggyback the application onto its own operating system. Taylor would be responsible for converting the software and maintaining the final package. But how well this would work wasn't at all clear when Warehouse Manager became available in April 1987.

Most of the early indications, as evidenced by customers' letters to NCR, were negative. In May, for instance, Vogue Tyre & Rubber Co., an auto parts distributor in Skokie, Ill., complained about long delays, sloppy service, inattention to detail and "Band-Aid solutions" to problems with its system.

In August, a wood-laminating company in Franklin Park, Ill., complained that it hadn't been able to place a purchase order in the five weeks since it had switched over to Warehouse Manager. The backlog was costing $2,000 a day. "We are shocked and dismayed at this crisis that NCR and its software vendor have created," wrote William E. Schierer, president of the company, E. Kinast Distributors Inc.

'Deadly Embrace'

Some of the problems flagged early by NCR seemed to recur at every site where Warehouse Manager was installed. During busy periods, for example, NCR field technicians noted in internal documents that the system's response time would slow to a crawl. Commands that were supposed to take seconds would take minutes. Operators at different terminals would find that when they tried to get simultaneous access to the central computer, both their terminals would lock up. NCR engineers referred to this as the "deadly embrace."

The only solution was to log off the central computer and log back on again. But when the terminals went back on line, information stored in the central computer often came back altered. Sometimes it was destroyed. The deadly embrace between terminals was corrupting data stored in the central computer, a phenomenon NCR referred to internally as the "silent death."

At Burgman Industries, a Jacksonville, Fla., supplier of heavy construction parts, company President John W. Shearer complained in December 1987 that corrupted files in his Warehouse Manager had infected his general ledger with inaccurate numbers. In one instance, a machine part that had cost him $114 was listed for sale at 54 cents.

"This software is so unprofessional and is riddled with so many bugs that it may actually put us out of business," Mr. Shearer wrote NCR.

Moreover, despite NCR's promise of a "single source solution," customers who called for technical help were bounced between NCR and Taylor Management. By mid-January 1988, it had become clear that Taylor's software and NCR's operating equipment weren't compatible. That's why NCR finally ordered a halt to further sales until an updated version of the application was developed by Taylor and tested by NCR.

Delays and Lockups

Hopper Specialty says it knew none of this. Despite the sales freeze, NCR began installing hardware and countertop terminals the following month for Hopper. During sales demonstrations, Mr. Hopper had been impressed that the terminals could punch up a customer invoice in a fraction of a second. But when Hopper Specialty actually switched on its new system in September 1988, the response time ranged from half a minute to several minutes, leaving Hopper's customers waiting in increasingly long lines. Additional delays were caused by 20 to 30 terminal lockups a day.

At Hopper, Warehouse Manager couldn't even be relied on to keep prices straight. A piece of industrial hose that should have been listed at $17 a foot showed up as costing $30 a foot. "Our counter people didn't know it was the wrong price by looking at it," says Charles Brannin, Hopper Specialty's general manager. "Customers would go ahead and pay it, and then we lost their business."

By far the most damaging problem stemmed from huge gaps between what the computer told Hopper Specialty was in stock and what actually was there. The Warehouse Manager might show 50 parts in stock, for instance, when in fact Hopper needed to order 50. Other times, it would show that items were on order when they were sitting on the shelf.

The chaos seemed to feed on itself. Six times in two months during 1989, Hopper employees hand-counted every item in the building, only to find the tally didn't match what NCR's computer said was there.

NCR kept records of complaints from Hopper and the nearly identical ones from many others using Warehouse Manager. But at Hopper and other locations, users say NCR told them that their problems were isolated. When he called for technical help, Mr. Hopper says, NCR blamed his employees' inexperience in using the system. In one instance, Mr. Hopper says, NCR technicians blamed problems on static electricity from office manager Tracy Irwin's nylon stockings.

Was It Stocking Static?

"They kept telling us everyone else was doing great with this thing, it's just you," says Mr. Hopper. NCR's Mr. Siegel says he has "no idea whether or why that took place," but says NCR didn't "intentionally deceive" customers. He adds that there is no way he can reconstruct whether Ms. Irwin's nylons were mentioned, but he says, "we plainly could have served customers better throughout the process."

By early 1989, Warehouse Manager was turning into an albatross for NCR as well as for customers as the problems worsened. NCR's forecast of 443 sales a year for the system was far off; after resuming sales following a debugging effort in mid-1988, the company was processing only four to five orders a month.

And its relations with Taylor Management, the software provider, were becoming strained. The two companies were feuding in particular over what was causing the deadly embrace and silent death. NCR blamed Taylor's software; Taylor blamed NCR's operating equipment. The dispute would later result in litigation over royalties.

Mr. Hopper, meanwhile, was getting desperate. Some days after making his morning sales calls, he would pull into the parking lot and see customers lined up through the door and along the front of his building. "You would pull your hair out," he says. "You know, you come in here after making sales calls, and there's people waiting, sitting here, and the computer's down and we're handwriting invoices. Damned right I'm upset."

Customers Go Elsewhere

Ms. Irwin, the office manager, began logging 14-hour days and coming in on weekends with her children to work out problems with the system. But she couldn't keep customers from taking their business two doors down, to Advance Supply & Pump Co., which now was boasting superior inventory and service. As Hopper Specialty's customer base eroded, it couldn't afford to carry as big an inventory. The shrinking inventory and confusion over what was in stock, in turn, further hurt Hopper's reputation for reliability. "The whole thing just snowballed," says Mr. Hopper.

Back at NCR, Taylor Management's new version of its software, Release.2, was billed as the answer to everybody's problems. It was an improvement, but it, too, turned out to be full of bugs.

By early 1991, Hopper Specialty called in its outside accounting firm to try to straighten out the books. Warehouse Manager, it turned out, had randomly erased information that fed into the firm's general ledger. Britton Smith, Hopper's accountant, was dismayed.

"Records were in terrible shape. Nothing was ever right . . . We were continually trying to get inventory correct for financial statements and their income-tax returns," says Mr. Smith. Hopper had always struck him as one of the better-managed businesses in town; now, as he struggled to reconcile its books, he saw that Mr. Hopper had put up $350,000 of his own money to keep the business afloat.

Largest Contract Canceled

The biggest blow came in April of 1993: Hopper's largest customer, BHP Mineral International Inc., canceled its contract, worth $350,000 to $500,000 a year. Hopper's contract required it to fill 90% of any parts order from BHP, a strip-mine operator, within 48 hours. Increasingly, it could barely meet half the quota. "I met with them personally three times," says BHP purchasing agent Richard Richter. "They told us at that time they were trying to get a new computer system up and running. The longer it went, the worse it got."

With the loss of BHP's business, Mr. Hopper found he had no choice but to start laying off employees and slashing healthcare benefits; today, 10 of the 19 people who were in place when Warehouse Manager was installed still have their jobs. Since 1988, gross annual sales have dropped to $1.9 million from $3.5 million, according to Mr. Hopper. Inventory now is so low that Hopper Specialty doesn't need a computer to keep track of it.

As for NCR, it is publicly contrite. Mr. Siegel, the spokesman, maintains that AT&T Global Information Services is assuming full responsibility for what went wrong with Warehouse Manager and is bending over backward to accommodate the needs of its customers. "That's very much our focus as we look at these case by case," he says. Of the more than two dozen suits that have been filed alleging fraud, negligence or misrepresentation, about half have been settled. The plaintiffs were required not to discuss any aspect of their dealings with NCR.

Restrictive Sales Agreement

But NCR's stance toward companies that don't settle has been far from generous. In Hopper's suit, filed in U.S. District Court in Albuquerque, NCR is relying on its so-called Universal Sales Agreement signed by Ms. Irwin, the Hopper office manager, to limit damages. Hopper claims Warehouse Manager cost it $4.2 million in lost profit, but the Universal Agreement caps damages at the cost of the computer. (The two sides don't even agree on that. Hopper says it spent $284,821 on the system; NCR says it was $184,567.)

Further, the Universal Agreement requires that all disputes, "including any claims of misrepresentation," be arbitrated instead of litigated in court, and courts—including the one hearing Hopper's case—have refused to vacate it. While speedier and less expensive, arbitration places limits on pretrial fact-finding and interviews that can make it harder for plaintiffs to prove their cases, particularly allegations of fraud. Restrictions such as these are common in many computer sales agreements, though experts in computer performance law say NCR's version goes further than most.

NCR isn't conceding anything in the contested cases. In legal papers drafted in Hopper's case, NCR contends it "had every reason to believe" that Taylor Management's software worked on NCR equipment, despite NCR's own internal communications to the contrary. "When NCR sold Hopper its system in 1987, NCR did not yet know that problems would arise with TMS's software," NCR asserts.

On narrow legal grounds alone, NCR has contended, Hopper's suit should be dismissed. It wasn't filed until after New Mexico's four-year statute of limitations expired, according to NCR. "Because

Hopper knew of its alleged system problems shortly after installation," the company argues in defense pleadings, "its fraud, unfair trade practice and negligence claims are barred."

The case is scheduled to be arbitrated later this year. In settlement talks, the company has offered discounts on future AT&T phone rates and held out the possibility of replacing Hopper's Warehouse Manager with a new system. But Mr. Hopper won't hear of that.

"We told them," he says, "' 'We don't want any more of your equipment.' "

2.7.2   *LISP FLAW SCUTTLES MCC CAD PROJECT*

by Robert Ristelhueber

Micro-electronics & Computer Technology Corp. is scrapping nearly four years of development work on a large-scale prototype CAD system because of performance problems that will require conversion of the Lisp-based system into the Unix environment, it was learned.

The decision to discard development which has cost MCC millions of dollars and occupied most of the efforts of its VLSI/CAD program since its inception resulted from pressure by member companies who were dismayed with the performance of the recently-delivered CAD system.

Problems with the program were recently judged serious enough to require MCC chairman and chief executive Grant Dove to step in as acting program director. John Hanne, a vice-president who had headed the operation, has been shifted to deputy program director and his future status with MCC is uncertain.

Of the 750,000 lines of code delivered for the CAD system, 80 percent will either have to be rewritten in the C language or discarded. Revision of the system platform and tools could take years to complete.

MCC has ordered an undisclosed number of Sun Microsystems workstations for future development of the system. The Sun workstations will perform tasks that have been done until now on some 80 systems purchased from Symbolics Inc.

Mr. Dove, who joined MCC last spring, called the shift a "pragmatic move. We said 'OK' there are things we need to change. Let's take a fresh look and see what makes sense for the next 3 years."

"I am listening to our shareholders very hard," he said. "They are sending very strong signals that they want workstations that use the predominant open Unix environments."

About 20 percent of the 750,000 lines of code were originally written in C and can be used by shareholders fairly quickly, Mr. Dove

This article was originally published in Electronic News, April 11, 1988. Reprinted with permission.

said. "In some of the other areas we'll take the Lisp prototype and do conversion. We're still deciding how much of that to take to operational status."

Mr. Dove declined to say he was disappointed in the results of the CAD program. "We took on a tough task to put together a very large system. We learned a lot, and now we have to take the knowledge we gained and put it to work."

He stressed that the VLSI/CAD operation is a 6-to-10 year program. "This can be considered a mid-term exam. We've done a lot of very good work, according to outside consultants who have looked at the program."

John Hanne said the prototype CAD system developed by MCC "didn't have the performance or the stability we wanted. Instead of finishing it we decided to slow down and take the hit here, and redo it in C."

A number of shareholders have agitated to abandon Lisp all along, he said. "There was pressure to do that. Some people never liked Lisp."

While the CAD tools could be rewritten in less than a year, revising the system platform could take years, he said. A large part of the development work may not be converted to C, however. "The way we're looking at it, most of it may not reappear," Mr. Hanne said.

Lisp Future

"Lisp hung us out to dry in performance," he added. 'Lisp has a future, but it might not necessarily be in large systems."

When MCC began the CAD development in 1984, a number of companies and research organizations were developing systems using Lisp, Mr. Hanne said. "All of a sudden, we're alone."

The recent decision to scrap the Lisp-based system came in the midst of a restructuring of the VLSI/CAD program, one of five research programs carried on by the consortium. The reorganization will likely follow the path of earlier revisions of the Advanced Computer Architecture (ACA) and Packaging programs, which permitted shareholders to fund only portions of research instead of all activities as before.

Mr. Dove said the goal was to complete the restructuring by mid-year. Asked what role Mr. Hanne would play in the CAD program at that point, he called it "an open question. That's part of what I'm looking at."

To facilitate the restructuring, Mr. Dove has also named as deputy program directors John Pinkston, vice-president and chief MCC scientist, and Carroll Hall, who was in integration manager at the ACA program.

Open Unix

Adopting the open Unix architecture "should allow us to work more closely with universities, CAD vendors and the Semiconductor Research Corp.," Mr. Dove said. He also said he hoped that a CAD hardware vendor would join the current nine shareholders in the VLSI/CAD program. "We have had almost zero interface with them," he said.

Mr. Dove said MCC wasn't abandoning Lisp. "It's still the language of preference in our ACA and software programs, and we'll still be using it in research and fast prototyping work."

3

Software Runaway Remedies

"At last I've found the secret that guarantees success.
To err, and err, and err again, but less, and less, and less."

—Ogden Nash

In this chapter, we present several remedies for warding off the software runaway. Section 3.1 discusses risk management, an approach to be used both at the outset of a project and as the project proceeds. Section 3.2 discusses issue management, an approach to be used as unexpected obstacles arise during the course of a project. Because both Sections 3.1 and 3.2 are somewhat theoretical, we will then present in Section 3.3 the remedies actually attempted during the projects described in the research study previously presented in Section 1.4.

3.1   RISK MANAGEMENT

There is increasingly strong belief in the computing community that
the best way to rein in runaways is to manage project risks from the
very beginning. Many books have been written (e.g., [Boehm 1989],
[Charette 1989], [Charette 1990], [Jones 1994]) and a great deal of
research has been performed on the subject of software risk management.

What is a risk? My dictionary says it is:

> the possibility of meeting danger or suffering harm or
> loss, or exposure to harm or loss

Given that, risk management is about the anticipation of the most serious problems (harms and losses) that could occur on a project, and
the necessary steps to handle them.

It is particularly important to note that in the KPMG study of runaway projects mentioned in earlier sections of this book [KPMG
1995], there was little attempt in the runaway enterprises cited to
anticipate subsequent risks, or to manage those risks that had been
anticipated. Thus, although that study does not show evidence that
risk management can ward off runaways, it certainly can and does
show that the absence of risk management may contribute to runaway occurrences.

This book is not the place for an in-depth analysis on the subject
of risk management. The books cited in the first paragraph of this
section do that rather nicely, and in considerably more depth than
anything we might attempt here. However, there is a place in this
book to further discuss one of those references, in view of the fact
that the book is most unusual and far from the mainstream of the
computing field.

Imagine that you are the manager of a large-scale software project,
and that you suspect it may be a runaway in the making. Suddenly,
the subject of risk management has become more than an academic
exercise; you could use some good, specific advice on what it means
to manage risks *now*. What risks should you be concerned about?
What can you do about those risks?

It is the intention of one of the above mentioned books [Jones 1994] to answer these kinds of questions. In that book, Jones attempts to present a medical handbook approach to software projects. In medicine, because of the commonality of many types of diseases and problems, there exists a handbook that provides doctors with rudimentary diagnoses and cures for such problems. That handbook covers a standard nine topics for each potential medical problem, including how to identify the problem as well as methods of controlling it. It is easy to imagine that *Control of Communicable Diseases in Man* is an indispensable part of the medical professional's library.

The Jones book tries to follow in these footsteps. It identifies roughly 60 software risks, and for each risk presents the following pieces of information:

1. Definition of the risk

2. Its severity

3. The frequency of its occurrence

4. Examples of places where it occurs

5. Susceptibility/resistance to it

6. Its root causes

7. Problems associated with it

8. Its cost impact

9. Methods of prevention

10. Methods of control

So far, so good. This book is attempting to be a thorough, easily used reference handbook for the problem of software risks.

Let's talk about Jones's book a little more. As an example of what it is about, let us examine what Jones calls the "most serious software risks," the ones you as a budding manager of a potential runaway project must be especially careful to look out for. (A word of caution is important here. Jones's "most serious software risks" are of necessity project-independent. Your own potential runaway project may well encounter the risks he labels most serious, but you may also encounter some others unique to your project. The use of a handbook of common risks is no substitute for a project-specific risk analysis conducted in the context of your own project.)

Here is what Jones identifies as the most serious risks (and remember that, for each of these risks and 50 or so others, he provides the information listed above):

1. *Inaccurate metrics*—Metrics are the measurement of various attributes of a project. Jones's concern here is that there are bad as well as good things to measure, and bad and good ways of measuring them.

2. *Inadequate measurement*—This is a twin to Item 1, pertaining more to omitted measures than the first, which concerns poorly-chosen measures.

3. *Excessive schedule pressure*—Recall that the second most common cause of runaways, as identified in Part 2 of this book, is "bad planning and estimating." Poor planning/ estimation is one of the prime causes of excessive schedule pressure, the situation where the project developers are given insufficient time to do their job correctly.

4. *Management malpractice*—This concern correlates with Part 2's "Bad Planning," "Inadequate/No Project Management Methodology," and perhaps "Insufficient Senior Staff on the Team." Jones points a finger at academe for this problem, saying that it provides inadequate education for software project managers.

5. *Inaccurate cost estimating*—Here we return to Part 2's "Bad Planning and Estimating," but from the point of view of cost rather than schedule.

6. *Silver bullet syndrome*—It has been all too common in the software development world for new solution approaches to be hyped as "breakthroughs" (one noted software author refers to those kinds of approaches derisively as "silver bullets," where a silver bullet was the mythical tool for slaying the mythical werewolf). Management naiveté, Jones says, allows them to place too much unwarranted credence on

those approaches. This topic correlates to some degree with Part 2's "Technology New to the Organization."

7. *Creeping user requirements*—Requirements are, of course, the definition of what the system to be built is to do. In Part 2, we spoke of "Project Objectives Not Fully Specified." Jones is speaking of the requirements changing during the course of a project, whereas we speak of projects that are never quite pinned down successfully. The two topics are nearly the same.

8. *Low quality*—Jones equates quality to product errors; when he speaks of low quality, he means an unreliable product. There is nothing comparable to this risk in the section titles of Part 2. The reason may be that most runaways self-destruct before they get to the point of finding out how many errors they contain. Some of our runaway projects, in fact, had a plague of errors; that problem did not, however, emerge as a dominant cause.

9. *Low productivity*—Jones's concern here is that software producers generate a software product at a measurably slow rate. He measures products in "function points," where a function point is the satisfaction of a significant elemental part of the problem such as processing an information file. His data suggests that programmers produce about five function points per-staff month, which he believes is insufficient, in general, to meet project schedule targets. There is nothing comparable to this risk in our Part 2.

10. *Canceled projects*—Cancellation is, of course, an effect rather than a cause of project problems. Although the risks inherent in cancellation are huge, it is curious that Jones includes them in his list of top risks to be managed, since most of his book is about managing causes rather than effects. However, one explanation for Jones's choice is his belief that most canceled projects are huge—a belief that most experienced software engineers would share. When he speaks of managing the risk of cancellation, he is actually speaking of the risks of huge projects. Because of the effect/cause factor, cancellation is not considered in our Part 2 material.

Although the Jones book is a significant step forward in the prevention and cure of software runaway projects, there are some anomalies about it that make it an important first, rather than final, step. For one thing, Jones's focus on metrics as the most serious software risks is not one that most software experts would agree with (recall that his top two most serious risks were about inaccurate and inadequate metrics). Most surveys of software practice show that metrics are dramatically underused—that is, it is rare to find projects measuring anything. Therefore, it seems unlikely that "inaccurate metrics" are the most serious software risk; it would be easier to make a case for their inadequacy given that they often do not exist!

For another thing, Jones's concern about "low productivity" is also arguable. One notable software expert, Tom DeMarco, has been known to respond to the statement that programmers are relatively unproductive with the question "compared to what?" We do know one thing about the production of software; it is a deeply intellectual exercise, using no raw materials, producing a product that is constructed purely out of intellect. There are few if any comparable disciplines; although it is easy to say that five function points per month seem low, it is not at all easy to suggest that it should be, or could be made, higher. Certainly a risk-concerned manager will need to be on the lookout for obstacles to programmer productivity in order to remove them, but it is unclear how that manager is to know whether he has or has not done an adequate job.

Given all of that, Jones's book is still an excellent starting place for the manager concerned with warding off a runaway project. The manager using that book must apply a few filters to select out some of Jones's unique beliefs and biases, but once that is done this material can be invaluable. And to increase its value, Jones does one more thing that is unique and worthwhile.

Recall our warning at the beginning of this section that software risks may be both generic—the ones Jones tends to deal with—and project-specific. Jones takes an interesting half-step toward the problem of project-specific risks. He defines six major classes of software projects, and relates his top risks to those classes. His classes are:

1. *Management information systems*—the business system, the most common of software applications

2. *Systems software*—the software that facilitates applications software, such as the operating system

3. *Commercially marketed software*—packaged software, such as spreadsheets and word processors

4. *Military systems*—software built to military procurement standards

5. *Contracted/outsourced software*—software built for, rather than by, the enterprise that needs it

6. *End-user software*—software built by the intended user rather than professional software producers

Jones's list of classes is an interesting contribution to the field; the lack of such an "application taxonomy" has been cited as a serious problem inhibiting the maturity of the field ([Glass 1992] and [Glass 1995]). However, as with his list of top risks, there are some curious biases and omissions in Jones's list. He has left out scientific/engineering applications, which constitute the second most common type of application after management information systems. And he has mixed the manner of building the system (by end users, outsource firms, or by military standards) with the type of system being produced (management information system, systems software). Nevertheless, Jones's follow-through on his classes of projects is impressive. He speaks of the kinds of risks inherently different across these classes and identifies particular risks that particular classes should be looking out for.

REFERENCES

Boehm 1989, *Software Risk Management*, IEEE Computer Society Press, 1989, Barry W. Boehm.

Charette 1989, *Software Engineering Risk Analysis and Measurement*, McGraw-Hill, 1989, Robert N. Charette.

Charette 1990, *Application Strategies for Risk Analysis*, McGraw-Hill, 1990, Robert N. Charette.

Glass 1992, "Towards a Taxonomy of Software Application Domains: History," *Journal of Systems and Software*, February 1992, Robert L. Glass and Iris Vessey.

Glass 1995, "Contemporary Application-Domain Taxonomies," *IEEE Software,* July 1995, Robert L. Glass and Iris Vessey.

Jones 1994, *Assessment and Control of Software Risks*, Yourdon Press, 1994, Capers Jones.

KPMG 1995, "Runaway Projects—Causes and Effects," *Software World*, Vol. 26, No. 3, 1995, Andy Cole of KPMG.

3.2 ISSUE MANAGEMENT

Risks are problems that are (or at least may be) anticipated prior to the beginning of project work. Issues, on the other hand, are problems that arise while the project is in process. If all issues could be identified in advance, they would probably be addressed as risks. But, given the complexity of software construction, there will always be plenty of (surprise) issues arising as work proceeds.

What is an issue? My dictionary says it is:

The point in question, an important topic for discussion.

In the context of a software project, by issues we mean obstacles that tend to arise that threaten to disrupt project progress. And issue management is project management by responding to issues.

It may strike you that issue management is a bit like "crisis management," the usually-derided practice of firefighting (addressing problems as they arise on a helter-skelter basis) rather than planning. But there are some significant differences:

1. There are some generic issues that project managers must watch for, and can plan for.

2. There are some measurement techniques that can be used to evaluate the status of both the generic issues as well as some project-specific issues.

3. There are some management techniques that can be applied to management by issue. Issue management works best in a climate of openness and helpfulness. That is, for issue management to work well, technologists must feel open to discuss issues with their managers as they arise, and the managers must demonstrate that they are capable of helping resolve the issues that are brought to their attention. In some organizations, the management response to issues is blame. Blame kills openness, which makes issue management impossible. In a climate of blame rather than openness, lying to management is a common reaction (to learn more about the unfortunately widespread practice of lying to management in the software field, see [Glass 1993]). One of the war stories in

Part 2 of this book, the story of the CONFIRM reservation systems failure, is a classic example of the problems of blame and lying.

Of course, issue management alone is insufficient. Managers must also oversee the development process and the emerging software product. But with management of issues, process, and product, the software manager, of necessity, is overseeing the schedule as well, without the onerous problems that so often arise when only management by schedule is employed. (For a more complete discussion of issue management, see [Glass 1997].)

It is not simple, of course, to manage by issues. There is no one management approach that those who manage by issue can utilize, because the issues that arise typically are extremely project-specific. Managers who manage by issue must be nimble, reacting to ongoing events rather than relying on a formula or methodology that will tell them what to do next.

But at the same time, as the (somewhat profane) bumper sticker says, "Shit happens." Issues are the excrement that threaten to derail the software project; the manager who is not managing issues is probably not managing terribly well at all.

Fortunately, there is some advice regarding issues to supplement what might otherwise be an essentially ad hoc approach. In a military-funded guidebook [JLC 1996], issues form the basis for the management approach it proposes (the guidebook says, "Program issues and objectives guide the measurement process."). The guidebook suggests this taxonomy of issues:

1. schedule/progress (this is where "management by schedule" comes in, but as an issue)

2. resource/cost

3. growth/stability

4. product quality (here is where managing the product comes in)

5. development performance (this, growth/stability, and resource/cost subsume process)

6. technical adequacy

The guidebook also suggests the importance of prioritizing issues and focusing on the important ones (the guidebook calls them "primary issues") first. (The next two prioritized levels are called "secondary issues" and "peripheral issues." These approaches seem very much like the medical approach of "triage," dividing problems into three prioritized categories.)

Although issues are always project-specific, the above taxonomy suggests that there are some generic patterns of issues that an alert software manager should be watching for.

The guidebook goes on to propose the intertwining of metrics and issues; that is, according to the guidebook, metrics should be driven by the issues to be measured (the guidebook says that 95 percent of software measurement plans fail to identify the issues driving the measurement), and the issues should then be managed with the aid of the metrics so identified.

For any project, the guidebook states, there will be a unique selection and prioritization of these generic issues. (That is what we have meant when using the phrase "project-specific issues".) The bulk of the guidebook is then spent in listing three or four categories of measurement for each generic issue, and for each category a longer list of possible specific measures. Thus the somewhat ad hoc approach of management by (project-specific) issue is made quantifiable and at least somewhat predictable by the notion of intertwining issues and metrics.

REFERENCES

Glass 1993, "Lying to Management," special issue, *Software Practitioner*, September 1993, Robert L. Glass.

Glass 1997, "The Date Wars, and Management by Issue," *Software 2020*, Computing Trends, 1997, Robert L. Glass.

JLC 1996, "Practical Software Measurement: A Guide to Objective Program Insight," March 27, 1996, Joint Logistics Commanders (Joint Group on Systems Engineering); available from John McGarry, Naval Undersea Warfare Center Code 2252, 1176 Howell St., Newport RI 02841, prepared by Elizabeth Bailey, David Card, Joseph Dean, Cheryl Jones, Beth Layman, and John McGarry.

3.3 REMEDIES ATTEMPTED DURING RUNAWAYS

Risk and issue management are textbook approaches to the problem of a budding runaway project. That is, they are easy remedies to propose in a textbook, and in fact risk management, at least, is frequently found there. But what do those in the midst of an actual runaway use as approaches to attempt to emerge from that status?

There is a collection of answers to that question in the research study we have frequently referred to in this book, [KPMG 1995]. In the survey presented in that study, respondees were asked what remedies they had tried. Their answers, in order of decreasing commonality, were:

1. Extending the schedule (the paper's authors called this "more time")—85 percent

2. Better project management procedures—54 percent

3. More people—53 percent

4. More funds—43 percent

5. Pressure on suppliers by withholding payment—38 percent

6. Reduction in scope of project—28 percent

7. New outside help—27 percent

8. Better development methodologies—25 percent

9. Pressure on suppliers by threat of litigation—20 percent

10. Change of technology used on the project—13 percent

11. Abandoning the project—9 percent

12. Other—9 percent

(Percentages above were readings from the graph presented in [KPMG 1995]. The paper did not contain the actual numbers.)

Those remedies pretty well cover the spectrum of topics that one might address in attempting to curb a runaway. Because of that, let's talk about them in a bit more depth.

1. *Extending the schedule.* Note that this is by far the most common remedy, exceeding its next closest competitor by 30

something percent. It is an interesting remedy, in that it suggests one or perhaps two things—either the productivity of the developers has been too low (we have already seen that suggested as a major risk in Capers Jones's book discussed earlier), or the original schedule was too ambitious (and I have noted that my personal belief is that this is usually the prime cause of schedule overrun). Extending the schedule may or may not be a simple remedy, of course. If there was a substantive reason for setting the schedule in the first place, such as a market opportunity that will be missed if it is not met, or a need to integrate the results of this project with another where delay is expensive, or the fact that the year 2000 is approaching and the system in question must operate correctly in that time frame, then this remedy may be an exceedingly painful one. But, if (as is often the case) the schedule was somewhat arbitrary in the first place, then this remedy is easy and relatively painless.

2. *Better management procedures.* This remedy, one can imagine, covers a multitude of sins. It suggests that inferior management procedures were used on the project up to the point of applying the remedy, and that in turn causes one to wonder why that happened. Perhaps the managers in question had their attention diverted by too many other activities, or perhaps an inept manager was in charge and is now being supplemented or replaced by a more effective one. In any case, the remedy is relatively easy to apply. [It is interesting to note that "improved project management" was the remedy most often suggested as a step to be taken to ward off future runaways, as we will see in the next section of this book. This suggests that the survey respondees either (a) were aware of some common project management problems with a way to fix them, or (b) used this response as a generic one to which they attributed little specific meaning. The study offers no clue as to which might be the case.]

3. *More people.* This is a particularly interesting remedy. What makes it interesting is that Fred Brooks, a well-known

software engineering expert, has taken the position that adding more people to a late project makes it even later (in fact, his book *The Mythical Man-Month* uses that concept as its title and as a main theme). The reason that happens, of course, is that integrating new people into a project adds training and learning-curve costs (where costs are both time and money), and diverts the present project participants from their assigned tasks in order to accomplish such training and learning curves. Nevertheless, the survey finding is an accurate one—regardless of the advice of the Brooks's of the world, adding people is an easily applied remedy. If the people added happen to be knowledgeable and experienced in the project in question, then of course those training costs and learning curves are diminished—the new people can "hit the ground running."

4. *More money.* This remedy can be paired with the first, extending the schedule. That is, more time costs more money. But there is another way that more money can be spent on a runaway without extending the schedule—adding resources, in the form of people (as we saw above) or equipment or outside services or . . . In fact, no matter what remedy approaches are taken, they will usually result in spending more money. Consider the remedies in this list—all but two, "reduction in scope of project" and "abandoning the project" will result in increased cost!

5. *Pressure on suppliers by withholding payment and*
9. *Pressure on suppliers by threat of litigation.* These two remedies both imply that the runaway project was dependent on one or more outside suppliers. These are the only two remedies for which the research study provides some words of explanation. "A remarkably high number of organizations became involved in disputes with their outside suppliers," the authors say. It is remarkable for two reasons (1) in the first study in 1989, none of the organizations in question had been involved in formal disputes; and (2) in this newer (1995) study, 38 percent withheld payments, 20 percent threatened

litigation, and 4 percent actually sued. Apparently there is a dramatic increase in the involvement of the legal system in remedies for runaway software projects.

6. *Reduction in scope of project.* It is not always possible to reduce the scope of a project—that is, to eliminate requirements in order to make the task manageable. But it is usually possible to defer some requirements or features in order to meet other targets. Because of that, it is surprising that this remedy was not among the top five remedies used. The implication of its position at number six is that most of the projects in question could not, or would not, defer or eliminate any requirements.

7. *New outside help.* There is an increasing trend in the computing business toward the use of outside suppliers to assist with, or take over, internal projects. In fact, the term "outsourcing" has been coined in the last few years to cover this increasing trend. (There were earlier terms used to describe the trend, such as "facilities management"). Academics often note that the best students in their graduating classes are increasingly being hired, not by the companies that use computing solutions, but by consulting firms (e.g., KPMG or Andersen Consulting), software houses (e.g., Microsoft or Computer Associates), or service vendors (e.g., Computer Sciences Corp. or EDS) who provide services for hire. This will likely become an increasingly common remedy in the future. Note that this remedy automatically invokes several of the other remedies, such as "More people" and "More money" and (probably) "More time."

8. *Better development methodologies* and 10. *Change of technology used in the project.* These remedies pair, in my mind, with each other and also with the number 2 remedy, "better management procedures," in the sense that it implies that the project in question was using poor procedures, methodologies, or technologies. I find it hard to get past the question, "Why were those procedures, methodologies, and technologies poor in the first place?" I also find this remedy troubling. Changing methodologies or technologies in

midstream may be an effective remedy, but it could also traumatize a project and guarantee that the runaway becomes a failure. The time to switch methodologies and technologies, I would assert, is not at midproject, but at the project's outset. The exception to that rule would, of course, be when a damaging methodology or technology was being used (for whatever reason—perhaps the project had been sold on some experimental and untried process, for example), and its use needed to be discontinued immediately. In any case, changing methodologies is not an easy remedy to apply. There are, as with adding more people, training costs and learning curves to be absorbed. It might be somewhat easier to change technologies, since the scope of impact of a technology is often less than that of a methodology.

9. *Pressure on suppliers by threat of litigation.* (This remedy was discussed under number 5, above.)

10. *Change of technology used in the project.* (This remedy was discussed under number 8, above.)

11. *Abandoning the project.* Some remedy! The only way in which this is a remedy, of course, is that it stops or rapidly slows project bloodletting, such as money and resources. But abandoning the project means returning to the previous status quo, which presumably was found faulty in some way, or the new project would never have been undertaken. What is interesting and perhaps surprising about this "remedy" is that it is found to be used so seldom in this study, and is the last one (aside from the ever-popular "other") on the list. You may recall from earlier in this book that this particular research study used a more lenient definition of "runaway" than we do in this book. For example, this study called a project a runaway if it was more than 30 percent over schedule, whereas our definition required the schedule overrun to be 100 percent or more. Whereas most of our case studies in Part 2 resulted in some form of project cancellation, clearly that was an unusual option (at the 10 percent level) in the KPMG study. Recall also the earlier discussion of a software crisis in

which various percentages of project failures were reported by various authors. It is particularly interesting that in this study of projects known to be runaways, only 10 percent actually failed!

12. *Other.* The study gave no indication of what other remedies this category might imply.

REFERENCE:

KPMG 1995, "Runaway Projects—Cause and Effects," *Software World,* Vol. 26, No. 3, 1995, Andy Cole of KPMG.

3.4 REMEDIES ENVISIONED FOR THE FUTURE

In the heat of battle, the remedies for a runaway project are limited. Any remedies tried must fit within the envelope of the progress (or lack thereof) the project has made to date. But once the battle is over, it is time to translate the lessons learned from that runaway into better practices for the future.

Unfortunately, one of the failings of the software field is that it is very poor at learning those lessons. A few industry projects follow project conclusion with some sort of "post-mortem" review (the name is ironic—the review is appropriate whether the project has experienced "death" or not!), but the large majority do not. The same excessive schedule pressure that we have discussed many times earlier in this book seems to argue for taking this project's team and quickly assigning its members to another, taking no time at all to ruminate over just what went right—and wrong.

That same failing extends to the research community. There are far too few research studies of projects in process, or projects that have concluded, or of collections of projects. The computing and software research communities, in spite of recent exhortations to change, seem little interested in its pursuit.

There are a few exceptions, but what is discouraging is that they can be counted on the fingers of one hand. The most noted is the Software Engineering Lab (SEL) at NASA-Goddard, where NASA projects are studied by researchers from the triumvirate of the University of Maryland Computer Science department, Computer Sciences Corp., and NASA-Goddard. The aggregation of academe, industry, and government was deliberate. There, over 15 years worth of short- and long-term, practice-relevant studies have been conducted. Their findings are presented each year at their Software Engineering Workshop.

The reach of the SEL is being extended. Similar programs are being established at places like Linkoping University in Sweden (at that institution, in-depth case studies of industry projects have been conducted for several years) and Kaiserslautern University in Germany.

Similar work is being done at a university consortium, the Software Engineering Research Center (SERC), consisting of universities in In-diana, Florida, and Oregon. Other centers of at least somewhat practical software study are: the Software Engineering Institute (SEI) at Carnegie Mellon University, funded largely by the U.S. Department of Defense, and the Software Productivity Consortium (SPC), a center funded by industry and located in the Washington, D.C. area. But these latter institutions seem more focused on the transfer of new technology to industry, rather than the study of industry projects to see what they will need in the future or how to determine the project-specific merits of the technology they are attempting to transfer.

Because of this lack of adequate, practice-focused research, the findings of the research study we have been mentioning throughout this book [KPMG 1995] are especially important. In the previous section we reported on the findings of that study regarding remedies attempted during runaway projects. Here, we report on what the study learned about the future plans of those companies that had suffered runaways.

The companies in question proposed (in decreasing order of importance) the following long-term solutions:

1. Improved project management—86 percent

2. Feasibility study—84 percent

3. More user involvement—68 percent

4. More external advice—56 percent

5. None of the above—4 percent

(Percentages are derived from a reading of the graphs in the paper; findings were not presented in the form of numbers.)

There are some particularly interesting aspects of this list, and we will explore them in more depth in what follows.

The first interesting fact is that the list is quite short. There were 12 remedies attempted during the runaway projects, but there are only five proposed after the fact. In some ways, that is understandable. Some of the remedies that were attempted during the project make no sense as a long-term cure—examples would include more time, more people, more money, pressure on suppliers, or abandoning the project. Clearly these are efforts of expediency only.

But some of the other remedies tried during the runaways would seem to have longer-term corollaries. For example, during the projects some remedies focused on technology—better development methodologies and change of technology used in the project. Neither of them appears in any form whatsoever in the list of longer-term ideas. It is as if technology is a problem of the moment, not one to be focused on long-term. And that seems very short-sighted.

The same thing is true of the remedies regarding working with suppliers. Note that there is nothing in the long-term remedies regarding better acquisition management. Of course, that could be buried under the long-term focus on "improved project management," but there is reason to question that; acquisition is often performed by senior technical people rather than by management.

Another interesting difference between the lists regards user involvement. It is seen as a long-term remedy, but nothing analogous to it was tried during the projects themselves. One wonders if the users could not have helped by reining in a runaway project in some way. Of course, one remedy attempted during the projects was reducing the project scope, something that could not—or at least should not—be attempted without consulting with the users. Still, there is the feeling that the respondees who saw more user involvement as a long-term solution may be repeating a mantra rather than speaking from experience.

Perhaps the most interesting idea in the long-term concepts, falling at a strong number 2 position, is the notion of the need for a feasibility study. The implication is that feasibility studies were often *not* conducted on the projects that became runaways. Certainly, the earlier data that we reported regarding the lack of risk analysis, while not quite the same subject, has relevance here. There seems to have been a sort of unrealistic optimism present at the outset of the projects that became runaways, and that sobering experience is leading management to follow a more realistic approach in the future.

But the strongest theme, running across both the in-progress remedies and the long-term remedies, is better project management. There seems to have been a very strong belief among these companies that project management is, and will continue to be, the prime cause of software runaways until something is done about it. But what does improved project management really mean? It is discouraging that it is not broken down into some constituent steps. There are many tasks that managers perform. Which are the ones that need improving? How are they to be improved? These questions, begged by the research study findings, are not answered there. Perhaps it is finding answers to those questions that could provide us with the most progress toward stemming software runaways in the future.

REFERENCE

KPMG 1995, "Runaway Projects—Cause and Effects," *Software World*, Vol. 26, No. 3, 1995, Andy Cole of KPMG.

PART

4

Conclusions

"Success covers a multitude of blunders."

—*George Bernard Shaw*

Los Angeles is a land of many things, but one of those things is calamity.

During the year I lived there, we experienced earthquakes, fires, killings, and floods. And not just your tiny little earthquakes, fires, killings, and floods. These were large-scale, highly-visible, major earthquakes, fires, killings, and floods.

I remember vividly one visit to Malibu shortly after the fires and floods ravaged that beautiful community. On a narrow, winding road descending from the Santa Monica Mountains to the ocean, there were remnants of destruction visibly surrounding us. Deeply trenched ravines, carved by the force of the water that flows so rapidly in its short span from mountaintop to sea. Buildings washed into those ravines, tilting crazily at angles that God found suitable, but that mankind had never envisaged. Remains from the awesome destruction caused by fire. Foundations with no houses rising above them, on lot after lot—and acreage after acreage (these calamities are an equal opportunity destroyer!). Fireplaces reaching 10 or 20 or 30 feet above those foundations, reaching eerily toward the sky from a platform of empty destruction.

There is an incredible sadness that comes from wandering among the aftereffects of calamity. It doesn't matter that these were not my buildings, my foundations, my chimneys. They were someone's building or foundation or chimney, and they were worthless now. Plenty of someones had no doubt shed tears over those remains, and over the memories once formed there.

Software runaways are somewhat like those calamities. Oh, there are no physical structures that get torn down during a software runaway, and there is no one killed. But there is plenty of emotional destruction. A team of people, probably operating in crunch mode on a death march quest, went down to defeat. Their hopes and plans for the future were probably dashed. There was probably blame and recrimination as the end approached, and relationships were bent or broken. Self-belief came under attack, and for some participants it was probably plowed under.

I have participated on a lot of software projects. A small percentage of them have failed. I have lived through the loss of those hopes and plans, that blame and recrimination, that loss of self-belief. I have empathy for every single participant on every single runaway war story found in this book. Perhaps because software is a product built from no physical resources, a product constructed purely out of intellect, it is especially devastating to the psyche when it fails. For many of us in the software business, what we bring to the table of our profession is our intellect. We software nerds may or may not be good with our hands; we may or may not be strong enough to excel in sports; we may or may not be socially adept; but, doggone it, we are artists with our minds! And when such people have a major failure of the intellect, it is also a major failure of the self.

In this book we have sifted through the artifacts of those failed software runaway projects. We have seen those hopes and plans, that blame and recrimination, that loss of self-belief scattered about like flotsam from a flood and ashes from a fire. We have analyzed the feelings and the facts that have emerged from those projects. We have tried to derive lessons learned, lessons about what to look out for at the beginning of software projects, about how to extricate ourselves from a runaway in progress, about how to avoid getting involved in a runaway in the future. It has been, for the most part, an intellectual exercise.

But in the background—always there to remind us that the failure could have been about us, and in any case was about real software human beings—has been an emotional component. Our intellectual analysis can't quite damp out those feelings, the sadness at failure, the mourning of the memories that must have been left behind.

Los Angeles may have suffered a lot of calamities. And so have lots of other places in our country, in our world.

But so has the software profession. And it hurts.

Index